Advisor-Consultants

Vincent J. Altamuro
Assistant Principal,
Thomas Jefferson School
Queens, New York

Sandra Pryor Clarkson
Associate Professor
of Mathematical Sciences
Hunter College of CUNY
New York, New York

Jeanette Gann
Mathematics and Science
Coordinator, High Point
Public Schools
High Point, North Carolina

Zelda Gold
Mathematics Advisor,
Los Angeles Unified
School District
Los Angeles, California

Dorothy Keane
Professor of Education
California State University,
Los Angeles
Los Angeles, California

Joel Levin
Teacher, Chicago Public Schools
Chicago, Illinois

Gail Lowe
Principal, Conejo Valley
Unified School District
Thousand Oaks, California

Kozo Nishifue
Administrator of Mathematics,
Oakland Unified School District
Oakland, California

James A. Peters, Jr.
Elementary Mathematics
Resource Teacher,
Samuel Powel School
Philadelphia, Pennsylvania

Andria P. Troutman
Professor, University
of South Florida
Tampa, Florida

LAIDLAW
Mathematics

LAIDLAW BROTHERS • PUBLISHERS

RIVER FOREST, ILLINOIS
Sacramento, California • Chamblee, Georgia • Dallas, Texas

Acknowledgments

Developed by Kirchoff/Wohlberg, Inc.,
in cooperation with Laidlaw Brothers, Publishers

Editorial Director   Mary Jane Martin

Laidlaw Editorial Staff

Editorial Manager   David B. Spangler

Editor/Consultant   Barbara J. Huffman

Editors   Robert C. Mudd, Judith A. Witt

Educator/Reviewers
  Deborah Abbott, Carole Bauer, Lynn Cohn, Cynthia Frederick,
  Patricia A. Schwartz, Helene Silverman, Larry A. Tagle,
  Josephine Wraith

The colored rods depicted in this series are Cuisenaire® rods. The name Cuisenaire® and the color sequence of the rods are trademarks of Cuisenaire Company of America, Inc.

TABLE OF CONTENTS

CHAPTER 7   METRIC MEASUREMENT: MASS AND CAPACITY

CHAPTER 8   GEOMETRY

CHAPTER 9   MULTIPLICATION FACTS: 2 AND 3 AS FACTORS

CHAPTER 10   MULTIPLICATION FACTS: 4 AND 5 AS FACTORS

CHAPTER 11   DIVISION FACTS: 2 AND 3 AS DIVISORS

CHAPTER 12   DIVISION FACTS: 4 AND 5 AS DIVISORS

CHAPTER 13   MULTIPLICATION AND DIVISION

CHAPTER 14   TIME AND TEMPERATURE

CHAPTER 15   MULTIPLICATION FACTS: 6 AND 7 AS FACTORS

CHAPTER 19   PLACE VALUE: LARGER NUMBERS

CHAPTER 20   ADDITION AND SUBTRACTION OF LARGER NUMBERS

CHAPTER 21   MEANING OF FRACTIONS

CHAPTER 22   ADDITION AND SUBTRACTION OF FRACTIONS

CHAPTER 23   MEANING OF DECIMALS

CHAPTER 24   ADDITION AND SUBTRACTION OF DECIMALS

CHAPTER 25   GEOMETRY

CHAPTER 26   MULTIPLICATION BY A ONE-DIGIT NUMBER

CHAPTER 27   DIVISION BY A ONE-DIGIT DIVISOR

CHAPTER 28   CUSTOMARY MEASUREMENT: LENGTH AND TEMPERATURE

CHAPTER 29   CUSTOMARY MEASUREMENT: WEIGHT AND CAPACITY

CHAPTER 30   PROBABILITY

LAIDLAW
Mathematics

CHAPTER 1

Using Mathematics

These people love their jobs. All of them worked hard to learn how to do their jobs. They use math skills they learned in school.

One person is a vet. This is a short way of saying veterinarian. She takes care of sick animals. Animal doctors use math when they decide how much medicine an animal needs. The vet knows how much medicine to give a horse. Would she give the same amount to a pony or a dog?

The person driving the bulldozer is helping to build a skyscraper. He must follow a written plan. This has math problems for the driver to solve.

The pet store owner buys and sells many kinds of pets. He keeps records of the money people pay him. He also keeps records of the animals in the store. He needs to know how much food to buy for them. He uses numbers every day.

This skater is making geometric shapes on the ice. This is called doing school figures. Ice skaters make circles, figure eights, and other shapes. Skaters count as they do school figures. Figure skaters work for points. A high score is given for perfect patterns.

The children you see here all have something in common: they are all using mathematics skills in their lives outside of school.

People use mathematics all of the time to make their lives easier. You know that people use math when they pay for clothes or cook meals. You know that math is a big part of sports, as in keeping score or measuring distance. Do you know that you are also using math when you knit a sweater or pack a bag for a weekend trip?

Mathematics is more than adding, subtracting, multiplying, and dividing. In a way, math is like a river formed by lots of little streams flowing together. Each stream adds to the strength and size of the river. Like the little streams that form a river, math is formed by separate topics, called strands. The strands work together. In this book you will be using seven math strands:

1. NUMBER SKILLS When you add, subtract, multiply, or divide, you use number skills.

2. MEASUREMENT When you use money, tell time, or find the length of an object, you use measurement skills.

3. GEOMETRY When you deal with shapes and lines, you use geometry skills.

4. PATTERNS AND FUNCTIONS When you find a pattern or write a rule, you use patterns and functions skills.

5. STATISTICS AND PROBABILITY When you use or make a graph, you use statistics skills. When you use a spinner to see how often a certain color comes up, you use probability skills.

6. LOGIC When you reason things out before making a guess, you use logic skills.

7. ALGEBRA When you write a number sentence, you use algebra skills.

NUMBER SKILLS

Getting Started

Every time you add, subtract, multiply, or divide, you are using number skills. Number skills are used with whole numbers, fractions, and other kinds of numbers you will be learning about.

The exercises that follow will help you review some of the number skills you have already studied. If you need help look at the addition table in the Data Bank on page 425.

Add or subtract.

1. $\begin{array}{r} 5 \\ +4 \\ \hline \end{array}$	**2.** $\begin{array}{r} 6 \\ +7 \\ \hline \end{array}$	**3.** $\begin{array}{r} 9 \\ +8 \\ \hline \end{array}$	**4.** $\begin{array}{r} 13 \\ -\ 5 \\ \hline \end{array}$	**5.** $\begin{array}{r} 18 \\ -\ 9 \\ \hline \end{array}$	**6.** $\begin{array}{r} 15 \\ -\ 7 \\ \hline \end{array}$
7. $\begin{array}{r} 33 \\ +22 \\ \hline \end{array}$	**8.** $\begin{array}{r} 74 \\ +\ 4 \\ \hline \end{array}$	**9.** $\begin{array}{r} 156 \\ +232 \\ \hline \end{array}$	**10.** $\begin{array}{r} 89 \\ -24 \\ \hline \end{array}$	**11.** $\begin{array}{r} 67 \\ -\ 6 \\ \hline \end{array}$	**12.** $\begin{array}{r} 989 \\ -782 \\ \hline \end{array}$

13. 7 + 4   **14.** 18 + 21   **15.** 340 + 149   **16.** 26 − 15   **17.** 572 − 560

Write the missing number.

18. ■, 66, 67   **19.** 52, ■, 54   **20.** 79, 80, ■

21. 109, ■, 111   **22.** 326, 327, ■   **23.** ■, 430, 431

24. 417, 418, ■   **25.** 679, ■, 681   **26.** ■, 300, 301

Solve each problem.

27. A stamp album with 187 pages has 63 pages full of stamps. How many pages are left?

28. Cal spends 65¢ on some stickers and 32¢ on baseball cards. How much is spent in all?

FOCUS | Review NUMBER skills.

MEASUREMENT

Getting Started

If you tell the time, use money, or find the length or weight of an object, you are using measurement skills.

Doing the following exercises will help you remember some of the measurement skills you have already studied. Look at pages 426 and 427 of the Data Bank to review measurement facts.

Write the time.

29.    30.    31.    32.

Solve the problem.

33. Nicky has

He buys some clay for 83¢.
How much does Nicky have left?

Does each one weigh more or less than a pound?
Write *more* or *less*.

34.    35.   36.    37.

GEOMETRY
Getting Started

You are using geometry skills whenever you deal with shapes, sides, and corners.

Doing these exercises will give you a chance to go over some of the geometry skills you have studied. Turn to page 425 in the Data Bank if you need help.

Copy the chart. Write the name of each figure. Then complete the rest of the chart.

1.	Name of figure	◼	▲	●	▬
2.	Number of straight sides	▪	▪	▪	▪
3.	Number of corners	▪	▪	▪	▪

Look at the birds.

4. How many squares?

5. How many triangles?

6. How many circles?

7. How many rectangles?

PATTERNS AND FUNCTIONS

Getting Started

Each time you make a pattern and use a rule, you are working with patterns and functions skills.

Copy each pattern. Draw and color the next shape.

8.

9.

10.

Find each pattern. Then copy and complete each chart.

11.

2	4
3	6
4	■
5	10
6	12
7	■

12.

1	4
2	5
3	6
4	■
■	8
6	■

13.

50	48
46	44
43	41
31	■
■	26
22	20

14.

10	20
30	40
70	80
■	100
■	130
160	170

Write the next two numbers for each pattern.

15. 4, 6, 8, 10, 12, ■, ■

16. 7, 9, 11, 13, 15, ■, ■

Review PATTERNS AND FUNCTIONS.

9

STATISTICS AND PROBABILITY
Getting Started

If you make a graph or find the chance of picking an item from a group without looking, you are using statistics and probability skills.

There are 10 books in the Share-a-Book box.

3 mystery books   1 "how-to" book
2 poetry books   4 adventure books

If you put your hand in the box to choose one book without looking, the probability of your picking a mystery book would be 3 out of 10. What is the probability that you would pick

1. a how-to book?   **2.** an adventure book?   **3.** a book of poems?

Copy and complete the bar graph showing the different kinds of books in the box.

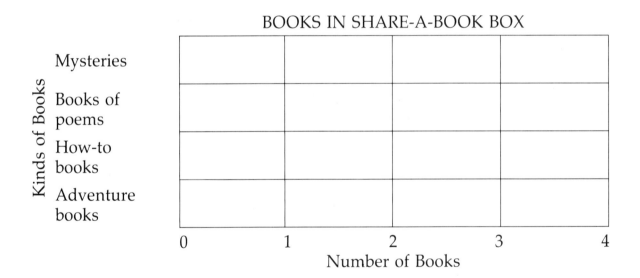

BOOKS IN SHARE-A-BOOK BOX

Kinds of Books: Mysteries, Books of poems, How-to books, Adventure books

Number of Books: 0 1 2 3 4

4. How many books are poems?

5. How many books are adventure stories?

FOCUS | Review STATISTICS AND PROBABILITY.

LOGIC
Getting Started

Each time you use reasoning before you make a guess or while you work out a problem, you are using logic skills.

Use the picture to answer each question.

6. How many flowers are in the shade?

7. How many flowers are in the sun?

8. How many more flowers are in the sun than in the shade?

9. How many flowers are in the window box or in the shade?

ALGEBRA
Getting Started

Whenever you write a number sentence using >, <, or =, you are using algebra skills. Remember that > means "greater than" and < means "less than."

Copy these number sentences. Write >, <, or = in the $\bigcirc$.

10. 8 $\bigcirc$ 5   **11.** 0 $\bigcirc$ 6   **12.** 9 $\bigcirc$ 11

13. 18 $\bigcirc$ 81   **14.** 55 $\bigcirc$ 45   **15.** 33 $\bigcirc$ 33

16. 25 $\bigcirc$ 19   **17.** 62 $\bigcirc$ 71   **18.** 86 $\bigcirc$ 86

19. 119 $\bigcirc$ 121   **20.** 304 $\bigcirc$ 304   **21.** 852 $\bigcirc$ 849

Review LOGIC and ALGEBRA.

USING THIS BOOK
Understanding How This Book Works

This book will always let you know the kind of lesson you are doing and why you are doing it. The titles above and below the line tell you what you will be learning. The FOCUS gives you the main idea of the lesson.

At the beginning of each chapter is a FORMULATING PROBLEMS lesson. Here, you will learn to form problems from data and other information.

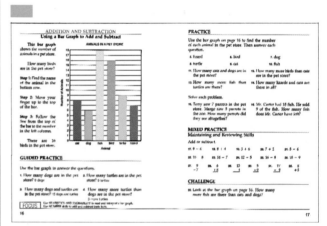

The two-page lesson that comes next is set up like this:
1. You look at the new skill and "walk through" a sample.
2. You practice the new skill with help in Guided Practice.
3. Then you PRACTICE on your own.
4. Next you do some MIXED PRACTICE. This keeps all your skills sharp.
5. You may do a CHALLENGE problem to use your skill in another way.

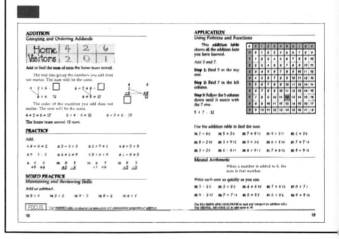

The next two pages give you more time to practice the skill.
1. First you go over the skill.
2. Then you PRACTICE it again.

FOCUS Understand how this book is organized.

12

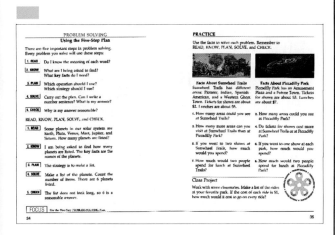

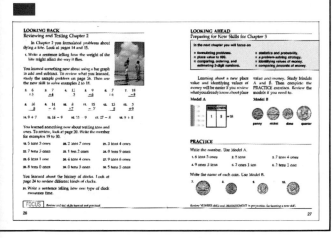

3. More MIXED PRACTICE is next.

4. You apply the new skill and use it with another math strand.

Your book has special PROBLEM - SOLVING lessons. These lessons show you a good 5-step plan for solving problems. The plan really helps.

In MATH IN THE CONTENT AREAS you will learn how math is used in art, music, and other subjects.

LOOKING BACK reviews and tests you on your new skills. This will help you know what you have learned well and what you need to keep working on.

LOOKING AHEAD ends the chapter. You will preview the skill coming up in the next chapter. You will be shown which old skills you will need to use with the new work. A few exercises will help you decide which skills you will need to sharpen. All this will help you get ready for the next step in math and will make learning math more fun.

FOCUS — Formulate problems using picture cues, text, and data.

DATA

Activity   Kite-flying contest

Number of children
with kites flying   9

Number of children
with broken kites   2

Minutes in contest   15

Wind speed   12 miles
an hour

Height of
highest kite   30 feet

Materials needed to make
a flat kite
     Two sticks, each 2 feet
         long, $\frac{3}{8}$ inch wide, and
         $\frac{1}{8}$ inch thick
     Glue
     Kite string
     Tissue paper or newspaper
     Paint or markers
     Strips of cloth about
         2 inches wide and
         6 inches long

CHAPTER 2

Basic Facts and Place Value

Making and flying a kite is an exciting activity. Kite flying is done on windy days in early spring or in the fall. On a windy day, these small delicate-looking forms, made of sticks and paper, become soaring birds. The kites dip and glide and can rise so high that they look like tiny specks against the sky. A kite behaves like the hawk-like bird called a *kite*. This bird gave the kite its name.

These two children are in a kite-flying contest. What problems did they solve before the contest? What problem did two other children have as they tried to fly their kites? What do you think the winner of the contest has to do to win?

Using a Bar Graph to Add and Subtract

This **bar graph** shows the number of animals in a pet store.

How many birds are in the pet store?

Step 1: Find the name of the animal in the bottom row.

Step 2: Move your finger up to the top of the bar.

Step 3: Follow the line from the top of the bar to the number in the left column.

There are 16 birds in the pet store.

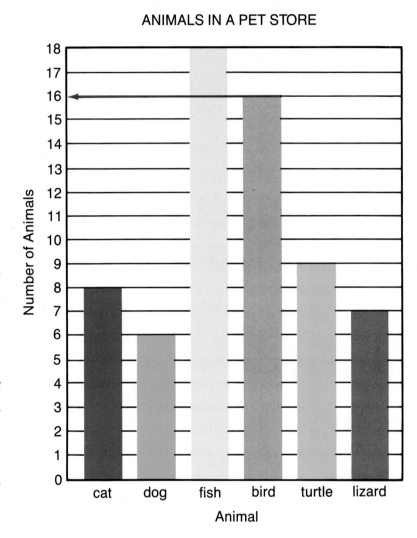

ANIMALS IN A PET STORE

GUIDED PRACTICE

Use the bar graph to answer the questions.

1. How many dogs are in the pet store?

2. How many turtles are in the pet store?

3. How many dogs and turtles are in the pet store?

4. How many more turtles than dogs are in the pet store?

| FOCUS | Use STATISTICS AND PROBABILITY to read and interpret a bar graph. Use NUMBER skills to add and subtract basic facts. |

PRACTICE

Use the bar graph on page 16 to find the number of each animal in the pet store. Then answer each question.

5. lizard   **6.** bird   **7.** dog

8. turtle   **9.** cat   **10.** fish

11. How many cats and dogs are in the pet store?

12. How many more birds than cats are in the pet store?

13. How many more fish than turtles are there?

14. How many lizards and cats are there in all?

Solve each problem.

15. Terry saw 7 parrots in the pet store. Marge saw 5 parrots in the zoo. How many parrots did they see altogether?

16. Mr. Carter had 18 fish. He sold 9 of the fish. How many fish does Mr. Carter have left?

MIXED PRACTICE
Maintaining and Reviewing Skills

Add or subtract.

17. $9 + 6$ **18.** $8 + 4$ **19.** $5 + 6$ **20.** $7 + 2$ **21.** $5 + 4$

22. $15 - 8$ **23.** $14 - 7$ **24.** $12 - 5$ **25.** $16 - 8$ **26.** $18 - 9$

27. $\begin{array}{r} 9 \\ -7 \\ \hline \end{array}$ **28.** $\begin{array}{r} 6 \\ +8 \\ \hline \end{array}$ **29.** $\begin{array}{r} 13 \\ -\ 4 \\ \hline \end{array}$ **30.** $\begin{array}{r} 5 \\ +9 \\ \hline \end{array}$ **31.** $\begin{array}{r} 17 \\ -\ 9 \\ \hline \end{array}$ **32.** $\begin{array}{r} 8 \\ +5 \\ \hline \end{array}$

CHALLENGE

33. Look at the bar graph on page 16. How many more fish are there than cats and dogs?

ADDITION
Grouping and Ordering Addends

Home	4	2	6
Visitors	2	0	1

Add to find the **sum** of runs the home team scored.

The way you group the numbers you add does not matter. The sum will be the same.

4 + 2 + 6 = ☐
6 + 6 = 12

4 + 2 + 6 = ☐
4 + 8 = 12

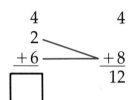

The order of the numbers you add does not matter. The sum will be the same.

4 + 2 + 6 = 12   2 + 4 + 6 = 12   6 + 2 + 4 = 12

The home team scored 12 runs.

PRACTICE

Add.

1. 4 + 6 + 2   **2.** 3 + 4 + 5   **3.** 2 + 7 + 1   **4.** 4 + 5 + 3

5. 5 + 1 + 3   **6.** 4 + 1 + 9   **7.** 3 + 6 + 8   **8.** 1 + 6 + 3

9. 4   9   **10.** 8   5   **11.** 6   7   **12.** 9   3
$+9$ $+4$ $+5$ $+8$ $+7$ $+6$ $+3$ $+9$

MIXED PRACTICE
Maintaining and Reviewing Skills

Add or subtract.

13. 3 + 4   **14.** 5 + 2   **15.** 9 − 3   **16.** 8 − 4   **17.** 6 + 4

FOCUS   Use NUMBER skills to observe the associative and commutative properties of addition.

18

APPLICATION

Using Patterns and Functions

This **addition table** shows all the addition facts you have learned.

Add 5 and 7.

Step 1: Find 5 in the top row.

Step 2: Find 7 in the left column.

Step 3: Follow the 5 column down until it meets with the 7 row.

$5 + 7 = 12$

+	0	1	2	3	4	5	6	7	8	9
0	0	1	2	3	4	5	6	7	8	9
1	1	2	3	4	5	6	7	8	9	10
2	2	3	4	5	6	7	8	9	10	11
3	3	4	5	6	7	8	9	10	11	12
4	4	5	6	7	8	9	10	11	12	13
5	5	6	7	8	9	10	11	12	13	14
6	6	7	8	9	10	11	12	13	14	15
7	7	8	9	10	11	12	13	14	15	16
8	8	9	10	11	12	13	14	15	16	17
9	9	10	11	12	13	14	15	16	17	18

Use the addition table to find the sum.

18. $2 + 6$ **19.** $5 + 3$ **20.** $7 + 8$ **21.** $9 + 2$ **22.** $4 + 5$

23. $8 + 2$ **24.** $1 + 9$ **25.** $3 + 5$ **26.** $6 + 4$ **27.** $7 + 7$

28. $3 + 2$ **29.** $6 + 8$ **30.** $8 + 9$ **31.** $7 + 6$ **32.** $9 + 9$

Mental Arithmetic

When a number and 0 are added, the sum is that number.

Write each sum as quickly as you can.

33. $3 + 2$ **34.** $5 + 0$ **35.** $4 + 6$ **36.** $7 + 8$ **37.** $0 + 7$

38. $9 + 3$ **39.** $7 + 7$ **40.** $0 + 8$ **41.** $6 + 0$ **42.** $9 + 9$

Use PATTERNS AND FUNCTIONS to read and interpret an addition table.
Use MENTAL ARITHMETIC to add sums to 18.

Writing Tens and Ones

Vonda is making strawberry pie. How many strawberries does she have in all?

The strawberries can be grouped by tens: 10 ones equal 1 ten.

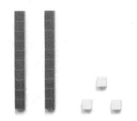

1 ten   3 ones   13

Vonda has 13 strawberries.

These cubes are grouped by tens. How many cubes are there in all?

Tens	Ones
2	3

There are 23 cubes in all.

GUIDED PRACTICE

Write the number of tens and ones.

1.

<u>2</u> tens <u>5</u> ones

2.

■ ten ■ ones

| FOCUS | Use NUMBER skills to identify the place values of two-digit numbers. |

PRACTICE

Copy and complete the charts.

3.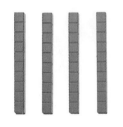

Tens	Ones

4.

Tens	Ones

Write the number.

5. 8 tens   4 ones   **6.** 4 tens   0 ones   **7.** 6 tens   6 ones

8. 3 tens   5 ones   **9.** 7 tens   2 ones   **10.** 4 tens   3 ones

11. 5 tens   7 ones   **12.** 2 tens   1 one   **13.** 9 tens   0 ones

14. 6 tens   1 one   **15.** 8 tens   8 ones   **16.** 6 tens   9 ones

MIXED PRACTICE

Maintaining and Reviewing Skills

Write the number.

17. 2 tens   3 ones   **18.** 8 tens   0 ones   **19.** 1 ten   6 ones

Add or subtract.

20. $2 + 9$ **21.** $11 - 4$ **22.** $7 + 8$ **23.** $18 - 9$ **24.** $8 + 9$

CHALLENGE

25. Look at the gate letters and the seat numbers. Mary has a ticket for seat 35. Which gate does she go to?

Gate A	Gate B	Gate C
seats:	seats:	seats:
0-25	26-50	51-75

PLACE VALUE
Comparing Tens and Ones

Doug has 25 blocks.   Ruth has 23 blocks.

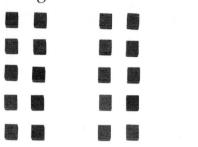  

Who has the greater number of blocks?

Compare 25 and 23.

First compare the tens. The tens are the same. Then compare the ones. Since 5 is greater than 3,

   25 **is greater than** 23   and   23 **is less than** 25.
        $25 > 23$ $23 < 25$

Doug has the greater number of blocks.

PRACTICE

Write $<$ or $>$ to show which number is greater.
The $<$ or $>$ always points to the lesser number.

1. 43 ● 21   2. 27 ● 12   3. 75 ● 86   4. 67 ● 32   5. 54 ● 96

6. 36 ● 62   7. 51 ● 49   8. 22 ● 27   9. 19 ● 18   10. 75 ● 57

11. 90 ● 87   12. 36 ● 29   13. 45 ● 54   14. 71 ● 73   15. 16 ● 14

MIXED PRACTICE
Maintaining and Reviewing Skills

Add or subtract.

16. $15 - 7$ 17. $16 - 9$ 18. $8 + 9$ 19. $6 + 7$ 20. $12 - 7$

FOCUS   Use NUMBER skills to compare two-digit numbers.

APPLICATION

Using Numbers

There are many different kinds of numbers.

Some numbers are **odd.** The ones digit of an **odd number** is 1, 3, 5, 7, or 9.

Some numbers are **even.** The ones digit of an **even number** is 0, 2, 4, 6, or 8.

Some numbers are used to show order. First, tenth, and twenty-third are **ordinal numbers.**

The Romans used letters to show numbers.

I is for 1.   V is for 5.   X is for 10.

VI is 5 + 1 or 6.   IV is 5 − 1 or 4.

XI is 10 + 1 or 11.   IX is 10 − 1 or 9.

XX is 10 + 10 or 20.   XIX is 10 + 9 or 19

Write *even* or *odd* for each number.

21. 12   **22.** 3   **23.** 74   **24.** 25   **25.** 8   **26.** 57

Write a number for each word.

27. third   **28.** fifteenth   **29.** twenty-fourth   **30.** thirty-first

Write a Roman numeral for each number.

31. 1   **32.** 5   **33.** 10   **34.** 12   **35.** 14   **36.** 19

37. 3   **38.** 9   **39.** 4   **40.** 15   **41.** 20   **42.** 17

43. Write a letter to a friend. Use even and odd numbers, ordinal numbers, and Roman numerals in the letter.

Use NUMBER skills to explore odd and even numbers, ordinal numbers, and Roman numerals.

Early Clocks

Time has been measured throughout history. Egyptians, over 4,000 years ago, used the sun and shadows. A stick was put straight up in the soil. The shadow, cast by the stick as the sun moved across the sky, was measured.

Sundials were built about 2,800 years ago. They also use the idea of measuring the shadow of an object as the sun moves from east to west during a day.

Water clocks were used to measure time at night or when it was cloudy. The first water clock was a bucket with a small hole at the bottom to let water out. Lines on the bucket showed how much time had passed.

Hourglasses have a measured amount of sand in them which pours through a narrow space at a steady rate.

Candle clocks were marked with 12 lines. It took an hour to burn from one line to the next.

Mechanical clocks were invented in the 1200s. In the 1600s the pendulum was developed, and the balancing spring was invented. These made measuring time more accurate. Minute and second hands were added. Today, digital clocks are quite common.

CRITICAL THINKING

1. Why was the sundial the first type of clock?

2. Give two reasons why the water clock might not have been accurate.

3. To tell time for a whole day, how many candle clocks would you need? How many times would an hourglass have to be turned?

FOCUS   Discover how people used MEASUREMENT to make early clocks.

This is the back of a 1688 English clock. It has a pendulum.

LOOKING BACK
Reviewing and Testing Chapter 2

In Chapter 2 you formulated problems about flying a kite. Look at pages 14 and 15.

1. Write a sentence telling how the weight of the kite might affect the way it flies.

You learned something new about using a bar graph to add and subtract. To review what you learned, study the sample problem on page 16. Then use the new skill to solve examples 2 to 18.

| 2. $\begin{array}{r} 6 \\ +5 \end{array}$ | 3. $\begin{array}{r} 7 \\ +4 \end{array}$ | 4. $\begin{array}{r} 11 \\ -5 \end{array}$ | 5. $\begin{array}{r} 9 \\ +6 \end{array}$ | 6. $\begin{array}{r} 7 \\ +6 \end{array}$ | 7. $\begin{array}{r} 18 \\ -9 \end{array}$ |

| 8. $\begin{array}{r} 16 \\ -8 \end{array}$ | 9. $\begin{array}{r} 14 \\ -6 \end{array}$ | 10. $\begin{array}{r} 8 \\ +7 \end{array}$ | 11. $\begin{array}{r} 15 \\ -7 \end{array}$ | 12. $\begin{array}{r} 13 \\ -8 \end{array}$ | 13. $\begin{array}{r} 5 \\ +9 \end{array}$ |

14. $9 + 7$ 15. $16 - 9$ 16. $15 - 9$ 17. $17 - 8$ 18. $9 + 8$

You learned something new about writing tens and ones. To review, look at page 20. Write the number for examples 19 to 30.

19. 5 tens 3 ones   20. 2 tens 7 ones   21. 3 tens 4 ones

22. 7 tens 5 ones   23. 1 ten 2 ones   24. 0 tens 9 ones

25. 6 tens 1 one   26. 4 tens 4 ones   27. 9 tens 6 ones

28. 8 tens 0 ones   29. 0 tens 3 ones   30. 5 tens 5 ones

You learned about the history of clocks. Look at page 24 to review different kinds of clocks.

31. Write a sentence telling how one type of clock measures time.

FOCUS | Review and test skills learned and practiced.

LOOKING AHEAD

Preparing for New Skills for Chapter 3

In the next chapter you will focus on

- formulating problems.
- place value to 999.
- comparing, ordering, and estimating 3-digit numbers.

- statistics and probability.
- a problem-solving strategy.
- identifying values of money.
- comparing amounts of money.

Learning about a new place value and identifying values of money will be easier if you review what you already know about place value and money. Study Models A and B. Then complete the PRACTICE exercises. Review the models if you need to.

Model A

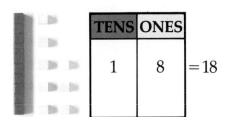

$= 18$

Model B

penny   nickel   dime   quarter

PRACTICE

Write the number. Use Model A.

1. 6 tens 3 ones

2. 8 tens

3. 7 tens 4 ones

4. 9 ones 5 tens

5. 2 ones 1 ten

6. 2 tens 1 one

Write the name of each coin. Use Model B.

7.

8.

9.

10.

Review NUMBER skills and MEASUREMENT in preparation for learning a new skill.

FOCUS   Formulate problems using picture cues, text, and data.

3

Place Value and Money

DATA

	Red Robins	Blue Jays
Game	Kickball	
Score	Red Robins	12
	Blue Jays	8

Inning	Red Robins	Blue Jays
1	4	0
2	3	0
3	3	0
4	1	0
5	1	1
6	0	2
7	0	2
8	0	3

Kickball is an exciting game. It lasts for nine innings and takes all the energy and skill a player has to try to win! Look at the data given for this game. As you can see, it is the last inning. The ninth inning is just starting.

Use this photo and the data given to tell how the game might end. What problem does the Red Robin team have? What problem does the Blue Jay team have? Finish the data for the last inning to show how the game ended.

PLACE VALUE
Writing Three-Digit Numbers

How many cubes are in the picture?

The cubes are grouped by hundreds and tens. 10 tens equal 1 hundred. 10 ones equal 1 ten.

2 hundreds 3 tens 5 ones ⟶

HUNDREDS	TENS	ONES
2	3	5

Two hundred thirty-five cubes are in the picture.

GUIDED PRACTICE

Write the letter of the picture that matches the number.

1. 478   **2.** three hundred sixteen   **3.** 147

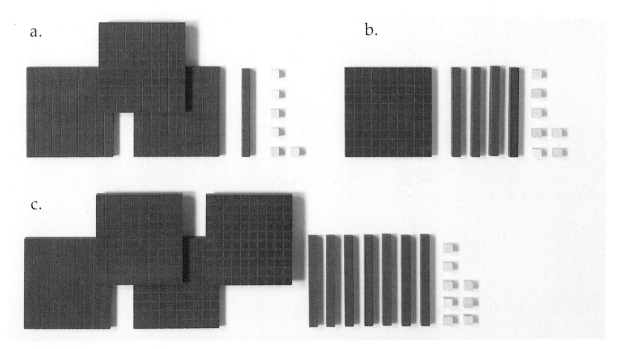

a.

b.

c.

FOCUS   Use NUMBER skills to identify the place value of three-digit numbers.

30

PRACTICE

Copy and complete the place-value chart. Then write
the number.

4.

HUNDREDS	TENS	ONES
▪	▪	▪

5.

HUNDREDS	TENS	ONES
▪	▪	▪

What is the place value of the underlined digit?
Write *hundreds*, *tens*, or *ones*.

6. 6̲32   7. 18̲0   8. 92̲4   9. 3̲00   10. 457̲   11. 77̲5

12. 209̲   13. 7̲46   14. 483̲   15. 16̲8   16. 5̲19   17. 891̲

MIXED PRACTICE
Maintaining and Reviewing Skills

Write the number.

18. 5 hundreds, 7 tens, 8 ones   19. 9 hundreds, 0 tens, 1 one

Add or subtract.

20. 4 + 8   21. 12 − 7   22. 9 + 5   23. 17 − 8   24. 6 + 7

CHALLENGE

Write each number.

25. 1 more than 912   26. 10 more than 672   27. 100 more than 838

PLACE VALUE

Comparing Three-Digit Numbers

Brittany drove for 175 miles. Anthony drove for 185 miles. Who drove less miles?

Compare 175 and 185.

- Compare the hundreds: The hundreds are the same.
- Compare the tens: 7 tens is less than 8 tens.

175 **is less than** 185   and   185 **is greater than** 175

$\qquad$ 175 < 185 $\qquad\qquad\qquad$ 185 > 175

Brittany drove less miles.

PRACTICE

Write < or > to show which number is less.
The < or > always points to the lesser number.

1. 451 ● 692   **2.** 716 ● 803   **3.** 264 ● 176   **4.** 885 ● 588

5. 137 ● 146   **6.** 902 ● 800   **7.** 498 ● 489   **8.** 540 ● 546

Write the numbers in order from greatest to least.

9. 247, 962, 654, 800, 379   **10.** 532, 423, 413, 550, 400

Write the numbers in order from least to greatest.

11. 794, 109, 190, 689, 200   **12.** 947, 892, 929, 996, 853

MIXED PRACTICE

Maintaining and Reviewing Skills

Add or subtract.

13. $18 - 9$ **14.** $17 - 6$ **15.** $8 + 5$ **16.** $4 + 7$ **17.** $14 - 8$

FOCUS   Use NUMBER skills to compare and order three-digit numbers.

APPLICATION
Using Statistics and Probability

Mr. Thompson has several orchards. He counted the number of trees in each orchard. He drew this picture for every one hundred trees he counted.

Apple Trees	Peach Trees	Cherry Trees	Pear Trees
(5 trees)	(2 trees)	(3 trees)	(1 tree)

Use the chart above to answer the questions.

18. How many apple trees did Mr. Thompson count?

19. How many pear trees did Mr. Thompson count?

20. How many hundreds of peach trees are there?

21. How many peach and pear trees are there in all?

22. How many apple and cherry trees are there in all?

Estimation

When you estimate, you are making a guess.

23. Copy this chart. Fill it in by estimating the number of words on the pages in this math book. Find the actual number of words by counting each word. Estimate and count the words only.

Page Number	Estimate	Actual
15		
29		

Use STATISTICS AND PROBABILITY to interpret picture symbols.
Use NUMBER skills to explore estimation.

PROBLEM SOLVING
Using the Five-Step Plan

There are five important steps in problem solving. Every problem you solve will use these steps:

1. READ	Do I know the meaning of each word?
2. KNOW	What am I being asked to find? What **key facts** do I need?
3. PLAN	Which operation should I use? Which strategy should I use?
4. SOLVE	Carry out the plan. Can I write a number sentence? What is my answer?
5. CHECK	Why is my answer reasonable?

READ, KNOW, PLAN, SOLVE, and CHECK.

1. READ	Some planets in our solar system are Earth, Pluto, Venus, Mars, Jupiter, and Saturn. How many planets are listed?
2. KNOW	I am being asked to find how many planets are listed. The **key facts** are the names of the planets.
3. PLAN	The strategy is to make a list.
4. SOLVE	Make a list of the planets. Count the number of items. There are 6 planets listed.
5. CHECK	The list does not look long, so 6 is a reasonable answer.

FOCUS	Use the Five-Step PROBLEM-SOLVING Plan.

PRACTICE

Use the facts to solve each problem. Remember to
READ, KNOW, PLAN, SOLVE, and CHECK.

Facts About Sunwheel Trails
Sunwheel Trails has different areas: Pioneer, Indian, Spanish–American, and a Western Ghost Town. Tickets for shows are about $2. Lunches are about $5.

Facts About Piccadilly Park
Piccadilly Park has an Amusement Plaza and a Future Town. Tickets for shows are about $3. Lunches are about $7.

1. How many areas could you see at Sunwheel Trails?

2. How many areas could you see at Piccadilly Park?

3. How many more areas can you visit at Sunwheel Trails than at Piccadilly Park?

4. Do tickets for shows cost more at Sunwheel Trails or at Piccadilly Park?

5. If you went to two shows at Sunwheel Trails, how much would you spend?

6. If you went to one show at each park, how much would you spend?

7. How much would two people spend for lunch at Sunwheel Trails?

8. How much would two people spend for lunch at Piccadilly Park?

Class Project

Work with some classmates. Make a list of the rides at your favorite park. If the cost of each ride is $1, how much would it cost to go on every ride?

MONEY
Identifying Values of Money

Look at the money Joey took out of his pocket.

Penny	Nickel	Dime
1¢ or $0.01	5¢ or $0.05	10¢ or $0.10

Quarter	Half dollar	Dollar

25¢ or $0.25	50¢ or $0.50	100¢ or $1.00

Gloria took some money out of her pocket. How much money does she have?

100 ⟶ 150 ⟶ 160 ⟶ 165 ⟶ 166

Gloria has 166¢ or $1.66.

GUIDED PRACTICE

Write the value in two ways.

1.
2.
3.

PRACTICE

Write the value in two ways.

4.

5.

6.

7.

8. 2 dollars, 1 quarter, 2 dimes

9. 5 dollars, 6 dimes, 3 nickels

Write *yes* or *no*.

10. Cindy has 10 pennies. Can she trade her pennies for a dime?

11. Stanley has 2 dimes and 1 nickel. Can he buy a toy that costs $0.35?

MIXED PRACTICE
Maintaining and Reviewing Skills

Write the value in two ways.

12.
13.
14.
15.
16.

What is the place value of the underlined digit?

17. 4<u>7</u>   18. 59<u>6</u>   19. <u>9</u>7   20. <u>4</u>82   21. 3<u>6</u>7   22. <u>6</u>89

CHALLENGE

23. Write 3 ways to pay for a 25¢ telephone call. You cannot use pennies.

MONEY
Comparing Values of Money

Here is Leo's money.

Here is Becky's money.

Who has more money?

Count and compare the values.

Leo has $0.25.   Becky has $0.17.

Twenty-five cents **is greater than** seventeen cents.
$$\$0.25 > \$0.17$$

Leo has more money than Becky.

PRACTICE

Write $<$, $>$, or $=$.

1. ●   2. ●

3.  ●   4. ●

MIXED PRACTICE
Maintaining and Reviewing Skills

Write $<$ or $>$.

5. 367 ● 954   **6.** 832 ● 797   **7.** 641 ● 654   **8.** 260 ● 206

FOCUS   Use NUMBER skills and MEASUREMENT to compare values of money.

APPLICATION

Problem Solving: Using the Five-Step Plan

Remember to READ, KNOW, PLAN, SOLVE, and CHECK all problems. See the Five-Step Plan on page 425 in the Data Bank.

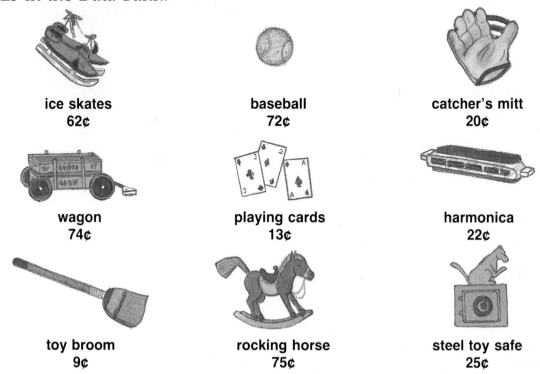

ice skates
62¢

baseball
72¢

catcher's mitt
20¢

wagon
74¢

playing cards
13¢

harmonica
22¢

toy broom
9¢

rocking horse
75¢

steel toy safe
25¢

Use the toys and their prices to help you solve the problems. They are in an 1897 toy catalog.

9. Sue has 2 quarters and 1 dime. Can she buy the harmonica?

10. Jo has 1 dollar and 1 quarter. Can she buy the rocking horse?

11. What toys can Eric buy with 2 dimes and 3 pennies?

12. Johanna has a dime. What can she buy?

13. Nicole has 2 dimes. Can she buy the catcher's mitt?

14. Robert has 6 nickels. Can he buy the ice skates?

15. Stephen has 6 pennies and 3 nickels. What toys can he buy?

16. Lou has 4 nickels and 4 dimes. Can he buy the wagon?

Use the Five-Step PROBLEM SOLVING Plan.

LOOKING BACK
Reviewing and Testing Chapter 3

In Chapter 3 you formulated problems about a kickball game. Look at pages 28 and 29.

1. Write a sentence telling what advantage the Blue Jays have.

You learned something new about writing three-digit numbers. To review what you learned, study the sample problem on page 30. Then use the new skill to write the place value of the underlined digit in examples 2 to 13. Write *hundreds*, *tens*, or *ones*.

2. 4<u>8</u>5   3. <u>7</u>92   4. 80<u>6</u>   5. <u>6</u>62   6. 1<u>2</u>7   7. <u>3</u>50

8. <u>5</u>38   9. 2<u>1</u>7   10. 91<u>1</u>   11. <u>3</u>82   12. 44<u>8</u>   13. 9<u>7</u>1

You learned how to use the Five-Step Plan. To review what you learned, look at pages 34 and 35. Use the facts to solve the problem.

14. There are 6 blue hats, 5 striped hats, 7 green hats, and 9 red scarves in a clothing store. How many hats are in the store?

You learned something new about identifying values of money. To review, look at pages 36 and 37. Write the value for examples 15 to 22 in two ways.

15. 3 dollars, 1 dime, 1 nickel

16. 1 quarter, 2 dimes, 3 pennies

17. 2 dollars, 6 dimes, 6 pennies

18. 7 dimes, 1 nickel, 4 pennies

19. 7 dollars, 4 nickels, 8 pennies

20. 5 dollars, 2 quarters, 3 nickels

21. 1 dollar, 4 quarters, 3 dimes, 2 pennies

22. 7 dollars, 4 quarters, 6 nickels, 1 penny

FOCUS   Review and test skills learned and practiced.

LOOKING AHEAD
Preparing for New Skills for Chapter 4

In the next chapter you will focus on

- formulating problems.
- adding two-digit numbers.
- rounding two-digit numbers.
- using measurement.

- adding three-digit numbers.
- rounding three-digit numbers.
- estimating sums.
- math in technology.

New addition skills will be easier to learn if you brush up on the skills you already know. Review the basic addition facts on page 425 in the Data Bank. Then study the model. Remember to keep the numbers in straight columns. Add the ones first and then the tens. Complete the PRACTICE exercises. Use the model to help you.

Model

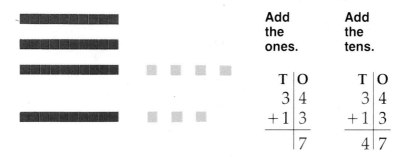

Add the ones.

```
  T | O
  3 | 4
+ 1 | 3
------
    | 7
```

Add the tens.

```
  T | O
  3 | 4
+ 1 | 3
------
  4 | 7
```

PRACTICE

Add. Review the model if you need to.

1. 3
   +4

2. 15
   +14

3. 7
   +6

4. 37
   +60

5. 9
   +0

6. 52
   +47

7. 28 + 31

8. 6 + 5

9. 73 + 22

10. 7 + 8

11. 49 + 40

12. 9 + 9

13. 82 + 17

14. 5 + 8

15. 30 + 56

16. 18 + 71

Review NUMBER skills in preparation for learning a new skill.

FOCUS   Formulate problems using picture cues, text, and data.

DATA

Hill City Zoo

Feeding times

3:00 P.M.	Giraffes
3:30 P.M.	Lions
4:00 P.M.	Seals
4:30 P.M.	Elephants
5:00 P.M.	Monkeys

Some foods the animals eat

Giraffes	Hay
Lions	Meat
Seals	Fish
Elephants	Hay
	Peanuts
Monkeys	Bananas

Pen numbers

1	Giraffes
2	Monkeys
3	Elephants
4	Lions
5	Seals

CHAPTER **4**

Addition

It's always fun to visit the zoo. A visitor can see wild animals from all over the world. Zoos not only give people a chance to see these animals. They also protect animals that are endangered in the wild.

The zookeeper is the person who takes care of the animals. It is the zookeeper's job to make sure the animals are well-fed, clean, and healthy.

This can be a very satisfying job, but it can also be dangerous. The zookeeper must be trained in the proper way to feed lions, tigers, and other wild animals.

Using the picture and the data, imagine what the zookeeper's day might be like. What problems might the zookeeper face?

ADDITION
Adding Two-Digit Numbers

Julio has 24 purple pencils and 12 blue pencils. How many pencils does Julio have in all?

Add to find the total number of pencils.

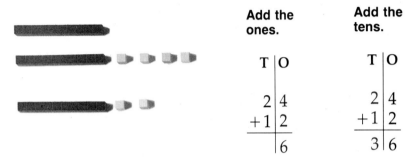

Add the ones.

```
T | O
  |
2 | 4
+1| 2
------
  | 6
```

Add the tens.

```
T | O
  |
2 | 4
+1| 2
------
3 | 6
```

Julio has 36 pencils.

There are 16 pencils in a red can and 9 pencils in a green can. How many pencils are there in both cans?

Add to find the total number of pencils.

Add the ones. Regroup.

```
T | O
 1|
1 | 6
+ | 9
------
  | 5
```

```
  6
 +9
-----
 1 5
```

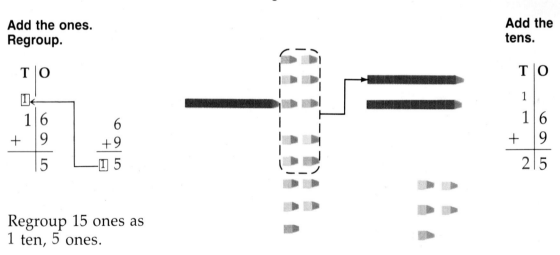

Add the tens.

```
   T | O
   1 |
   1 | 6
 + |   9
--------
   2 | 5
```

Regroup 15 ones as 1 ten, 5 ones.

There are 25 pencils in both cans.

| FOCUS | Use NUMBER skills to add two-digit numbers, with and without regrouping. |

GUIDED PRACTICE

Add. Sometimes you need to regroup.

1.	T	O
	1	6
+	1	2
	■	8

2.	T	O
		1
	2	3
+	4	9
	■	2

3.	T	O
	5	4
+		3
	■	■

4.	T	O
	■	
	3	8
+	4	7
	■	■

PRACTICE

Do you need to regroup? Write Y (yes) or N (no).
Then add to find the sum.

5. 22
   +15

6. 28
   +16

7. 42
   + 4

8. 36
   +13

9. 63
   + 8

10. 54
    +29

11. 23
    +12

12. 32
    +11

13. 54
    +31

14. 48
    +25

15. 35
    +27

16. 89
    + 6

17. 32 + 46

18. 27 + 56

19. 41 + 8

20. 58 + 9

21. Roy has 12 pens. Joy has 36 pens. How many pens do Roy and Joy have in all?

22. Mary has 26 pens. Rena gives Mary 7 pens. What is the total number of pens Mary now has?

MIXED PRACTICE

Maintaining and Reviewing Skills

Add or subtract.

23. 3 + 5

24. 6 + 0

25. 14 − 8

26. 5 + 9

27. 16 − 9

CHALLENGE

28. What number is added to 41 to equal 58?

ESTIMATION
Rounding Two-Digit Numbers

Nick has 23 chickens and 35 pigs. About how many chickens does he have? About how many pigs does he have?

Round to find *about* how many of each animal Nick has.

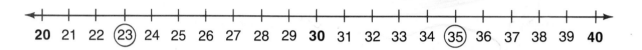

Round 23 to the nearest ten.
- 23 is between 20 and 30.
- 23 is closer to 20.
- 23 rounds down to 20.

Round 35 to the nearest ten.
- 35 is halfway between 30 and 40.
- A number halfway between two tens rounds up.
- 35 rounds up to 40.

Nick has about 20 chickens and about 40 pigs.

PRACTICE

Round each number to the nearest ten.

| 1. 24 | 2. 56 | 3. 87 | 4. 39 | 5. 62 | 6. 75 |
| 7. 48 | 8. 35 | 9. 91 | 10. 16 | 11. 54 | 12. 83 |

Round each price to the nearest ten cents.

| 13. 56¢ | 14. 12¢ | 15. 39¢ | 16. 71¢ | 17. 25¢ | 18. 44¢ |

MIXED PRACTICE
Maintaining and Reviewing Skills

Add or subtract.

19. 15 + 6   20. 17 − 8   21. 44 + 15   22. 8 + 3   23. 16 − 8

FOCUS | Use NUMBER skills to round two-digit numbers.

APPLICATION
Using Estimation

```
☀SCHOOL LUNCH MENU ☀
Yogurt  57¢   ☀   Juice   15¢
Fruit   35¢   ☀   Milk    11¢
Bread   32¢   ☀   Soup    38¢
```

Natalie orders juice and yogurt. About how much does Natalie spend?

Estimate to find *about* how much she spends.

Step 1: Round each price to the nearest ten cents.

Estimate

$$15¢ \longrightarrow \quad 20¢$$
$$57¢ \longrightarrow \quad +60¢$$

Step 2: Add the rounded prices.

$$80¢$$

Natalie spends *about* 80¢.

Use the menu above. Estimate each sum by rounding each price and adding.

24. Arnold orders soup and bread. About how much does he spend?

25. Yoko orders milk and fruit. About how much does she spend?

26. Pearl orders milk, soup, and bread. About how much does she spend?

27. Dory orders juice, bread, and fruit. About how much does he spend?

Mental Arithmetic

Write whether the sum is *odd* or *even*.

28.	29.	30.	31.	32.	33.
24	71	58	33	45	64
+32	+19	+27	+36	+17	+43

Use ESTIMATION and NUMBER skills to estimate sums.
Use MENTAL ARITHMETIC to distinguish between even and odd sums.

ADDITION
Adding Three-Digit Numbers

There are 352 baseballs and 215 bats in the sport store. How many baseballs and bats are in the sport store?

Add 352 and 215 to find the total number of baseballs and bats in the sport store.

Add the ones.

```
  H T O
  3 5 2
+ 2 1 5
------
      7
```

Add the tens.

```
  H T O
  3 5 2
+ 2 1 5
------
    6 7
```

Add the hundreds.

```
  H T O
  3 5 2
+ 2 1 5
------
  5 6 7
```

There are 567 baseballs and bats in the sport store.

The shoe store has 68 sneakers. It has 156 more moccasins than sneakers. How many moccasins does the shoe store have?

Add 156 and 68 to find the total number of moccasins the shoe store has.

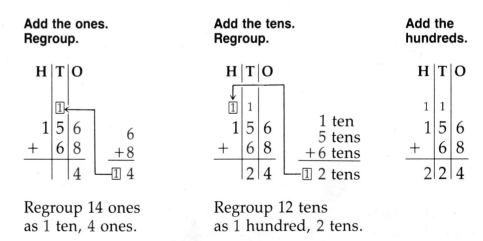

Add the ones. Regroup.

```
    H T O
      1
    1 5 6      6
  +   6 8    + 8
  -------    ----
        4      1 4
```

Regroup 14 ones as 1 ten, 4 ones.

Add the tens. Regroup.

```
    H T O
    1   1
    1 5 6      1 ten
  +   6 8      5 tens
  -------    + 6 tens
      2 4    --------
              1 2 tens
```

Regroup 12 tens as 1 hundred, 2 tens.

Add the hundreds.

```
    H T O
    1 1
    1 5 6
  +   6 8
  -------
    2 2 4
```

The shoe store has 224 moccasins.

| FOCUS | Use NUMBER skills to add three-digit numbers, with and without regrouping. |

48

GUIDED PRACTICE

Add. Sometimes you need to regroup.

1.
H	T	O
4	2	3
+1	5	6
■	7	9

2.
H	T	O
	1	
6	5	8
+2	3	7
■	■	5

3.
H	T	O
■	■	
3	7	9
+	8	4
■	■	■

PRACTICE

Add.

4. 231
   +142

5. 622
   +347

6. 456
   +238

7. 374
   +142

8. 538
   +285

9. 772
   + 26

10. 938
   + 31

11. 567
   + 19

12. 192
   + 79

13. 465
   + 57

14. 533 + 226

15. 746 + 32

16. 476 + 25

17. 659 + 174

18. There are 368 pink sneakers and 226 red sneakers. How many sneakers are there in all?

19. There are 59 bats. There are 137 more balls than bats. How many balls are there?

MIXED PRACTICE
Maintaining and Reviewing Skills

Add or subtract.

20. 6 + 7

21. 37 + 8

22. 9 − 0

23. 15 − 7

24. 43 + 5

CHALLENGE

25. Saul has 185 marbles. Marge has 352 more marbles than Saul. Eliot has 196 more than Marge. How many marbles does Eliot have?

ESTIMATION
Rounding Three-Digit Numbers

Jill picked 130 strawberries. **Round** to the **nearest hundred** to find *about* how many berries she picked.

- 130 is between 100 and 200
- 130 is closer to 100
- 130 rounds down to 100

100 110 120 (130) 140 150 160 170 180 190 **200**

Jill picked *about* 100 strawberries.

Jack paid $2.50 for a pint of blueberries. **Round** to the **nearest dollar** to find *about* how much Jack spent.

- $2.50 is halfway between $2.00 and $3.00
- $2.50 rounds up to $3.00

Jack spent *about* $3.00 for the blueberries.

PRACTICE

Round each number to the nearest hundred.

1. 260	**2.** 370	**3.** 910	**4.** 590	**5.** 150	**6.** 480
7. 620	**8.** 550	**9.** 180	**10.** 730	**11.** 290	**12.** 840

Round each price to the nearest dollar.

13. $4.90   **14.** $7.10   **15.** $5.20   **16.** $8.50   **17.** $3.70   **18.** $6.90

MIXED PRACTICE
Maintaining and Reviewing Skills

Add or subtract.

19. 26 + 17   **20.** 29 + 8   **21.** 15 − 8   **22.** 173 + 146   **23.** 344 + 77

FOCUS | Use NUMBER skills to round three-digit numbers.

APPLICATION
Using Estimation

> ## ✦ CATALOG ✦
> Shirt $8.20   Shoes $9.30
> Pants $9.40   Sneakers $8.50
> Skirt $7.60   Slippers $6.70

Warren buys a pair of pants and a pair of sneakers. About how much does Warren spend?

Estimate to find *about* how much he spends.

Step 1: Round each price to the nearest dollar.

		Estimate
$9.40	$\longrightarrow$	$9.00
$8.50	$\longrightarrow$	$+$ $9.00

Step 2: Add the rounded prices. $18.00

Warren spends *about* $18.00.

Use the catalog above. Estimate each sum by rounding each price and adding.

24. Lucille buys a skirt and a shirt. About how much does she spend?

25. Lewis buys a pair of shoes and a pair of slippers. About how much does he spend?

26. Murray buys two shirts. About how much does he spend?

27. Gertrude buys two skirts. About how much does she spend?

28. Sophia buys a pair of pants, a pair of shoes, and a shirt. About how much does she spend?

29. Jonas buys two pairs of pants and a pair of sneakers. About how much does he spend?

Use ESTIMATION and NUMBER skills to estimate sums.

Where Are Computers Found?

Computers affect our lives every day in many ways. All around us, computers make slow, hard jobs faster and easier to do. Computers are very good at receiving and saving large amounts of information and at recalling it quickly. So in places like libraries, airports, and police stations, computers are an important help. Computers are also able to do hard math problems easily.

Factories receive materials and fit parts together, making finished products over and over again. Computers are often used to control the repeated movements of factory machines.

Stores must keep track of the things they have to sell and the prices they charge. Computers are used to record sales and the changing number of items.

Hospitals save information describing the progress of their patients. At any moment, a patient's entire medical history or billing history might be needed. A hospital computer finds this information easily. Doctors also use computers to recall cases and to perform medical tests.

From school to home and even at all the traffic lights in between, we benefit from the help of computers. The development of **personal computers** or **PCs** has been very important in bringing computers into our classrooms and homes. The possibilities for using computers are only beginning to be explored.

CRITICAL THINKING

1. In which of the following could you use a computer?
   a. studying math homework
   b. buying soap at the supermarket
   c. walking a dog
   d. keeping a record of baseball scores

2. How would a computer be helpful in doing the things chosen above?

3. What jobs might computers do for NASA scientists?

FOCUS   Use LOGIC to study the uses of computers.

This farmer uses a computer to manage his hog farm.

New York City's traffic lights are computer controlled.

LOOKING BACK
Reviewing and Testing Chapter 4

In Chapter 4 you formulated problems about a zoo. Look at pages 42 and 43.

1. Write a sentence telling some of the dangers of being a zookeeper.

You learned something new about adding two-digit numbers. To review what you learned, study the sample problem on page 44. Then use the new skill to find each sum for examples 2 to 17.

2.	13	3.	12	4.	35	5.	11	6.	34	7.	27
	+18		+ 7		+15		+17		+ 8		+12

8. 14 + 12   9. 22 + 6   10. 43 + 13   11. 19 + 11   12. 36 + 28

13. 55 + 9   14. 31 + 48   15. 67 + 8   16. 29 + 52   17. 94 + 5

You learned something new about adding three-digit numbers. To review, look at pages 48 and 49. Then use the new skill to find each sum for examples 18 to 31.

18.	614	19.	314	20.	514	21.	173	22.	450	23.	627
	+228		+211		+237		+ 82		+126		+ 72

24. 218 + 411   25. 327 + 85   26. 532 + 117   27. 214 + 211

28. 137 + 37   29. 412 + 550   30. 608 + 89   31. 773 + 96

You learned about computers. Look at page 52 to review the ways computers help us.

32. Why is it important to have computers in a hospital?

FOCUS	Review and test skills learned and practiced.

LOOKING AHEAD

Preparing for New Skills for Chapter 5

In the next chapter you will focus on

- formulating problems.
- subtracting two-digit numbers.
- using measurement.

- a problem-solving strategy.
- subtracting three-digit numbers.
- estimating differences.

New subtraction skills will be easier to learn if you brush up on the skills you already know. Review the basic subtraction facts on page 425 in the Data Bank. Then study the model. Remember to keep the numbers in straight columns and to subtract the ones first and then the tens. Complete the PRACTICE exercises. Use the model to help you.

Model

Subtract
the ones.

```
 T | O
 2 | 4
-1 | 2
───────
   | 2
```

Subtract
the tens.

```
 T | O
 2 | 4
-1 | 2
───────
 1 | 2
```

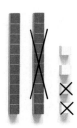

PRACTICE

Subtract. Review the model if you need to.

1. 18
   − 9

2. 84
   −23

3. 15
   − 6

4. 68
   −20

5. 12
   − 5

6. 79
   −56

7. 55 − 33
8. 17 − 9
9. 37 − 15
10. 14 − 6
11. 98 − 27

12. 16 − 7
13. 46 − 36
14. 13 − 8
15. 88 − 33
16. 62 − 40

Review NUMBER skills in preparation for learning a new skill.

FOCUS   Formulate problems using picture cues, text, and data.

Subtraction

DATA

Bird	Flamingo
Home	Lake Nakuru, Kenya, Africa

Features of Lake Nakuru

Size	10,000 acres
Depth	3–4 feet

Population of Nakuru

1963	25,000 people
1977	70,000 people
1985	100,000 people

Number of flamingos on lake

Best conditions	1,000,000
Worst conditions	50,000

One of Africa's greatest treasures is a glorious bird, the flamingo. Long-necked like the swan, but pink in color, the flamingo has always lived along the shores of Lake Nakuru. Once there were over one million of these beautiful birds on the lake. But today their number is few.

Look at the picture of the flamingos. Now look at the data. As you can see, the town of Nakuru has a growing population. How do you think the increasing number of people has affected the birds along the lake?

What problems do you think the birds have faced in recent years? What might **BEST** and **WORST conditions** mean?

SUBTRACTION

Subtracting Two-Digit Numbers

It is 23 miles from the Louisa Mae Alcott School to the Benjamin Franklin School. It is 13 miles from the Benjamin Franklin School to the Elizabeth Blackwell School. What is the difference between the two distances?

Subtract to find the difference.

Subtract the ones.

```
 T | O
 2 | 3
-1 | 3
---|---
   | 0
```

Subtract the tens.

```
 T | O
 2 | 3
-1 | 3
---|---
 1 | 0
```

The difference between the distances is 10 miles.

A hiking trail on Mount Desert Island is 23 miles long. Sharon walked 8 miles along the trail. How many miles does Sharon have left to walk?

Subtract to find how many miles Sharon has left to walk.

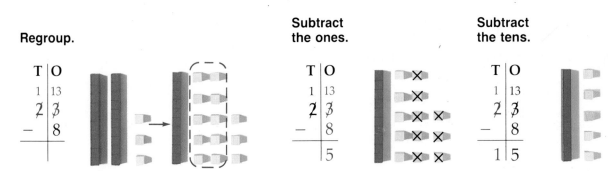

Regroup.

```
   T | O
   1 | 13
   2̶ | 3̶
 -   | 8
```

Subtract the ones.

```
   T | O
   1 | 13
   2̶ | 3̶
 -   | 8
  ---|---
     | 5
```

Subtract the tens.

```
   T | O
   1 | 13
   2̶ | 3̶
 -   | 8
  ---|---
   1 | 5
```

Regroup 2 tens, 3 ones as 1 ten, 13 ones.

Sharon has 15 miles left to walk.

| FOCUS | Use NUMBER skills to subtract two-digit numbers, with and without regrouping. |

GUIDED PRACTICE

Subtract. Sometimes you will need to regroup.

1.
T	O
3	4
−1	2
■	2

2.
	4	12
T	O
5̸	2̸
−3	6
■	6

3.
T	O
6	8
−	5
■	■

4.
T	O
□	□
4̸	5̸
−2	9
■	■

PRACTICE

Do you need to regroup? Write *Y* or *N*. Subtract.

5.
$$43 \\ -12$$

6.
$$76 \\ -52$$

7.
$$95 \\ -79$$

8.
$$37 \\ -\ 8$$

9.
$$24 \\ -13$$

10.
$$50 \\ -\ 7$$

11.
$$96 \\ -48$$

12.
$$69 \\ -35$$

13.
$$21 \\ -\ 6$$

14.
$$59 \\ -39$$

15.
$$82 \\ -\ 7$$

16.
$$78 \\ -59$$

17. $85 - 32$
18. $77 - 6$
19. $32 - 19$
20. $63 - 8$

21. Lois biked 35 miles. Clark biked 19 miles. How much further did Lois bike?

22. Lonny hiked 22 miles. Esther hiked 8 miles. How many more miles did Lonny hike?

MIXED PRACTICE
Maintaining and Reviewing Skills

Add or subtract.

23. $16 - 7$
24. $48 + 5$
25. $14 - 6$
26. $27 + 9$
27. $12 - 8$

CHALLENGE

28. When this number is subtracted from 84, the difference is 55. What is the number?

SUBTRACTION
Estimating Differences

Paul buys a comic book that costs 63¢. He gives the clerk 75¢. About how much money does Paul get back?

Estimate to find *about* how much he gets back.

Step 1: Round each amount to the nearest ten cents.

$$
\begin{array}{rcr}
 & & \text{Estimate} \\
75¢ & \longrightarrow & 80¢ \\
63¢ & \longrightarrow & -60¢ \\
\hline
\end{array}
$$

Step 2: Subtract the rounded amounts. $20¢$

Paul gets back *about* 20¢.

PRACTICE

Round each amount. Then estimate the difference.

1. $72¢ \longrightarrow$ ■
   $56¢ \longrightarrow -$ ■
   ————
   ■

2. $89¢ \longrightarrow$ ■
   $72¢ \longrightarrow -$ ■
   ————
   ■

3. $94¢ \longrightarrow$ ■
   $35¢ \longrightarrow -$ ■
   ————
   ■

Estimate to solve.

4. Kay has 86¢. She buys a book for 58¢. About how much does she have left?

5. Stanley has 93¢. He buys a bookmark for 71¢. About how much does he have left?

6. Jacob buys a newspaper for 19¢. He gives the clerk 25¢. About how much does he get back?

7. Rudy buys a magazine for 42¢. She gives the clerk 50¢. About how much does she get back?

MIXED PRACTICE
Maintaining and Reviewing Skills

Add or subtract.

8. $17 - 8$ 9. $5 + 6$ 10. $33 - 9$ 11. $7 + 3$ 12. $54 - 6$

FOCUS Use NUMBER skills and MEASUREMENT to estimate differences.

APPLICATION

Using Measurement

The **map** shows the distance between places.

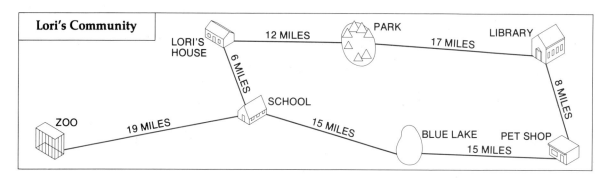

Use the map to find the shortest distance between places. Then complete the problems.

13. from Lori's house to the park   12 miles
    from the park to the library   + 17 miles
    from Lori's house to the library   29 miles

14. from the library to the pet shop   8 miles
    from Lori's house to school   − 6 miles
    difference between the distances   14 miles

Use addition or subtraction to solve each problem.

15. How far is it from Lori's house to Blue Lake? 21 miles

16. How far is it from Lori's house to the zoo? 25 miles

17. How much farther is it from Lori's house to the zoo than from Lori's house to Blue Lake?

Mental Arithmetic

Write whether the difference is *odd* or *even*.

18.	19.	20.	21.	22.	23.
36	57	94	41	65	78
−22	−29	−35	−18	−47	−53

Use MEASUREMENT to read and interpret a map.
Use MENTAL ARITHMETIC to distinguish between odd and even differences.

Exploring READ and KNOW

The first two steps of the problem-solving plan, READ and KNOW, are important. You must understand a problem before you can solve it. Find the **key facts**. Do not solve the problem.

> **1. READ**
>
> Mary found the word *quadrumvirate* in a book. It means "a group of four people." How many consonants are in Mary's word?
>
> Ask yourself: Do I know the meaning of each word? Do I know what a consonant is?

> **2. KNOW**
>
> Ask yourself: What am I being asked to find? How many consonants are in Mary's word? What **key facts** do I need?

Some problems have information which you do not need. It is best to find the **key facts** to solve each problem. Making a table will help you.

Facts I Know	What I Need to Find	Key Fact
meaning of Mary's word spelling of Mary's word	number of consonants in Mary's word	spelling of Mary's word

Look at the Facts I Know to find the **Key Fact**.
- Does knowing the meaning of Mary's word help to find the number of consonants?
- Is the spelling of Mary's word enough information to answer the question?

> FOCUS | Use the READ and KNOW steps of the Five-Step PROBLEM-SOLVING Plan.

PRACTICE

For each problem, think about the READ and KNOW steps. Make a table like the one on page 62 to find the **key facts**. Do not solve the problems.

1. In English *sesquipedalian* means "a long word." In Latin it means "a foot-and-a-half long." How many letters of the alphabet after *m* are in this word?

2. The word *antidisestablishmentarianism* was used once by a British Prime Minister about 100 years ago. Give the total number of each vowel in this word.

3. *Foretopgallantmast* is the highest place on a ship where a sailor can sit to look out. How many letters are used more than once in this word?

4. *Diphenylaminechlorarsine* is sometimes used to make dyes. How many vowels and consonants are there in this word?

5. An *environmentalist* is a person who studies and protects nature. How many vowels are not in this word?

Class Project

Work in small groups. Look through the books in your classroom (you cannot use dictionaries). Make a list of the ten longest words you can find. Can you find any word with more vowels than consonants? Trade lists with another group. Did they write any of the words that your group wrote?

SUBTRACTION
Subtracting Three-Digit Numbers

Mr. Miller weighs 197 pounds. Mrs. Miller weighs 126 pounds. How much less does Mrs. Miller weigh?

Subtract to find how much less Mrs. Miller weighs.

Subtract the ones.	Subtract the tens.	Subtract the hundreds.

H T O
1 9 7
− 1 2 6
‗‗‗
      1
	H T O
	1 9 7
	− 1 2 6
	‗‗‗
	   7 1
		H T O
		1 9 7
		− 1 2 6
		‗‗‗
		   7 1

Mrs. Miller weighs 71 pounds less than Mr. Miller.

Mr. Simpson weighed 200 pounds. He lost 56 pounds. How much does Mr. Simpson weigh now?

Subtract to find how many pounds Mr. Simpson now weighs.

Regroup to get some tens.	Regroup again to get some ones.	Subtract.

H T O
1 10
2̸ 0̸ 0
−   5 6
	H T O
	  9 10
	1 1̸0̸
	2̸ 0̸ 0̸
	− 5 6
		H T O
		  9 10
		1 1̸0̸
		2̸ 0̸ 0̸
		− 5 6
		‗‗‗
		1 4 4

Regroup 2 hundreds, 0 tens as 1 hundred, 10 tens.

Regroup 10 tens, 0 ones as 9 tens, 10 ones.

Mr. Simpson now weighs 144 pounds.

FOCUS | Use NUMBER skills to subtract three-digit numbers, with and without regrouping.

GUIDED PRACTICE

Subtract. Sometimes you will need to regroup.

1.
```
   H | T | O
   5 | 7 | 9
-  3 | 6 | 5
   ▪ | ▪▪| ▪
```

2.
```
         H | T | O
             □
       2 | 5 | 15
       3 | 6 | 5
-        | 7 | 8
       ▪ | ▪▪| ▪
```

3.
```
       H | T | O
           □
       □ | □ | □
       8 | 0 | 0
-      1 | 4 | 9
       ▪ | ▪▪| ▪
```

PRACTICE

Do you need to regroup? Write *Y* or *N*. Subtract.

4. 368   5. 674   6. 829   7. 245   8. 796
  − 134   − 438   − 576   − 132   − 268

9. 700   10. 535   11. 900   12. 414   13. 600
  − 164   − 73   − 248   − 26   − 355

14. Ed weighs 56 pounds. His father weighs 194 pounds. How much more does his father weigh?

MIXED PRACTICE
Maintaining and Reviewing Skills

Add or subtract.

15. 10 − 7   16. 8 + 4   17. 13 − 5   18. 9 + 6   19. 16 − 7

CHALLENGE

Write the missing digits.

20. 54▪   21. 371   22. 4▪5   23. 6▪0   24. 9▪▪
   − 235   − 11▪   − ▪3▪   − ▪27   − 465
     ▪▪4   ▪▪8   251   18▪   ▪35

SUBTRACTION
Estimating Differences

Lisa buys a towel for $7.60. She gives the clerk $8.50. About how much money does she get back?

Estimate to find *about* how much she gets back.

Step 1: Round each amount to the nearest dollar.

$$
\begin{array}{rcr}
 & & \text{Estimate} \\
\$8.50 & \longrightarrow & \$9.00 \\
\$7.60 & \longrightarrow & -\ \$8.00 \\
\hline
\end{array}
$$

Step 2: Subtract the rounded amounts. $1.00

Lisa gets back *about* $1.00.

PRACTICE

Round each amount. Then estimate the difference.

1. $4.60 → ⬛ 5
   $1.30 → − ⬛
   ⬛ 4

2. $6.10 → ⬛ 6
   $3.70 → − ⬛ 4
   ⬛ 2

3. $5.80 → ⬛ 6
   $2.20 → − ⬛ 2
   ⬛ 4

Estimate to solve.

4. Bernardo has $3.60. He buys shampoo for $1.90. About how much does he have left?

5. Fran buys a brush for $4.50. She gives the clerk $7.00. About how much does she get back?

6. Ann buys soap for $2.10. She gives the clerk $3.50. About how much does she get back?

7. Roy has $9.20. He spends $6.60. About how much does he have left?

MIXED PRACTICE
Maintaining and Reviewing Skills

Add or subtract.

8. $15 - 6$ 9. $8 + 7$ 10. $11 - 4$ 11. $9 + 9$ 12. $13 - 9$

FOCUS | Use NUMBER skills and MEASUREMENT to estimate differences.

APPLICATION
Using a Calculator

ON/OFF key

Press ⬜ O once to turn the calculator on.
When you are finished, press ⬜ O to turn the calculator off.

CLEAR key

Press ⬜ C to erase a number on the display screen.

EQUAL key

Press ⬜ = to finish a problem. You will then see the answer on the display screen.

DISPLAY SCREEN
When you enter a number you will see it on the display screen.

13. Use a calculator to find the sum of 5 and 3.

● Turn the calculator ON. What do you see on the display screen?

● Press ⬜ 5 . What do you see on the display screen?

● Press ⬜ + . What do you see on the display screen?

● Press ⬜ 3 . What do you see on the display screen?

● Press ⬜ = . What do you see on the display screen?

● The sum of 5 and 3 is ■.

Enter each exercise into a calculator. Write the answer. Press CLEAR after you finish each exercise.

14. 2 + 3 = ■ **15.** 6 − 4 = ■ **16.** 9 + 5 = ■ **17.** 17 − 8 = ■ **18.** 7 + 6 = ■

Use a CALCULATOR to identify the keys on a calculator and to add and subtract using a calculator.

LOOKING BACK
Reviewing and Testing Chapter 5

In Chapter 5 you formulated problems about flamingos. Look at pages 56 and 57.

1. Write a sentence telling what a flamingo looks like.

You learned something new about subtracting two-digit numbers. To review what you learned, study the sample problem on page 58. Then use the new skill to find each difference for examples 2 to 12.

2. 36	3. 45	4. 33	5. 82	6. 73	7. 67
−14	−23	−17	−47	−54	−43

8. 52 − 9   9. 74 − 38   10. 26 − 17   11. 39 − 22   12. 94 − 59

You have learned how to READ and KNOW to solve problems. To review what you learned, look at pages 62 and 63. Find the **key facts.** Do not solve the problem.

13. Ellie was on vacation for 2 weeks. She left home on July 1. She drove 1,025 miles from Chicago to Denver. What date did Ellie arrive home?

You learned something new about subtracting three-digit numbers. To review, look at pages 64 and 65. Then use the new skill to find each difference for examples 14 to 23.

14. 763	15. 417	16. 596	17. 196	18. 982	19. 217
−152	−308	−377	− 78	−873	− 86

20. 676 − 83   21. 832 − 619   22. 388 − 92   23. 409 − 120

FOCUS | Review and test skills learned and practiced.

LOOKING AHEAD
Preparing for New Skills for Chapter 6

In the next chapter you will focus on

- formulating problems.
- centimeters and meters.
- estimating measures.
- statistics and probability.
- finding area.
- area and perimeter.
- geometry and patterns.
- math in science.

Learning about centimeters and meters will be easier if you review what you know about length. Study the model. Review the facts about metric measurement on page 426 in the Data Bank. Then complete the PRACTICE exercises. Review the model if you need to.

Model
Centimeters and **meters** are used to measure the length of objects.

A **centimeter** is used to measure the length of short objects. Use a centimeter to measure the length of a book.

A **meter** is used to measure the length of long objects. Use a meter to measure the length of a bookshelf.

PRACTICE

Write whether each object is *long* or *short*. Then write whether you would use *centimeters* or *meters* to measure each length.

1. an airplane

2. a sneaker

3. a bridge

4. your desk

5. a baseball bat

6. your thumb

7. a fence

8. a worm

9. a ladder

Review MEASUREMENT in preparation for learning a new skill.

Formulate problems using picture cues, text, and data.

CHAPTER **6**

Measurement of Length and Area

DATA

Time spent working in garden

| Per day | 1 period |
| Per week | 2 days |

Dimensions of garden

| Length | 30 feet |
| Width | 30 feet |

Number of sections in garden — 4

Plants grown in each section

Beans
Peas
Tomatoes
Flowers

There was a vacant lot across the street from the Lincoln School. The students in the third grade class thought it would be a good idea to start a garden there. Their teacher helped them get permission from the town to use the lot. A garden supply store donated seeds, fertilizer, and some tools.

As soon as the weather was warm enough, the class started to work on the garden. They spent one period a day, two days a week, working in the garden. The garden was 30 feet long and 30 feet wide. They divided the garden into four sections—one for beans, one for peas, one for tomatoes, and one for flowers.

What problems might the students have solved? What problems might the teacher have solved? Draw a picture to show how they might have divided the garden into parts.

MEASUREMENT
Measuring in Centimeters and Meters

Centimeters and **meters** are units used to measure length.

A centimeter is about as wide as a large paper clip.

We measure short lengths in centimeters.

100 centimeters = 1 meter

A meter is about as long as a baseball bat.

Meters are used to measure long lengths.

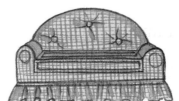

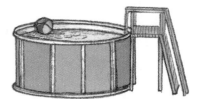

1 centimeter

cm stands for centimeter   **m** stands for meter

GUIDED PRACTICE

Choose *centimeters* or *meters* as the better unit for finding the length of each object.

1.    2.    3.

4. a pen   5. a playground   6. a truck

FOCUS   Use MEASUREMENT to find length.

PRACTICE

Use your centimeter ruler to find each length.

7.

▦ cm

8.

▦ cm

9.

▦ cm

Choose the better answer.

10. The height of a flagpole is about ■.

10 meters   10 centimeters

11. The length of a book is about ■.

25 centimeters   2 meters

12. The width of a door is about ■.

5 centimeters   1 meter

13. The length of a car is about ■.

4 meters   40 centimeters

MIXED PRACTICE
Maintaining and Reviewing Skills

Add or subtract.

14. $24 + 36$ 15. $92 - 63$ 16. $508 + 396$ 17. $871 - 348$ 18. $460 - 135$

CHALLENGE

19. The Kickers began on their own goal line and moved the ball 50 meters down the soccer field. The field is 100 meters long. How far must they go to score a goal?

EXTRA PRACTICE—page 419

MEASUREMENT
Estimating Length

When you measure *about* how long an object is, you make an **estimate.**

The length of the butterfly is between 9 and 10 centimeters. It is closer to 10 cm. We **estimate** that the length is *about* 10 cm.

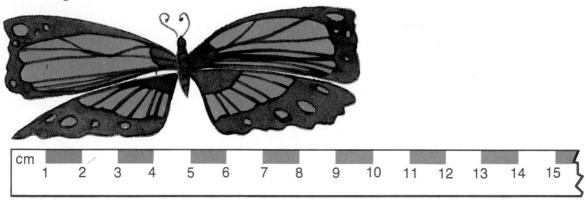

PRACTICE

Use a centimeter ruler to estimate each length.

1. The caterpillar is about ■ cm long.

2. The beetle is about ■ cm long.

3. The grasshopper is about ■ cm long.

MIXED PRACTICE
Maintaining and Reviewing Skills

Add or subtract.

4. $19 - 12$ **5.** $35 + 8$ **6.** $763 - 204$ **7.** $355 + 35$ **8.** $609 - 54$

FOCUS   Use MEASUREMENT to estimate length.

74

APPLICATION

Using Statistics and Probability

9. Measure the right hand of five classmates. Estimate each length to the nearest centimeter. Then make a bar graph to show the lengths of your classmates' hands. Your graph might look something like this:

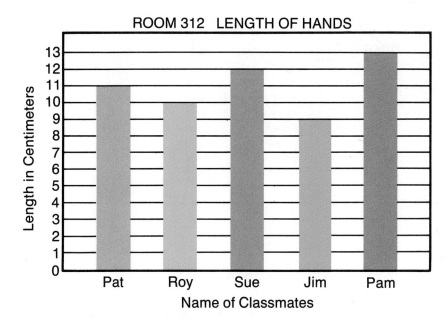

ROOM 312   LENGTH OF HANDS

Use your bar graph to answer the questions.

10. Who has the longest hand?

11. Who has the shortest hand?

12. What is the sum of the lengths of your classmates' hands?

13. What is the difference in length between the longest and the shortest hands?

14. Write the lengths of hands in order from longest to shortest.

Use STATISTICS AND PROBABILITY to make a bar graph.

Finding Area

Mr. James is using square tiles to cover a kitchen wall.

Square units are used to measure the inside or **area** of a flat shape.

The **area** of this rectangle is shaded.

This is a square centimeter.

Five square centimeters can cover this shape.

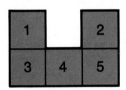
The area of this shape is 5 square centimeters.

GUIDED PRACTICE

Find the area of each object. Count the square centimeters.

1.

1	2	3	4
5	6	7	8

2.
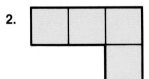

3.
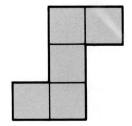

FOCUS | Use MEASUREMENT to find area.

76

PRACTICE

Find the area. Count the square centimeters.

4.

5.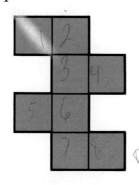

6.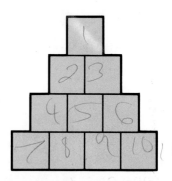

7.

8.

9.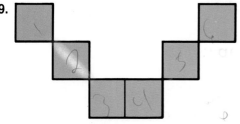

10.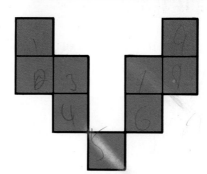

MIXED PRACTICE

Maintaining and Reviewing Skills

Add or subtract.

| 11. 52
+39 | 12. 26
+44 | 13. 76
−55 | 14. 53
−34 | 15. 27
+16 | 16. 44
−19 |

CHALLENGE

17. Draw different figures with an area of 12 square centimeters.

MEASUREMENT

Finding Area and Perimeter

Every shape has both an **area** and a **perimeter**.

The area of this window is 6 square centimeters.

The perimeter of the window is 10 centimeters.

The perimeter is the distance around the window.

$2 + 3 + 2 + 3 = 10$

PRACTICE

Give the area in square centimeters and the perimeter in centimeters.

1.   2.   3. 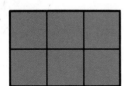   4.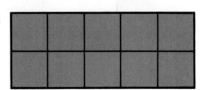

5. 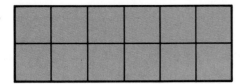   6.

MIXED PRACTICE

Maintaining and Reviewing Skills

Add or subtract.

7. $9 + 7$ **8.** $17 - 8$ **9.** $35 + 62$ **10.** $94 - 25$ **11.** $43 + 18$

APPLICATION
Using Geometry and Patterns

Each shape has two numbers **above** it. One number is the perimeter of the shape. One number is the area of the shape. Fill in the blanks with either *perimeter* or *area*. Then write the label, *centimeters* or *square centimeters*.

12. The ■ = 15 ■. The ■ = 18 ■. **13.** The ■ = 22 ■. The ■ = 18 ■.

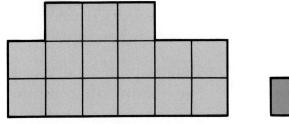 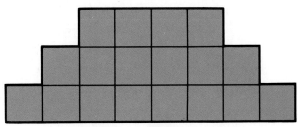

14. The ■ = 18 ■. The ■ = 6 ■. **15.** The ■ = 20 ■. The ■ = 13 ■.

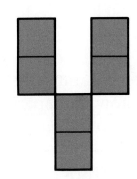 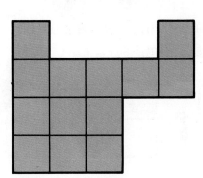

16. This shape grew. Can you draw the next size?

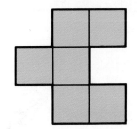 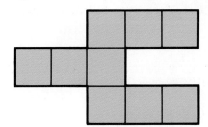

Use GEOMETRY and PATTERNS to distinguish between area and perimeter.

Seeds

Most plants begin their life as seeds. When there is enough soil, water, and sun, a seed will sprout, and a new little plant will begin to grow. The new plant will form seeds and the cycle will begin again.

If all the seeds of a plant grew in the same place, there would not be enough soil and water for them.

Seeds use many ways to travel to new places. Maple tree seeds have wings that can be carried by the wind. Some seeds are pushed out by their pods. Violet seeds leave the plant this way.

This young coconut plant sends leaves up and roots down from its large seed. When a coconut falls off a tree into water, it can float to a place where it can grow.

Gardeners plan where to put seeds. They know that different kinds of seeds grow best at a certain distance from each other.

The chart tells how to plant some seeds. Two distances are given. The first tells how far apart the rows of seeds must be. The second tells how far apart each seed should be from the next seed.

CRITICAL THINKING

Look at the chart on page 81.

1. Which two vegetables need the most growing space?

2. Why do you think that these vegetables need more space?

3. Which two vegetables need the least growing space? Why?

These strawberry plants use runners as well as seed-bearing fruit to insure new plant growth.

PLANTING DIRECTIONS		
Vegetable	Inches Between	
	Rows	Seeds
Brussels sprouts	24 inches	18 inches
Cucumber	48 inches	48 inches
Cauliflower	24 inches	15 inches
Eggplant	24 inches	24 inches
Tomato	36 inches	48 inches

LOOKING BACK
Reviewing and Testing Chapter 6

In Chapter 6 you formulated problems about planting a garden. Look at pages 70 and 71.

1. Write a sentence telling what you might plant in your garden.

You learned something new about measuring length with centimeters and meters. To review what you learned, study the sample problem on page 72. Then use the new skill to find the proper unit to measure length for examples 2 to 13.

2. pencil

3. wall

4. your height

5. key

6. paint brush

7. car

8. shoe

9. eraser

10. door

11. flagpole

12. fire engine

13. book

You learned something new about finding area. To review, look at pages 76 and 77. Then use the new skill to find the area for examples 14 to 16.

14.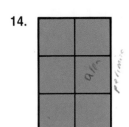

15.

16.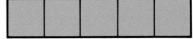

You learned about seeds. Look at page 80 to review what you learned.

17. Why is it important to space seeds properly when planting?

LOOKING AHEAD
Preparing for New Skills for Chapter 7

In the next chapter you will focus on

- formulating problems.
- grams and kilograms.
- milliliters and liters.

- finding volume.
- choosing an appropriate unit of measurement.

New measurement skills will be easier to learn if you brush up on the measurement skills that you already know. Study Models A and B. You can review the facts about metric measurement on page 426 in the Data Bank. Complete the PRACTICE exercises. Check your work with the models.

Model A
Grams and **kilograms** are used to measure the mass of objects. A paper clip has a mass of about 1 gram.

Model B
Milliliters and **liters** are used to measure how much liquid is in a container. A milk bottle holds about 1 liter.

PRACTICE

What is being measured? Write *mass* or *liquid*.

1. How much does a jar hold?

2. How heavy is a suitcase?

3. How light is a feather?

4. How much is in that glass?

5. How much juice is in the can?

6. How many grams is the pencil?

7. How much meat is in the freezer?

8. How many liters are in the bottle?

9. How many milliliters of juice are in the can?

10. How many kilograms is the crate of books?

Review MEASUREMENT in preparation for learning a new skill.

CHAPTER 7

Measurement of Mass and Capacity

DATA

Dates	February 16–19
Days	Wednesday–Saturday
Place	Sugar Falls
Predicted snowfall	25 inches
Actual snowfall	38 inches
Temperature	20°F
Wind	40 miles per hour
Windchill factor	−21°F
Checklist	Milk Bread Candles Sweaters Boots

A blizzard is a harsh snowstorm. Strong winds blow, and heavy snow falls. Winds of over 30 miles per hour bring cold temperatures. As much as 30 inches of snow can fall. It's not safe to go outside during a dangerous snowstorm. It can trap you inside for days. Most schools and offices close when there is a blizzard.

During a blizzard, the temperature can drop below 20°F, and the wind can gust to 40 miles per hour. This makes the air feel like it's 21°F below zero. That's enough to keep anyone indoors.

When the weather report forecasts a blizzard, you need to prepare for it. Look at the data on this page. What problems would you have to solve during this kind of weather?

MEASUREMENT
Using Grams and Kilograms

Grams and **kilograms** are used to measure mass.

A leaf has a mass of about
1 gram.

A small branch has a mass of about
1 kilogram.

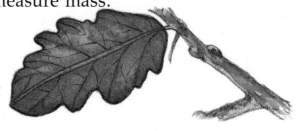

kg stands for kilogram.   **g** stands for gram.

Use grams to measure the mass of light things.

1 000 grams = 1 kilogram

Use kilograms to measure the mass of heavy things.

GUIDED PRACTICE

Choose *grams* or *kilograms* to measure mass.

1.    2.    3.

4.    5.    6.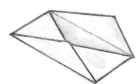

FOCUS | Use MEASUREMENT to measure mass in grams or kilograms.

PRACTICE

Choose *grams* or *kilograms* to measure the mass of each object.

7. 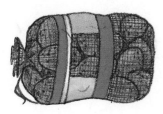   8.    9.

10. a pencil   11. a chair   12. a button

Choose the better answer.

13. The mass of a sparrow is about

     100 g   100 kg

14. The mass of a table is about

     300 g   30 kg

15. The mass of a pen is about

     500 g   50 g

16. The mass of a pan is about

     10 kg   1 kg

MIXED PRACTICE
Maintaining and Reviewing Skills

Choose *centimeters* or *meters* to measure the length of each object.

17. a truck   18. a worm   19. a light bulb

20. a whale   21. a kitchen   22. a cucumber

CHALLENGE

23. Hassan stood on a scale holding his bookbag. The scale showed 81 kilograms. Hassan knows he has a mass of 75 kilograms. His shoes have a mass of 1 kilogram. What is the mass of his bookbag?

EXTRA PRACTICE—page 419

MEASUREMENT
Using Liters and Milliliters

Milliliter and **liter** are used to measure amounts of liquid.

Five drops of water are about 1 milliliter.

A pitcher of milk is about 1 liter.

mL stands for milliliter.

L stands for liter.

1 000 milliliters = 1 liter

PRACTICE

Choose the better answer.

1.

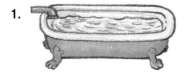

milliliter

liter

2.

milliliter

liter

3.

milliliter

liter

4. A bowl of soup is about

    300 mL   300 L

5. A can of paint is about

    2 L 2 mL

6. The water in a fish bowl is about

    3 mL 3 L

MIXED PRACTICE
Maintaining and Reviewing Skills

Choose *grams* or *kilograms* to measure mass.

7. a crayon

8. a watermelon

9. a flower

FOCUS   Use MEASUREMENT to identify liter and milliliter.

APPLICATION
Using Measurement

Choose the appropriate unit of measure.

10.

centimeter

liter

gram

11.

milliliter

centimeter

kilogram

12.

kilogram

meter

liter

13.

kilogram

liter

gram

14.

milliliter

gram

meter

15.

milliliter

gram

centimeter

Choose the appropriate unit of measure. Write
centimeter, meter, liter, or *kilogram.*

16. Jack and Ann want to find out who has the longest pencil. Which unit of measure will they use?

17. Two third grade classrooms bought new aquariums. Which unit of measure did they use to fill the tanks?

18. If you wanted to measure your classroom, which unit of measure would you use?

19. The science class found the mass of apples and pumpkins. Which unit of measure did they use?

Use MEASUREMENT to choose the appropriate unit of measure.

MEASUREMENT
Finding Volume

Cubic units are used to measure volume.

1 cubic unit

Volume is the number of cubic units needed to fill a space.

This box contains 3 cubic units.

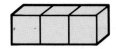

The volume of the box is 3 cubic units.

Jen filled a shoebox with blocks.

The volume of the shoebox is 10 cubic units.

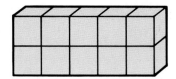

GUIDED PRACTICE

Find each volume. Give the number of cubic units.

1.

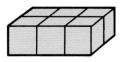

6 cubic units

2.

3.

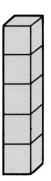

4.

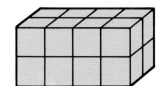

FOCUS   Use MEASUREMENT to find volume in cubic units.

PRACTICE

Give each volume in cubic units.

5.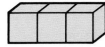

6.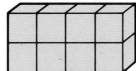

7.

8.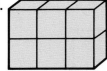

9.

10.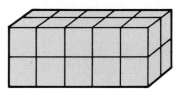

11.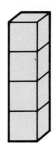

12.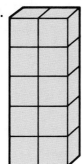

13.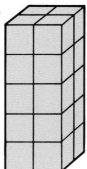

14.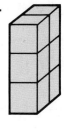

MIXED PRACTICE
Maintaining and Reviewing Skills

Add or subtract.

15. $17 + 12$ **16.** $98 - 23$ **17.** $146 - 132$ **18.** $650 + 152$ **19.** $706 - 536$

CHALLENGE

Give each volume in cubic units.

20.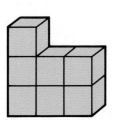

21.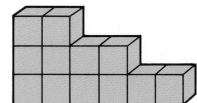

MEASUREMENT

Finding Volume in Cubic Centimeters

Cubic centimeters are used to measure **volume.**

1 cubic centimeter

The volume of this box is 8 cubic centimeters.

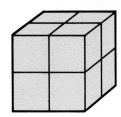

PRACTICE

Give each volume in cubic centimeters.

1.
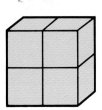

2.
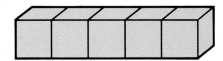

3.
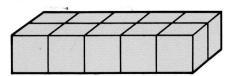

4.
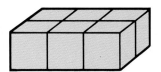

MIXED PRACTICE

Maintaining and Reviewing Skills

Choose *milliliters* or *liters* to measure the amount of liquid.

5. a teaspoon of juice   6. a jar of water   7. a cup of milk

FOCUS   Use MEASUREMENT to find volume in cubic centimeters.

APPLICATION
Using Measurement

Choose the correct unit of measure.

8. Kathleen poured herself a glass of apple juice from the liter jug. How much juice did she drink?

   250 centimeters   250 milliliters   250 grams

9. Sylvester built a fence around his garden. How long was his fence?

   30 grams   30 cubic centimeters   30 meters

10. Nona couldn't move the rock. What was its mass?

   800 kilograms   800 square meters   800 liters

11. Manuel filled the bucket at the pump. How much water will he carry?

   6 liters   6 grams   6 meters

12. Jo used her building blocks to build something. What is its volume?

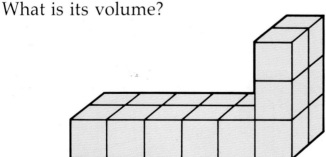

   16 grams   16 cubic centimeters   16 liters

Use MEASUREMENT to choose the appropriate unit of measure.

LOOKING BACK
Reviewing and Testing Chapter 7

In Chapter 7 you formulated problems about a blizzard. Look at pages 84 and 85.

1. Write a sentence telling how the wind affects the temperature.

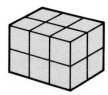

You learned something new about finding mass in grams or kilograms. To review what you learned, study the sample problem on page 86. Then use the new skill to find the proper unit to measure mass for examples 2 to 9.

2. dog

3. paperclip

4. bowling ball

5. feather

6. pen

7. brick

8. plate

9. stamp

You learned something new about finding volume in cubic units. To review, look at pages 90 and 91. Then use the new skill to find the volume for examples 10 to 15.

10.

11.

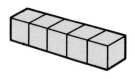

12.

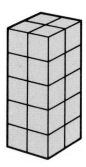

13.

14.

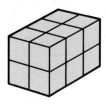

15.

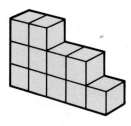

LOOKING AHEAD

Preparing for New Skills for Chapter 8

In the next chapter you will focus on

- formulating problems.
- exploring solid figures.
- using patterns and functions.

- identifying congruent figures.
- identifying similar figures.
- how math is used in art.

New geometry skills will be easier to learn if you brush up on skills you already know. Study Models A and B. Then complete the PRACTICE exercises. Review the models if you need to.

Model A

circle

square

triangle

rectangle

Model B

cube

cone

sphere

cylinder

PRACTICE

Write the name of each figure. Review Models A and B if you need to.

1.

2.

3.

4.

5.

6.

7.

8.

Review GEOMETRY in preparation for learning a new skill.

QUARTERLY REVIEW/TEST

Write the letter of the correct answer.

Add or subtract.

1. $7 + 5$
   A. 2   B. 35   C. 13   D. 12

2. $9 + 8$
   E. 17   F. 16   G. 1   H. 18

3. $6 + 7$
   A. 1   B. 13   C. 12   D. 14

4. $16 - 7$
   E. 23   F. 11   G. 9   H. 8

5. $17 - 9$
   A. 9   B. 26   C. 11   D. 8

6. $14 - 6$
   E. 8   F. 10   G. 20   H. 9

What is the number?

7. eighty-five
   A. 35   B. 58   C. 48   D. 85

8. 4 tens, 6 ones
   E. 61   F. 46   G. 31   H. 64

9. nine hundred twenty-three
   A. 293   B. 923   C. 329   D. 239

10. 4 hundreds, 0 tens, 1 one
    E. 401   F. 41   G. 104   H. 14

What is the value?

11. 1 dime, 1 quarter
    A. 10¢   B. 35¢   C. 25¢   D. 50¢

12. 1 nickel, 1 dime, 1 penny
    E. 51¢   F. 3¢   G. 21¢   H. 16¢

13. 3 dollars, 2 quarters, 1 dime
    A. $3.21   B. $3.30   C. $3.60   D. $3.51

14. 5 dollars, 6 dimes, 10 pennies
    E. $5.61   F. $5.70   G. $5.10   H. $5.60

Round to the nearest 10.

15. 48
    A. 50   B. 70   C. 80   D. 40

16. 25
    E. 20   F. 50   G. 60   H. 30

17. 73
    A. 60   B. 80   C. 70   D. 30

Round to the nearest 100.

18. 840
    E. 900   F. 400   G. 700   H. 800

19. 391
    A. 100   B. 200   C. 400   D. 300

20. 754
    E. 800   F. 400   G. 500   H. 700

FOCUS   Review concepts and skills taught in Chapters 2 to 7.

96

Add or subtract.

21. 64
    +23
      A. 41   B. 77
      C. 87   D. 47

22. 257
    + 19
      E. 266   F. 276
      G. 366   H. 238

23. 99
    −47
      A. 52   B. 32
      C. 58   D. 47

24. 32
    − 8
      E. 34   F. 40
      G. 22   H. 24

25. 706
    −543
      A. 263   B. 163
      C. 309   D. 243

What is the correct unit of measure?

26. the length of a bus
      E. cm   F. kg   G. m   H. g

27. the mass of a horse
      A. kg   B. cm   C. g   D. m

28. the length of a book
      E. m   F. mL   G. g   H. cm

29. the water in a bathtub
      A. m   B. L   C. mL   D. cm

30. the mass of a leaf
      E. g   F. cm   G. kg   H. mL

31. the juice in a glass
      A. cm   B. mL   C. g   D. L

What is the area?

32.
      E. 4 cubic units
      F. 8 square units
      G. 4 square units
      H. 8 cubic units

33.
      A. 3 cubic units
      B. 6 square units
      C. 6 cubic units
      D. 3 square units

What is the volume?

34.
      E. 4 cubic units
      F. 2 square units
      G. 4 square units
      H. 2 cubic units

35.
      A. 12 cubic units
      B. 6 cubic units
      C. 12 square units
      D. 6 square units

Solve each problem.

36. Ralph's mass is 36 kg. Pearl's mass is 42 kg. How much heavier is Pearl?
      E. 8 kg F. 4 kg G. 6 kg H. 78 kg

37. Lonny read 46 pages today and 28 pages yesterday. How many pages did he read in all?
      A. 62 pages   B. 18 pages
      C. 72 pages   D. 74 pages

FOCUS Formulate problems using picture cues, text, and data.

Geometry

DATA

Event	Costume party
Activity	Planning a costume
Today's date	October 21
Party's date	October 22
Planners	Lisa Roberta

Things they found in closets

- Skating outfit
- Baggy pants
- Ballet slippers
- Rubber nose
- Orange wig
- Crown
- Striped shirt
- Magic wand
- Suspenders
- White gloves
- Pointed hat

Parties are fun, but costume parties are something special! A guest at a costume party may see a robot, a comic book character, and a dancing pineapple all in one moment. Costumes can be bought in a store, or they can be made from things found at home.

Lisa was invited to a costume party. She forgot all about it until the day before! Her sister, Roberta, had gone to many costume parties. Roberta offered to help Lisa come up with an idea. Using the data and the picture, think about why it might not be easy to put together a costume. What problems might Lisa and Roberta have? Predict how Lisa's costume will turn out. Draw a picture of how you think Lisa will look at the party. Be sure to use the data.

GEOMETRY
Exploring Solid Figures

Here are some solid geometric figures.

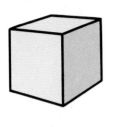   

Cube   **Cylinder**   **Cone**   **Sphere**

A cube has 6 flat surfaces or **faces**.
Two faces of a cube meet at an **edge**.
The edges of a cube meet at a **corner**.

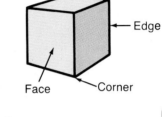

A cylinder has 1 **curved surface** and 2 **faces**.
A cylinder has no edges or corners.

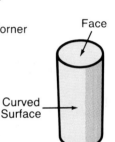

GUIDED PRACTICE

Write the name of the shape of each object.

1.

2.

3.

4.

5.

6.

PRACTICE

Copy and complete the chart. Then answer the questions.

	7.	8.	9.	10.
Curved surfaces	0	1	1	1
Faces	6	2	1	0
Edges	12	0	0	0
Corners				

11. Which figure has only flat surfaces?

12. Which figure has only a curved surface?

13. Which figures have flat and curved surfaces?

MIXED PRACTICE
Maintaining and Reviewing Skills

Add or subtract.

14. $17 + 12$ **15.** $38 - 16$ **16.** $562 + 219$ **17.** $793 - 355$ **18.** $340 + 78$

CHALLENGE

19. Name the solid figure that the folded pattern forms.

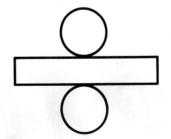

EXTRA PRACTICE—page 419

GEOMETRY
Recognizing Plane Figures Within Solid Figures

The face of a solid figure is a **plane figure.**

Each face of a cube is a **square.**   The face of a cone is a **circle.**

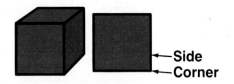

-Side
-Corner

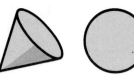

No corners
No sides

PRACTICE

Write the name of each figure. Then write the number of sides and corners each figure has.

1.   2.   3.   4.

Write the shape of the face of each solid figure.

5.   6.   7.

8. If a sphere is cut in half, what is the shape of each face?

MIXED PRACTICE
Maintaining and Reviewing Skills

Write the number of sides and corners.   Write the number of edges, corners, and faces.

9.   10.   11.   12.

FOCUS   Use GEOMETRY to recognize plane figures within solid figures.

102

APPLICATION
Using Patterns and Functions

Draw the next figure in the pattern.

13.

14.

15.

16.

Write the next figure in the pattern.

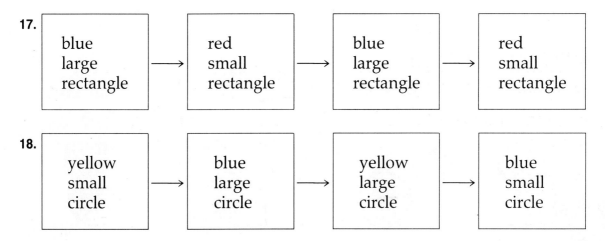

17.
| blue large rectangle | → | red small rectangle | → | blue large rectangle | → | red small rectangle |

18.
| yellow small circle | → | blue large circle | → | yellow large circle | → | blue small circle |

Use PATTERNS AND FUNCTIONS to extend geometric patterns.

GEOMETRY
Identifying Congruent Figures

If the two circles were cut out, they would fit exactly on top of each other.

Congruent circles

When two plane figures are the exact same size and shape they are **congruent** to each other.

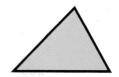 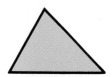

Congruent triangles

These two squares are not congruent. They are not the same size.

These two figures are not congruent. They are not the same shape.

GUIDED PRACTICE

Are the two figures congruent? Write *Y* (yes) or *N* (no).

1.

2.

3.  (large circle)

4.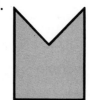

PRACTICE

Choose the figure in each group which is congruent
to the first figure in the row.

5.   a.    b.   c.

6.   a.   b.   c.

7.   a.   b.   c.

8. 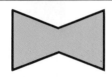   a.    b.    c.

9. Congruent figures are the same ▇ and ▇.

MIXED PRACTICE
Maintaining and Reviewing Skills

Write the name of each figure.

10.   11.    12.   13.

CHALLENGE

14. Trace the square. Draw two
    lines to divide the square into
    4 congruent triangles.

GEOMETRY
Identifying Similar Figures

Similar figures are always the exact same shape but not always the same size.

PRACTICE

Choose the two similar figures in each row.

1. a.   b.   c.   d.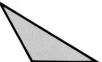

2. a.   b.   c.    d.

3. a.   b.   c.   d.

4. a.   b.   c.   d.

5. Similar figures have the same ■ but not always the same ■.

MIXED PRACTICE
Maintaining and Reviewing Skills

Are the two figures congruent? Write *Y* or *N*.

6.   7.

APPLICATION
Using Patterns

These are pictures of **tiling patterns.** The shapes fit together with no space between them.

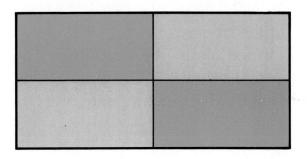 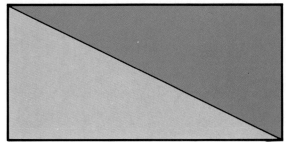

Copy and color each tiling pattern.

8.
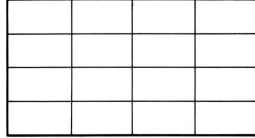

9.
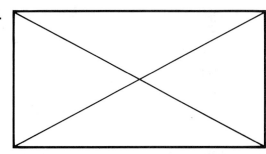

10.
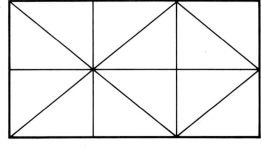

11.
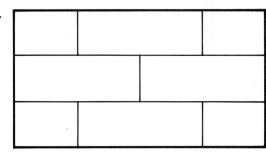

12.
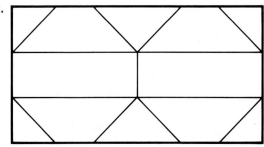

13.
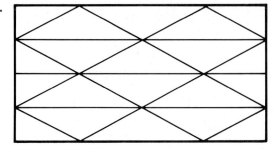

Use GEOMETRY to recognize tiling patterns.

Beadwork Patterns

Some American Indians used wampum beads as money. Wampum beads are white and purple. They are made from clam shells. Wampum was also woven into belts that were given as presents at peace parties.

Today, glass beads are used to decorate shirts, moccasins, bags, and knife cases. The designs often have special meanings.

Squares, rectangles, triangles, and other shapes were used. A design might be copied in different parts of the pattern, or repeated many times in a row. The Indians had to count and measure carefully.

The Washington Covenant belt was used for the peace treaty between the six nations of the Iroquois Confederacy and the thirteen colonies. The figure of a person is repeated many times.

The Hiawatha belt is a record of the Iroquois League of Nations, formed about the year 1570. The design below is in the center. What shapes are on either side of it?

CRITICAL THINKING

1. Look at the Washington Covenant belt. How many figures are on the left side and on the right side of the house?

2. Look at the Hiawatha belt. How many rectangles are there?

3. Look at the To-Ta-Da-Ho belt. If an imaginary line were drawn across the middle of the diamond shape, what shape would be formed twice?

FOCUS   Understanding PATTERNS and shapes in designs.

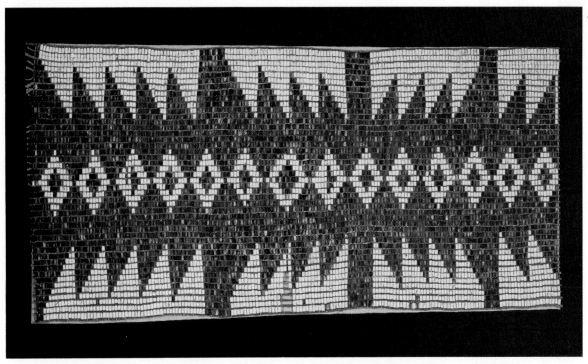

The To-Ta-Da-Ho belt was made by the Onondaga tribe of New York.

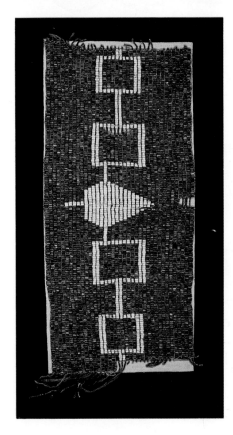

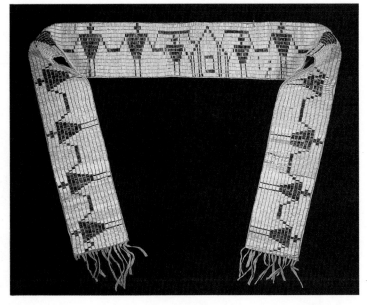

The Iroquois used the color white to represent peace and health, as shown in the Washington Covenant belt above.

This belt is named for the hero, Hiawatha. The purple beads show that it is an important article.

LOOKING BACK

Reviewing and Testing Chapter 8

In Chapter 8 you formulated problems about costume parties. Look at pages 98 and 99.

1. Draw a picture of a costume you would like to wear.

You learned something new about exploring solid figures. To review what you learned, study the sample problem on page 100. Then use the new skill to write the name of each shape for examples 2 to 5.

2.   3.    4.    5.

You learned something new about identifying congruent figures. To review, look at pages 104 and 105. Then use the new skill to write if the two figures in examples 6 to 9 are congruent.

6.

7.

8.

9.

You learned about beadwork patterns. Look at page 108 to review the patterns.

10. Draw your own beaded belt with a pattern.

FOCUS   Review and test skills learned and practiced.

LOOKING AHEAD
Preparing for New Skills for Chapter 9

In the next chapter you will focus on

- formulating problems.
- multiplying twos.
- statistics and probability.

- a problem-solving strategy.
- multiplying threes.
- multiplying money.

New multiplication skills will be easier to learn if you brush up on the addition skills you already know. Study the model. Then complete the PRACTICE exercises. Check your work with the model.

Model
There are 6 glasses. Each glass has 2 straws. How many straws are there in all?

$$2 + 2 + 2 + 2 + 2 + 2 = 12$$

There are 12 straws in all.

PRACTICE

Complete. Review the model if you need to.

1.

   $2 + 2 = \blacksquare$

2.

   $3 + 3 + 3 = \blacksquare$

3.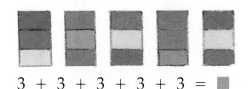

   $3 + 3 + 3 + 3 + 3 = \blacksquare$

4.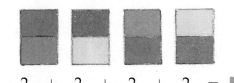

   $2 + 2 + 2 + 2 = \blacksquare$

Review NUMBER skills in preparation for learning a new skill.

Formulate problems using picture cues, text, and data.

CHAPTER 9

Multiplication Facts for Twos and Threes

DATA

Game	Hide-and-Seek
Place	Joy's house
Players	Joy
	Carol
	Bradley
	Steven
"It"	Bradley
Home base	Piano
Hiding places	Storeroom
	Garden
	Hall closet
	Coat closet
	Kitchen table

All players but "It" hide when the game of hide-and-seek is played. "It" counts to 100 and then looks for the other players. These hidden players leave their hiding places when the "coast is clear." They try to return to "home base," a place or thing that they have agreed on.

There are many places to hide. The data tell you what choices Joy and her friends have. Using the picture and the data, try to guess which hiding places are good ones and which are not. Remember that a good player keeps still and only leaves his or her hiding place when "It" is not nearby.

What do you think will happen when "It" goes looking for the other players? What problems might Joy and her friends face?

MULTIPLICATION
Multiplying Twos

Lisa has 4 pairs of socks. There are 2 socks in each pair.

Count by twos to find how many socks in all.

2 . . . 4 . . . 6 . . . 8 socks in all

Or add to find how many socks in all.

2 + 2 + 2 + 2 = 8 socks in all

Or **multiply** to find the total number of socks.

4 twos are 8:   4 × 2   =   8
                   ↑   ↑
         4 **times** 2 **is equal to** 8

There are 8 socks in all.

There are two ways to write a multiplication fact.

4	×	2	=	8		2 ← **Factor**
↑		↑		↑		×4 ← **Factor**
Factor		**Factor**		**Product**		8 ← **Product**

2	2	2	2	2	2	2	2	2
×1	×2	×3	×4	×5	×6	×7	×8	×9
2	4	6	8	10	12	14	16	18

GUIDED PRACTICE

Multiply to find how many there are in all.

1.

2 + 2 = 4
2 × 2 = 4

2.

2 + 2 + 2 + 2 + 2 = 10
5 × 2 = ■

3.

2 + 2 + 2 = ■
3 × 2 = ■

FOCUS   Use NUMBER skills to multiply twos.

114

PRACTICE

Find how many in all.

4. $2 + 2 + 2 + 2 + 2 + 2 + 2$
7×2

5. $2 + 2 + 2 + 2 + 2 + 2$
6×2

Write the factors and the product.

6. $1 \times 2 = 2$ **7.** $4 \times 2 = 8$ **8.** $5 \times 2 = 10$

9. $\begin{array}{r} 2 \\ \times 9 \\ \hline 18 \end{array}$ **10.** $\begin{array}{r} 2 \\ \times 8 \\ \hline 16 \end{array}$

Find each product.

11. 2×2 **12.** 1×2 **13.** 7×2 **14.** 5×2 **15.** 9×2

16. $\begin{array}{r} 2 \\ \times 3 \\ \hline \end{array}$ **17.** $\begin{array}{r} 2 \\ \times 9 \\ \hline \end{array}$ **18.** $\begin{array}{r} 2 \\ \times 6 \\ \hline \end{array}$ **19.** $\begin{array}{r} 2 \\ \times 5 \\ \hline \end{array}$ **20.** $\begin{array}{r} 2 \\ \times 8 \\ \hline \end{array}$ **21.** $\begin{array}{r} 2 \\ \times 4 \\ \hline \end{array}$

Solve each problem.

22. Bobby's closet has 3 shelves. There are 2 sweaters on each shelf. How many sweaters does Bobby have?

23. There are 4 pegs on the wall. There are 2 coats on each peg. How many coats are there?

MIXED PRACTICE
Maintaining and Reviewing Skills

Add, subtract, or multiply.

24. 3×2 **25.** 5×2 **26.** 1×2 **27.** $5 + 4$ **28.** $8 - 4$

29. $\begin{array}{r} 2 \\ \times 6 \\ \hline \end{array}$ **30.** $\begin{array}{r} 7 \\ +6 \\ \hline \end{array}$ **31.** $\begin{array}{r} 12 \\ -\ 9 \\ \hline \end{array}$ **32.** $\begin{array}{r} 45 \\ +21 \\ \hline \end{array}$ **33.** $\begin{array}{r} 35 \\ -22 \\ \hline \end{array}$ **34.** $\begin{array}{r} 2 \\ \times 9 \\ \hline \end{array}$

CHALLENGE

Complete the multiplication sentences.

35. $6 \times 2 = \blacksquare$ $2 \times \blacksquare = 12$

36. $2 \times 9 = \blacksquare$ $9 \times \blacksquare = 18$

MULTIPLICATION
Multiplying Twos

Kelly has 3 boxes of cars. Each box has 2 cars. How many cars does Kelly have in all?

Multiply to find how many cars Kelly has in all.

$3 \times 2 = 6$

Kelly has 6 cars in all.

Debra has 2 boxes of cars. Each box has 3 cars. Do Debra and Kelly have the same number of cars?

$2 \times 3 = 6$

**The order of the factors can change.
The product will be the same.**

$3 \times 2 = 2 \times 3$

Debra and Kelly have the same number of cars.

PRACTICE

Find each product.

1. 4×2
   2×4

2. 1×2
   2×1

3. 5×2
   2×5

4. 7×2
   2×7

5. 6×2
   2×6

6. $\begin{array}{cc} 2 & 3 \\ \times 3 & \times 2 \end{array}$

7. $\begin{array}{cc} 2 & 8 \\ \times 8 & \times 2 \end{array}$

8. $\begin{array}{cc} 2 & 1 \\ \times 1 & \times 2 \end{array}$

9. $\begin{array}{cc} 2 & 9 \\ \times 9 & \times 2 \end{array}$

MIXED PRACTICE
Maintaining and Reviewing Skills

Add, subtract, or multiply.

10. 4×2

11. 9×2

12. 2×5

13. $7 + 6$

14. $18 - 5$

| FOCUS | Use NUMBER skills to multiply twos. |

APPLICATION

Using Statistics and Probability

This is a **picture graph.** It shows the number of cars parked on the streets of Ellenville.

PARKED CARS IN ELLENVILLE

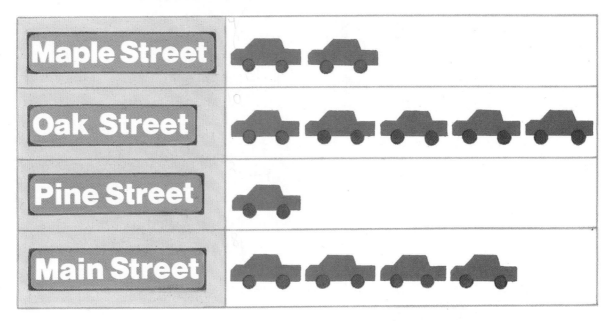

Each  stands for 2 cars.

Use the picture graph to answer the questions.

15. How many cars does each picture stand for?

16. Which streets are cars parked on?

17. How many cars are parked on Maple Street?

18. How many cars are parked on Main Street?

19. Which street has 10 cars parked on it?

20. Which street has 2 cars parked on it?

21. Which street has the most cars parked on it?

22. Which street has the fewest cars parked on it?

Use STATISTICS and PROBABILITY to count by twos showing 2 to 1 correspondence.

PROBLEM SOLVING
Exploring PLAN, SOLVE, and CHECK

The last three steps of the problem-solving plan show how to find the answer to a problem.

1. READ

King Kong was an ape. He was 50 feet tall. A King Kong balloon was put on the Empire State Building. The balloon was 120 feet tall. How much taller was the balloon than the ape?

2. KNOW

Facts I Know	What I Need to Find	Key Facts
King Kong: an ape 50 feet tall Balloon: on the Empire State Building 120 feet tall	How much taller is the balloon than King Kong?	King Kong: 50 feet tall Balloon: 120 feet tall

3. PLAN

Ask yourself: Which operation should I use? To find how much taller, I subtract.

4. SOLVE

Carry out the plan. Ask yourself: Can I write a number sentence?

$120 - 50 = $ ■ $120 - 50 = 70$

The balloon was 70 feet taller.

5. CHECK

Ask yourself: Why is my answer reasonable? Since $50 + 70 = 120$, my answer is reasonable.

FOCUS Use the PLAN, SOLVE, and CHECK steps of the Five-Step PROBLEM-SOLVING Plan.

PRACTICE

The **key facts** have been underlined. For each problem, copy and complete these steps:

3. PLAN   Choose an operation.

4. SOLVE   Carry out the plan. Write a number sentence. Write the answer.

5. CHECK   Check using another operation.

1. In the movie "King Kong" the ape climbed the Empire State Building. Fifty years later, a King Kong balloon was put on the <u>top 10 floors</u> of this building. <u>The Empire State Building has 102 floors.</u> On top of what floor were King Kong's feet?

2. King Kong was <u>50 feet tall</u> and his face was <u>7 feet tall.</u> How tall was he from his chin to his feet?

3. One of the taller buildings in Los Angeles is the First Interstate Bank Building. It has <u>62 floors.</u> How many more floors does the <u>102-floor</u> Empire State Building have than the First Interstate Bank Building?

Class Project

Work in small groups to PLAN, SOLVE, and CHECK. The Sears Tower Building in Chicago, Illinois, has <u>110 floors</u>. The King Kong balloon was <u>as tall as 10 floors</u>. If you put the balloon on the outside of the building, on what floors could King Kong's head and feet be?

MULTIPLICATION
Multiplying Threes

Mr. Taylor has 5 pots. Each pot has 3 flowers.
Add to find how many flowers in all.

3 + 3 + 3 + 3 + 3 = 15

Or **multiply** to find the total number of flowers.

5 threes are 15:

$$\text{number} \longrightarrow 5 \times 3 = 15$$
$$\text{of pots}$$
$$\uparrow$$
$$\text{flowers in each pot}$$

$$\begin{array}{r} 3 \\ \times 5 \\ \hline 15 \end{array}$$

Mr. Taylor has 15 flowers in all.

$1 \times 3 = 3$

$2 \times 3 = 6$

$3 \times 3 = 9$

$4 \times 3 = 12$

$5 \times 3 = 15$

$6 \times 3 = 18$

$7 \times 3 = 21$

$8 \times 3 = 24$

$9 \times 3 = 27$

GUIDED PRACTICE

Multiply to show how many there are in all.

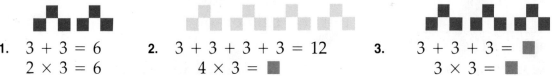

1. $3 + 3 = 6$
$2 \times 3 = 6$

2. $3 + 3 + 3 + 3 = 12$
$4 \times 3 = \blacksquare$

3. $3 + 3 + 3 = \blacksquare$
$3 \times 3 = \blacksquare$

PRACTICE

Find each product.

4. 2 × 3   **5.** 5 × 3   **6.** 4 × 3   **7.** 1 × 3   **8.** 6 × 3

9. 3 × 3   **10.** 7 × 3   **11.** 9 × 3   **12.** 8 × 3   **13.** 5 × 3

14.   3   **15.**   3   **16.**   6   **17.**   3   **18.**   7   **19.**   3
      ×4   ×1   ×3   ×9   ×3   ×3

20.   3   **21.**   3   **22.**   3   **23.**   9   **24.**   3   **25.**   8
      ×2   ×8   ×5   ×3   ×4   ×3

Solve each problem.

26. Mrs. Doe has 3 different kinds of trees. She has 3 of each kind of tree. How many trees does Mrs. Doe have?

27. Joann has 8 different vases. Each vase has 3 flowers. How many flowers does Joann have?

MIXED PRACTICE
Maintaining and Reviewing Skills

Add, subtract, or multiply.

28. 4 × 3   **29.** 8 × 3   **30.** 6 × 2   **31.**   24   **32.**   586
                                                   +36   −273

33. + +   **34.** +

CHALLENGE

Complete the number patterns.

35. 3, 6, 9, 12, ■, ■, ■

36. 21, 24, 27, ■, ■, ■

MULTIPLICATION
Multiplying Threes

Mario buys 6 pencils. He pays 3¢ for each pencil. How much does Mario spend?

Use multiplication to find how much Mario spends.

Multiply the cost of each pencil by the number of pencils.
Then write ¢ in the product.

$$6 \times 3¢ = 18¢$$

$$\begin{array}{r} 3¢ \\ \times 6 \\ \hline 18¢ \end{array}$$

Mario spends 18¢.

3¢ each

PRACTICE

Find each product. Remember the ¢.

1. $3 \times 3¢$ 2. $1 \times 3¢$ 3. $4 \times 3¢$ 4. $6 \times 3¢$ 5. $5 \times 3¢$

6. 2×3 7. 8×3 8. 3×3 9. 9×3 10. 7×3

11. $\begin{array}{r} 3¢ \\ \times 4 \\ \hline \end{array}$ 12. $\begin{array}{r} 3¢ \\ \times 1 \\ \hline \end{array}$ 13. $\begin{array}{r} 3¢ \\ \times 8 \\ \hline \end{array}$ 14. $\begin{array}{r} 3 \\ \times 5 \\ \hline \end{array}$ 15. $\begin{array}{r} 3 \\ \times 7 \\ \hline \end{array}$ 16. $\begin{array}{r} 3 \\ \times 9 \\ \hline \end{array}$

MIXED PRACTICE
Maintaining and Reviewing Skills

Add, subtract, or multiply.

17. $6 \times 3¢$ 18. $8 \times 3¢$ 19. 9×3 20. 7×2 21. 5×2

22. $\begin{array}{r} 8¢ \\ + 7¢ \\ \hline \end{array}$ 23. $\begin{array}{r} 17¢ \\ - 8¢ \\ \hline \end{array}$ 24. $\begin{array}{r} 25 \\ + 12 \\ \hline \end{array}$ 25. $\begin{array}{r} 37 \\ - 23 \\ \hline \end{array}$ 26. $\begin{array}{r} 146 \\ + 137 \\ \hline \end{array}$ 27. $\begin{array}{r} 764 \\ - 348 \\ \hline \end{array}$

FOCUS | Use MEASUREMENT and NUMBER skills to multiply threes.

122

APPLICATION

Problem Solving: Exploring PLAN, SOLVE, CHECK

READ, KNOW, PLAN, SOLVE, and CHECK. See the Five-Step Plan on page 425 in the Data Bank.

The **key facts** are underlined.

There are 362 students in Atlantic School. There are 127 third graders and 119 fourth graders. The rest are fifth graders. How many fifth graders are in the school?

3. PLAN — Add to find the total number of third and fourth graders. Then subtract to find the number of fifth graders.

4. SOLVE — 127 + 119 = 246   There are 246 third and fourth graders.
362 − 246 = 116   There are 116 fifth graders.

5. CHECK — 127 + 119 + 116 = 362
116 is a reasonable answer.

Use the **key facts** to solve each problem.

28. How many fewer third graders are there than fourth and fifth graders combined?

29. If 19 third graders leave, and 16 fourth graders and 18 fifth graders come to the school, how many students will Atlantic School have in all?

30. One day 27 third graders, 17 fourth graders, and 21 fifth graders were absent from school. How many students were at school that day?

Explore PLAN, SOLVE, and CHECK and apply the Five-Step PROBLEM-SOLVING Plan.

LOOKING BACK
Reviewing and Testing Chapter 9

In Chapter 9 you formulated problems about Hide and Seek. Look at pages 112 and 113.

1. Write a sentence telling what happens when "it" is not nearby.

You learned something new about multiplying twos. To review study the sample on page 114. Use the new skill to find each product for examples 2 to 12.

2. $\begin{array}{r} 2 \\ \times 3 \\ \hline \end{array}$
3. $\begin{array}{r} 2 \\ \times 5 \\ \hline \end{array}$
4. $\begin{array}{r} 2 \\ \times 9 \\ \hline \end{array}$
5. $\begin{array}{r} 2 \\ \times 6 \\ \hline \end{array}$
6. $\begin{array}{r} 2 \\ \times 2 \\ \hline \end{array}$
7. $\begin{array}{r} 2 \\ \times 4 \\ \hline \end{array}$

8. 7×2
9. 8×2
10. 5×2
11. 3×2
12. 9×2

You learned how to PLAN, SOLVE, and CHECK problems. To review, look at pages 118 and 119. PLAN, SOLVE, and CHECK the problem. The **key facts** have been underlined.

13. Judy built 3 towers. She used <u>12 blocks</u> for the first tower, <u>21 blocks</u> for the second tower, and <u>17 blocks</u> for the third tower. How many blocks did she use to build the 3 towers?

You learned something new about multiplying threes. To review what you learned, look at page 120. Then use the new skill to find each product for examples 14 to 24.

14. $\begin{array}{r} 3 \\ \times 4 \\ \hline \end{array}$
15. $\begin{array}{r} 3 \\ \times 9 \\ \hline \end{array}$
16. $\begin{array}{r} 3 \\ \times 3 \\ \hline \end{array}$
17. $\begin{array}{r} 3 \\ \times 8 \\ \hline \end{array}$
18. $\begin{array}{r} 3 \\ \times 6 \\ \hline \end{array}$
19. $\begin{array}{r} 3 \\ \times 7 \\ \hline \end{array}$

20. 5×3
21. 2×3
22. 6×3
23. 9×3
24. 8×3

FOCUS | Review and test skills learned and practiced.

LOOKING AHEAD
Preparing for New Skills for Chapter 10

In the next chapter you will focus on

- formulating problems.
- multiplying fours.
- using patterns and functions.

- using a calculator.
- multiplying fives.
- math in technology.

New multiplication skills will be easier to learn if you brush up on the addition skills you already know. Study the model. Then complete the PRACTICE exercises. Check your work with the model.

Model
There are 6 gloves. Each glove has 5 fingers. How many fingers are there in all?

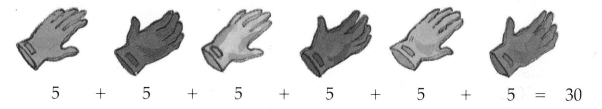

5 + 5 + 5 + 5 + 5 + 5 = 30

There are 30 fingers in all because 6 fives equal 30.

PRACTICE

Complete. Review the model if you need to.

1.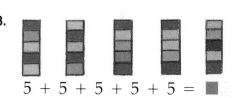

4 + 4 + 4 + 4 = ■

2.

5 + 5 = ■

3.

5 + 5 + 5 + 5 + 5 = ■

4.

4 + 4 + 4 + 4 + 4 + 4 = ■

Review NUMBER skills in preparation for learning a new skill.

FOCUS   Formulate problems using picture cues, text, and data.

10

Multiplication Facts for Fours and Fives

DATA

Time of year	Fall
Place	Tim's yard
Job	Raking leaves
Size of yard	Large
Number of trees	1 big 3 small
Tools	2 rakes 3 plastic bags 2 brooms
Helpers	Candace Joe Kathy
Time given	9:30 A.M.–noon
Colors of leaves	Red Orange Yellow Brown

In many parts of the country, the fall is a colorful season. Where the winters are cold, the green leaves on some trees change to red, yellow, orange, or gold. The cities and the countryside are filled with rich colors.

After the leaves change color, they begin to fall off the trees. Soon there are large piles of leaves on the ground. One job in the fall is to sweep up the fallen leaves with a rake. A rake is the same size as a broom, but it has long metal "fingers" instead of straw. Raking leaves can be hard work, but it can be fun, too! You can rake all of the leaves into one big pile and then jump onto it!

Using the photograph and the data, decide what Tim will need to do to get the leaves into piles. How will he get rid of them? Can you think of any ways to make the job easier?

MULTIPLICATION
Multiplying Fours

Ben has 6 pages of stamps. Each page has 4 stamps.

Multiply to find the total number of stamps.

6 fours are 24:   number ⟶ 6 × 4 = 24   4
                    of pages   ↑   ×6
                                                 ——
                    stamps on each page   24

Ben has 24 stamps altogether.

1 × 4 = 4

2 × 4 = 8

3 × 4 = 12

4 × 4 = 16

5 × 4 = 20

6 × 4 = 24

7 × 4 = 28

8 × 4 = 32

9 × 4 = 36

GUIDED PRACTICE

Multiply to show how many in all.

1.

   3 × 4 = 12

2.

   2 × 4 = ■

3.

   4 × 4 = ■

PRACTICE

Find each product.

4. 1×4 **5.** 5×4 **6.** 2×4 **7.** 4×4 **8.** 3×4

9. 7×4 **10.** 9×4 **11.** 6×4 **12.** 8×4 **13.** 1×4

14. $\begin{array}{r} 3 \\ \times 4 \\ \hline \end{array}$ **15.** $\begin{array}{r} 4 \\ \times 4 \\ \hline \end{array}$ **16.** $\begin{array}{r} 4 \\ \times 2 \\ \hline \end{array}$ **17.** $\begin{array}{r} 4 \\ \times 1 \\ \hline \end{array}$ **18.** $\begin{array}{r} 6 \\ \times 4 \\ \hline \end{array}$ **19.** $\begin{array}{r} 4 \\ \times 5 \\ \hline \end{array}$

20. $\begin{array}{r} 4 \\ \times 8 \\ \hline \end{array}$ **21.** $\begin{array}{r} 9 \\ \times 4 \\ \hline \end{array}$ **22.** $\begin{array}{r} 7 \\ \times 4 \\ \hline \end{array}$ **23.** $\begin{array}{r} 4 \\ \times 4 \\ \hline \end{array}$ **24.** $\begin{array}{r} 2 \\ \times 4 \\ \hline \end{array}$ **25.** $\begin{array}{r} 4 \\ \times 9 \\ \hline \end{array}$

Solve each problem.

26. Bob has 3 boxes of shells. There are 4 shells in each box. How many shells does Bob have altogether?

27. Sue's house has 7 rooms. Each room has 4 windows. How many windows are in Sue's house?

MIXED PRACTICE
Maintaining and Reviewing Skills

Add, subtract, or multiply.

28. 6×4 **29.** 2×4 **30.** 9×2 **31.** $\begin{array}{r} 253 \\ + 138 \\ \hline 391 \end{array}$ **32.** $\begin{array}{r} \overset{5}{6}29 \\ - 333 \\ \hline 296 \end{array}$

33. + +
     34. + +

CHALLENGE

35. Betty is thinking of a number. When you multiply it by 2 you get 10. When you multiply it by 4 you get 20. What is the number?

MULTIPLICATION
Multiplying Fours

Erin buys 7 cups of grape juice. She pays 4¢ for each cup. How much does Erin spend?

Use multiplication to find how much Erin spends.

Multiply the cost of each cup by the number of cups.
Then write ¢ in the product.

$$7 \times 4¢ = 28¢ \qquad \begin{array}{r} 4¢ \\ \times 7 \\ \hline 28¢ \end{array}$$

Erin spends 28¢.

PRACTICE

Find each product. Remember the ¢.

1. $5 \times 4¢$ **2.** $3 \times 4¢$ **3.** $6 \times 4¢$ **4.** $9 \times 4¢$ **5.** $1 \times 4¢$

6. 4×4 **7.** 8×4 **8.** 2×4 **9.** 7×4 **10.** 9×4

11. $\begin{array}{r} 4¢ \\ \times 3 \\ \hline \end{array}$ **12.** $\begin{array}{r} 4¢ \\ \times 6 \\ \hline \end{array}$ **13.** $\begin{array}{r} 4¢ \\ \times 7 \\ \hline \end{array}$ **14.** $\begin{array}{r} 4 \\ \times 9 \\ \hline \end{array}$ **15.** $\begin{array}{r} 4 \\ \times 1 \\ \hline \end{array}$ **16.** $\begin{array}{r} 4 \\ \times 4 \\ \hline \end{array}$

MIXED PRACTICE
Maintaining and Reviewing Skills

Add, subtract, or multiply.

17. $2 \times 4¢$ **18.** $8 \times 4¢$ **19.** 5×4 **20.** 9×3 **21.** 5×2

22. $\begin{array}{r} 7¢ \\ +9¢ \\ \hline \end{array}$ **23.** $\begin{array}{r} 16¢ \\ -\ 8¢ \\ \hline \end{array}$ **24.** $\begin{array}{r} 32 \\ +47 \\ \hline \end{array}$ **25.** $\begin{array}{r} 63 \\ -28 \\ \hline \end{array}$ **26.** $\begin{array}{r} 338 \\ +\ 52 \\ \hline \end{array}$ **27.** $\begin{array}{r} 971 \\ -\ 47 \\ \hline \end{array}$

FOCUS   Use MEASUREMENT and NUMBER skills to multiply fours.

APPLICATION

Using Patterns and Functions

The two factors in this multiplication function machine are 6 and 4. What is the product of the factors?

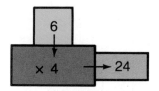

Find the product or the factor for each function machine.

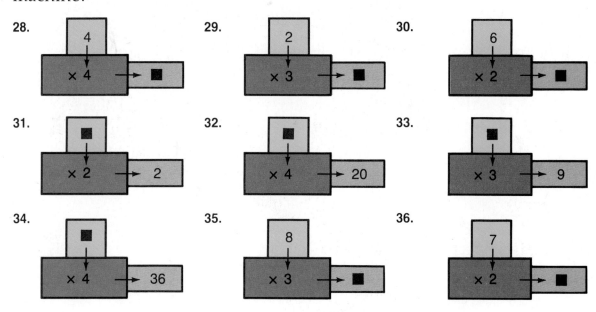

28. × 4 (input 4) → ■

29. × 3 (input 2) → ■

30. × 2 (input 6) → ■

31. × 2 (input ■) → 2

32. × 4 (input ■) → 20

33. × 3 (input ■) → 9

34. × 4 (input ■) → 36

35. × 3 (input 8) → ■

36. × 2 (input 7) → ■

Calculator

Use a calculator to add fours. First turn the calculator on and push the $+$ key. Then push the 4 key and the $=$ key. Every time you push the $=$ key 4 will be added to the number on the screen.

Use a calculator to complete the chart.

$=$ Key Pushes	1	2	3	4	5	6	7	8	9
Number on Screen	4	8	■	■	■	■	■	■	■

Use PATTERNS AND FUNCTIONS and a CALCULATOR to multiply twos, threes, and fours.

MULTIPLICATION
Multiplying Fives

Ming has 4 plates. Each plate has 5 cubes of gelatin.

Multiply to find the total number of cubes.

4 fives are 20:

number $\longrightarrow$ $4 \times 5 = 20$
of plates $\uparrow$
cubes on each plate

$$\begin{array}{r} 5 \\ \times 4 \\ \hline 20 \end{array}$$

Ming has 20 cubes of gelatin in all.

$1 \times 5 = 5$

$2 \times 5 = 10$

$3 \times 5 = 15$

$4 \times 5 = 20$

$5 \times 5 = 25$

$6 \times 5 = 30$

$7 \times 5 = 35$

$8 \times 5 = 40$

$9 \times 5 = 45$

GUIDED PRACTICE

Multiply to show how many in all.

1. $3 \times 5 = 15$

2. $1 \times 5 = \blacksquare$

3. $2 \times 5 = \blacksquare$

FOCUS   Use NUMBER skills to multiply fives.

132

PRACTICE

Find each product.

4. 2×5 **5.** 5×5 **6.** 1×5 **7.** 3×5 **8.** 4×5

9. 7×5 **10.** 9×5 **11.** 6×5 **12.** 8×5 **13.** 5×5

14. $\begin{array}{r} 5 \\ \times 2 \\ \hline \end{array}$ **15.** $\begin{array}{r} 5 \\ \times 5 \\ \hline \end{array}$ **16.** $\begin{array}{r} 1 \\ \times 5 \\ \hline \end{array}$ **17.** $\begin{array}{r} 5 \\ \times 4 \\ \hline \end{array}$ **18.** $\begin{array}{r} 5 \\ \times 3 \\ \hline \end{array}$ **19.** $\begin{array}{r} 5 \\ \times 6 \\ \hline \end{array}$

20. $\begin{array}{r} 5 \\ \times 8 \\ \hline \end{array}$ **21.** $\begin{array}{r} 6 \\ \times 5 \\ \hline \end{array}$ **22.** $\begin{array}{r} 5 \\ \times 7 \\ \hline \end{array}$ **23.** $\begin{array}{r} 9 \\ \times 5 \\ \hline \end{array}$ **24.** $\begin{array}{r} 5 \\ \times 1 \\ \hline \end{array}$ **25.** $\begin{array}{r} 5 \\ \times 9 \\ \hline \end{array}$

26. Write a word problem that could be solved by multiplying 5 and 8. Then solve the problem.

27. Write a word problem that could be solved by multiplying 5 and 3. Then solve the problem.

MIXED PRACTICE
Maintaining and Reviewing Skills

Add, subtract, or multiply.

28. 6×5 **29.** 9×5 **30.** 3×4 **31.** 8×3 **32.** 9×2

33. $12 - 7$ **34.** $9 + 8$ **35.** 9×3 **36.** 7×2 **37.** 9×4

38. $\begin{array}{r} 5 \\ \times 8 \\ \hline \end{array}$ **39.** $\begin{array}{r} 27 \\ + 35 \\ \hline \end{array}$ **40.** $\begin{array}{r} 4 \\ \times 6 \\ \hline \end{array}$ **41.** $\begin{array}{r} 56 \\ - 28 \\ \hline \end{array}$ **42.** $\begin{array}{r} 372 \\ + 154 \\ \hline \end{array}$ **43.** $\begin{array}{r} 968 \\ - 790 \\ \hline \end{array}$

CHALLENGE

44. Martha has 4 trays. Each tray has 2 plates. Each plate has 5 pieces of cheese. How many pieces of cheese does Martha have?

MULTIPLICATION
Multiplying Through Fives

This is a multiplication table. It shows all of the facts that have been learned so far.

Find the product of 5×4.

Step 1: Find 5 across on blue.
Step 2: Find 4 down on red.
Step 3: Follow the 5 column until it meets with the 4 row.

X	1	2	3	4	5	6	7	8	9
1	1	2	3	4	5	6	7	8	9
2	2	4	6	8	10	12	14	16	18
3	3	6	9	12	15	18	21	24	27
4	4	8	12	16	20	24	28	32	36
5	5	10	15	20	25	30	35	40	45

$$5 \times 4 = 20$$

$$\begin{array}{r} 4 \\ \times 5 \\ \hline 20 \end{array}$$

PRACTICE

Use the multiplication table to find the product.

1. 2×3 2. 3×1 3. 1×2 4. 3×5 5. 2×4

6. 4×1 7. 6×2 8. 5×3 9. 8×1 10. 3×3

11. $\begin{array}{r} 2 \\ \times 5 \\ \hline \end{array}$
12. $\begin{array}{r} 4 \\ \times 6 \\ \hline \end{array}$
13. $\begin{array}{r} 3 \\ \times 6 \\ \hline \end{array}$
14. $\begin{array}{r} 1 \\ \times 5 \\ \hline \end{array}$
15. $\begin{array}{r} 5 \\ \times 4 \\ \hline \end{array}$
16. $\begin{array}{r} 2 \\ \times 7 \\ \hline \end{array}$

17. $\begin{array}{r} 4 \\ \times 4 \\ \hline \end{array}$
18. $\begin{array}{r} 1 \\ \times 8 \\ \hline \end{array}$
19. $\begin{array}{r} 5 \\ \times 7 \\ \hline \end{array}$
20. $\begin{array}{r} 3 \\ \times 8 \\ \hline \end{array}$
21. $\begin{array}{r} 1 \\ \times 4 \\ \hline \end{array}$
22. $\begin{array}{r} 1 \\ \times 9 \\ \hline \end{array}$

MIXED PRACTICE
Maintaining and Reviewing Skills

Add, subtract, or multiply.

23. 5×5 24. 9×5 25. 7×4 26. $4 \times 3¢$ 27. $9 \times 2¢$

28. $\begin{array}{r} 9¢ \\ + 9¢ \\ \hline \end{array}$
29. $\begin{array}{r} 13¢ \\ - 8¢ \\ \hline \end{array}$
30. $\begin{array}{r} 42 \\ + 9 \\ \hline 51 \end{array}$
31. $\begin{array}{r} 56 \\ - 7 \\ \hline 49 \end{array}$
32. $\begin{array}{r} 957 \\ + 28 \\ \hline \end{array}$
33. $\begin{array}{r} 860 \\ - 751 \\ \hline 109 \end{array}$

| FOCUS | Use NUMBER skills to multiply through fives. |

APPLICATION

Using Patterns and Functions

Use the number line to find the next number in the **pattern.**
What is the rule for this number pattern?

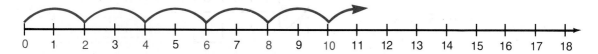

The next number in the pattern is 12.
The rule is *add 2.*

Use this number line to find the next number in the pattern.
What is the rule for this number pattern?

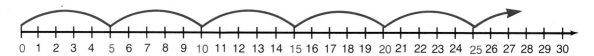

The next number in the pattern is 30.
The rule is *add 5.*

Use the correct number line to find the next number.

34. 2, 4, 6, ■   **35.** 5, 10, 15, ■

36. 12, 14, 16, ■   **37.** 15, 20, 25, ■

38. 1, 3, 5, ■   **39.** 1, 6, 11, ■

Continue the pattern. Write the rule.

40. 31, 36, 41, ■, ■, ■   **41.** 7, 9, 11, ■, ■, ■

42. 17, 19, 21, ■, ■, ■   **43.** 42, 47, 52, ■, ■, ■

44. 126, 131, 136, ■, ■, ■   **45.** 159, 161, 163 ■, ■, ■

Use NUMBER skills and PATTERNS AND FUNCTIONS to count by twos and fives.

Flowcharts

Do you want to go swimming? "Yes, if it's a nice day," you might reply. Imagine a friend who has never been swimming. How can you clearly describe the steps to take? "Get our swimsuits and go to the pool," could be a description. But you will need an even clearer picture to explain "going swimming"—especially if your friend is a computer.

A computer can be helpful only if it understands all the steps of the job. We can help describe the steps of a job by drawing a picture of them.

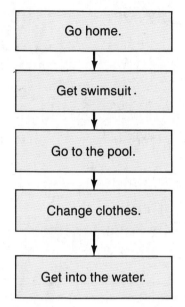

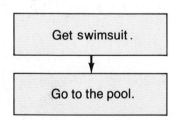

Use imagination to break down the idea into even smaller steps for a computer friend. For instance, you may have to go home for your swimsuit.

Here is a picture of the flow of steps. It is a **flowchart.**

Are there any more important details? (Hint: Would you swim outdoors on a stormy day?) Flowcharts have to show choices. So the "go to the pool" box is really a question box with 2 answers.

CRITICAL THINKING

1. How is a flowchart helpful?

2. What additional steps would make "go home" more detailed?

3. What step might come after "get into the water"?

4. Why are boxes different shapes?

FOCUS | Use LOGIC to understand computer flowcharts.

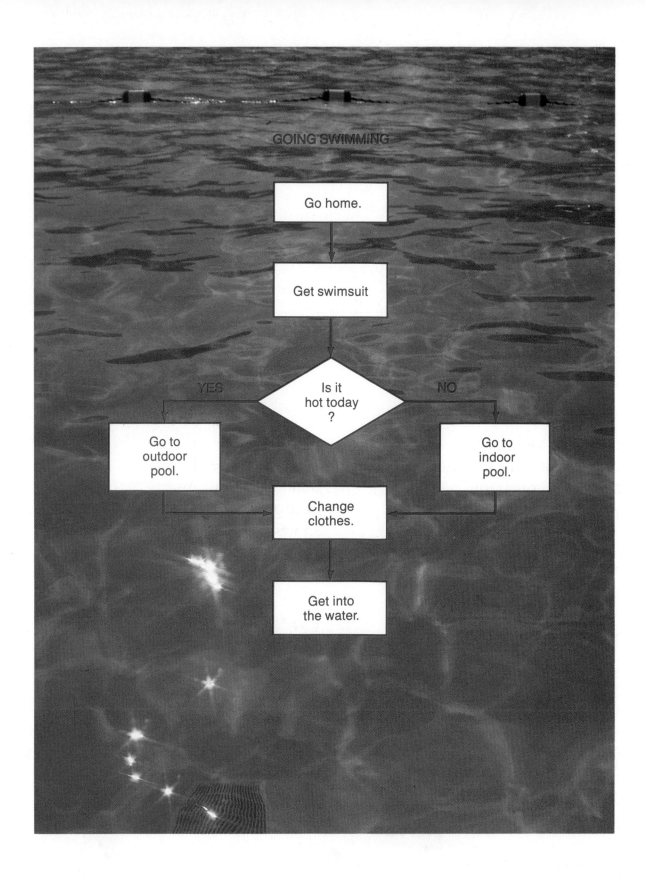

GOING SWIMMING

Go home.

Get swimsuit

Is it hot today ?

YES → Go to outdoor pool.

NO → Go to indoor pool.

Change clothes.

Get into the water.

LOOKING BACK
Reviewing and Testing Chapter 10

In Chapter 10 you formulated problems about fall. Look at pages 126 and 127.

1. Write a sentence telling what happens to leaves in fall.

You learned something new about multiplying fours. To review what you learned, study the sample problem on page 128. Then use the new skill to find each product for examples 2 to 12.

2. $\begin{array}{r} 4 \\ \times 3 \end{array}$
3. $\begin{array}{r} 4 \\ \times 4 \end{array}$
4. $\begin{array}{r} 4 \\ \times 2 \end{array}$
5. $\begin{array}{r} 4 \\ \times 6 \end{array}$
6. $\begin{array}{r} 4 \\ \times 9 \end{array}$
7. $\begin{array}{r} 4 \\ \times 5 \end{array}$

8. 9×4
9. 7×4
10. 8×4
11. 3×4
12. 2×4

You learned something new about multiplying fives. To review what you learned, look at page 132. Then use the new skill to find each product for examples 13 to 25.

13. $\begin{array}{r} 5 \\ \times 6 \end{array}$
14. $\begin{array}{r} 5 \\ \times 2 \end{array}$
15. $\begin{array}{r} 5 \\ \times 9 \end{array}$
16. $\begin{array}{r} 5 \\ \times 3 \end{array}$
17. $\begin{array}{r} 5 \\ \times 5 \end{array}$
18. $\begin{array}{r} 5 \\ \times 8 \end{array}$

19. 7×5
20. 8×5
21. 5×5
22. 4×5
23. 9×5

24. Write a word problem that could be solved by multiplying 4 and 5. Then solve the problem.

25. Write a word problem that could be solved by multiplying 7 and 5. Then solve the problem.

You learned about flowcharts. Look at page 136 to review what you learned.

26. Write a sentence to describe a flowchart.

FOCUS | Review and test skills learned and practiced.

LOOKING AHEAD

Preparing for New Skills for Chapter 11

In the next chapter you will focus on

- formulating problems.
- dividing by twos.
- a problem-solving strategy.

- dividing by threes.
- dividing money.
- using measurement.

New division skills will be easier to learn if you know how to find equal parts of a group. Study the model. Then complete the PRACTICE exercises. Check your work with the model.

Model

There are 10 baseballs. How many groups of 2 baseballs are there?

There are 5 groups of 2 baseballs.

PRACTICE

Answer the questions. Review the model.

1. There are 8 tennis balls. How many groups of 2 are there?

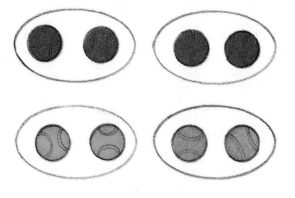

2. There are 9 soccer balls. How many groups of 3 are there?

Review NUMBER skills in preparation for learning a new skill.

139

The map shows: Parking, Discount Mart, Books Books Books, Ice Cream Shop, Longe Eyeland, Phred's Pharmacy, News Stand, Morrie's Shoes, Hard and Software, Helen's Sporting Goods, Dime Store, K.W. Grocery, Restaurant

FOCUS | Formulate problems using picture cues, text, and data.

Division Facts: 2 and 3 as Divisors

DATA

Shopper	Mrs. Gilligan
Items needed	Estimated cost
Bubblebath	$3.00
Basketball ✓	$18.00
Green necktie ✓	$10.00
Flyswatter	$1.00
White shoelaces	$2.00
Local newspaper ✓	$0.50
Birthday present for teenage daughter	$25.00

Shopping can be a lot of fun. But, if you have a lot of items to buy, it's important to plan ahead. Sometimes you can get an item at more than one store. And sometimes you have to start or end up in a certain place. Using the data and the photograph, tell at which stores Mrs. Gilligan might be able to get each item. In how many different stores is it possible that she could get a present for her daughter? What gift might she get at each of the stores you mentioned?

If Mrs. Gilligan parks in the lot, what is the shortest shopping route she could take and end up at her car? If she wants to end up at the restaurant, what should she do?

What problems must Mrs. Gilligan solve as she plans her shopping?

DIVISION
Dividing by Twos

How many toothbrushes are in the picture?

There are 12 toothbrushes in all. How many groups of 2 are there?

Divide to find how many groups of 2 there are. Divide the number of toothbrushes in all by the number of toothbrushes in each group.

12 toothbrushes in all   2 in each group   6 groups
$$12 \div 2 = 6$$
Twelve **divided by** two **is equal to** six.

There are 6 groups of 2 toothbrushes.

There are two ways to write a division fact.

$$12 \div 2 = 6 \qquad 2\overline{)12}^{\,6}$$

GUIDED PRACTICE

Divide to show how many groups there are.

1.

    How many 2s are in 6?

    $6 \div 2 = 3$

2.

    How many 2s are in 8?

    $8 \div 2 = \blacksquare$

3.

    How many 2s are in 4?

    $4 \div 2 = \blacksquare$

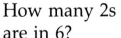 Use NUMBER skills to divide by twos.

PRACTICE

Divide.

4. 6 ÷ 2   **5.** 8 ÷ 2   **6.** 2 ÷ 2   **7.** 10 ÷ 2   **8.** 4 ÷ 2

9. 16 ÷ 2   **10.** 12 ÷ 2   **11.** 10 ÷ 2   **12.** 14 ÷ 2   **13.** 18 ÷ 2

14. $2\overline{)8}$ **15.** $2\overline{)2}$ **16.** $2\overline{)4}$ **17.** $2\overline{)12}$ **18.** $2\overline{)6}$ **19.** $2\overline{)10}$

20. $2\overline{)16}$ **21.** $2\overline{)14}$ **22.** $2\overline{)18}$ **23.** $2\overline{)8}$ **24.** $2\overline{)12}$ **25.** $2\overline{)18}$

26. $2\overline{)4}$ **27.** $2\overline{)10}$ **28.** $2\overline{)16}$ **29.** $2\overline{)6}$ **30.** $2\overline{)14}$ **31.** $2\overline{)8}$

Solve each problem.

32. Wilma has 14 bars of soap. She uses 2 bars every month. In how many months will Wilma finish all of the soap?

33. Randolf has 8 towels. He gives 2 towels to each of his brothers. How many brothers does Randolf have?

MIXED PRACTICE
Maintaining and Reviewing Skills

Add, subtract, multiply, or divide.

34. 10 ÷ 2   **35.** 6 ÷ 2   **36.** $2\overline{)18}$ **37.** 8 × 2   **38.** 6 × 2

39. $\begin{array}{r} 62 \\ -52 \\ \hline \end{array}$ **40.** $\begin{array}{r} 83 \\ -32 \\ \hline \end{array}$ **41.** $\begin{array}{r} 34 \\ +49 \\ \hline \end{array}$ **42.** $\begin{array}{r} 56 \\ +27 \\ \hline \end{array}$ **43.** $\begin{array}{r} 7 \\ \times 2 \\ \hline \end{array}$ **44.** $\begin{array}{r} 9 \\ \times 2 \\ \hline \end{array}$

CHALLENGE

45. Terry has 7 bags of walnuts. He buys 9 more bags. Then he gives each of his friends 2 bags. Terry keeps 2 bags for himself. How many friends does Terry give walnuts to?

DIVISION
Dividing by Twos

There are 8 roller skates in the window. There are 2 roller skates in each pair. How many pairs of roller skates are in the window?

Divide to find how many pairs of skates are in the window. Divide the number of skates in all by the number of skates in each pair.

$$\underset{\text{8 skates in all}}{8} \div \underset{\text{2 in each pair}}{2} = \underset{\text{4 pairs}}{4}$$

$8 \div 2 = 4$ can be written as $2\overline{)8}^{4}$

There are 4 pairs of skates in the window.

PRACTICE

Divide.

1. $6 \div 2$ **2.** $10 \div 2$ **3.** $4 \div 2$ **4.** $2 \div 2$ **5.** $8 \div 2$

6. $2\overline{)16}$ **7.** $2\overline{)8}$ **8.** $2\overline{)14}$ **9.** $2\overline{)12}$ **10.** $2\overline{)10}$ **11.** $2\overline{)18}$

Solve each problem.

12. There are 14 snowshoes in the shed. There are 2 snowshoes in each pair. How many pairs of snowshoes are in the shed?

13. There are 18 rubber boots in the shoe store. There are 2 boots in each box. How many boxes of boots are in the store?

MIXED PRACTICE
Maintaining and Reviewing Skills

Multiply or divide.

14. $14 \div 2$ **15.** $8 \div 2$ **16.** $2\overline{)18}$ **17.** 6×2 **18.** 3×2

FOCUS | Use NUMBER skills to divide by twos.

144

APPLICATION

Problem Solving: Exploring READ and KNOW

Remember to READ and KNOW all problems. See the Five-Step Plan on page 425 in the Data Bank.

You and a friend have gone shopping. The list shows the amount of fruit you bought.

bananas	2
strawberries	16
grapes	14
apples	12
grapefruit	4
plums	10
oranges	8
pears	6
cherries	18

Use the list to find the **key facts.** Do not solve the problems.

19. How many apples and oranges did you and your friend buy?
    Key facts:
    There are 12 apples.
    There are 8 oranges.

20. How many more cherries did you buy than plums?
    Key facts:
    There are 18 cherries.
    There are 10 plums.

21. You and your friend will share the grapes equally. How many grapes will your friend get?
    Key fact:
    There are 14 grapes.

22. If you buy twice as many bananas next time, how many bananas will you buy?
    Key fact:
    There are 2 bananas.

23. You and your friend will get the same number of strawberries. How many strawberries will you get?
    Key fact:
    There are 16 strawberries.

24. If you buy three times the number of grapefruit next time, how many grapefruit will you buy?
    Key fact:
    There are 4 grapefruit.

Explore the READ and KNOW steps of the Five-Step PROBLEM-SOLVING Plan.

DIVISION
Dividing by Threes

Look at the picture. How many muffins are there?

There are 15 muffins in all. How many groups of 3 are there?

Divide to find how many groups of 3 there are. Divide the number of muffins in all by the number of muffins in each group.

15 muffins in all   3 in each group   5 groups
     15   ÷   3   =   5
Fifteen **divided by** three **is equal to** five.

There are 5 groups of 3 muffins. $15 ÷ 3 = 5$ $3\overline{)15}$ (with 5 on top)

GUIDED PRACTICE

Divide to show how many groups there are.

1.

2.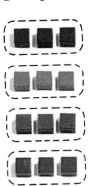

3.

How many 3s   How many 3s   How many 3s
are in 6?   are in 12?   are in 9?

$6 ÷ 3 = 2$ $12 ÷ 3 = \blacksquare$ $9 ÷ 3 = \blacksquare$

4. $3 ÷ 3$ **5.** $15 ÷ 3$ **6.** $21 ÷ 3$ **7.** $18 ÷ 3$ **8.** $27 ÷ 3$

9. $3\overline{)24}$ **10.** $3\overline{)12}$ **11.** $3\overline{)9}$ **12.** $3\overline{)18}$ **13.** $3\overline{)27}$ **14.** $3\overline{)15}$

FOCUS	Use NUMBER skills to divide by threes.

PRACTICE

Divide.

15. $3 \div 3$ **16.** $9 \div 3$ **17.** $15 \div 3$ **18.** $6 \div 3$ **19.** $12 \div 3$

20. $21 \div 3$ **21.** $18 \div 3$ **22.** $27 \div 3$ **23.** $24 \div 3$ **24.** $6 \div 3$

25. $3\overline{)9}$ **26.** $3\overline{)15}$ **27.** $3\overline{)3}$ **28.** $3\overline{)24}$ **29.** $3\overline{)12}$ **30.** $3\overline{)21}$

31. $3\overline{)27}$ **32.** $3\overline{)6}$ **33.** $3\overline{)12}$ **34.** $3\overline{)18}$ **35.** $3\overline{)21}$ **36.** $3\overline{)24}$

Solve each problem.

37. Michelle has 21 muffins. She will put 3 muffins in each bag. How many bags does Michelle need?

38. Ryan had 24 cherries. He put 3 cherries in each muffin. How many muffins did Ryan bake?

MIXED PRACTICE
Maintaining and Reviewing Skills

Add, subtract, multiply, or divide.

39. $24 \div 3$ **40.** $3\overline{)18}$ **41.** $16 \div 2$ **42.** $\begin{array}{r} 3 \\ \times 6 \\ \hline \end{array}$ **43.** $\begin{array}{r} 2 \\ \times 9 \\ \hline \end{array}$

44.

45.

CHALLENGE

Find the missing numbers.

46. ▪ $\times 3 = 12$
      ▪ $\div 3 = 4$

47. ▪ $\times 2 = 14$
      ▪ $\div 2 = 7$

48. ▪ $\times 3 = 15$
      ▪ $\div 3 = 5$

DIVISION
Dividing by Threes

Sonia spends 21¢ for 3 marbles. How much does each marble cost?

Use division to find the cost of each marble.

Divide the money Sonia spends by the number of marbles she buys. Then write ¢ in the answer.

$$21¢ \div 3 = 7¢ \qquad 3\overline{)21¢} \; {}^{7¢}$$

Each marble costs 7¢.

PRACTICE

Divide. Remember the ¢.

1. 9¢ ÷ 3   **2.** 21¢ ÷ 3   **3.** 12¢ ÷ 3   **4.** 24¢ ÷ 3   **5.** 15¢ ÷ 3

6. 3 ÷ 3   **7.** 18 ÷ 3   **8.** 6 ÷ 3   **9.** 21 ÷ 3   **10.** 27 ÷ 3

11. $3\overline{)6¢}$ **12.** $3\overline{)12¢}$ **13.** $3\overline{)3¢}$ **14.** $3\overline{)18¢}$ **15.** $3\overline{)9¢}$ **16.** $3\overline{)24¢}$

17. $3\overline{)15}$ **18.** $3\overline{)27}$ **19.** $3\overline{)21}$ **20.** $3\overline{)9}$ **21.** $3\overline{)12}$ **22.** $3\overline{)27}$

MIXED PRACTICE
Maintaining and Reviewing Skills

Multiply or divide.

23. 18 ÷ 3   **24.** $3\overline{)24¢}$ **25.** 16 ÷ 2   **26.** 7 × 3   **27.** 18 ÷ 9

FOCUS Use MEASUREMENT and NUMBER skills to divide by threes.

APPLICATION
Using Measurement

APRIL						
Sun.	Mon.	Tues.	Wed.	Thurs.	Fri.	Sat.
		1	2	3	4	5
6	7	8	9	10	11	12
13	14	15	16	17	18	19
20	21	22	23	24	25	26
27	28	29	30			

Look at the calendar. Then answer the questions.

28. Which dates in the Thursday column have numbers that can be evenly divided by 3? Which dates cannot be evenly divided by 3?

29. Which dates in the row that begins with 20 have numbers that can be divided evenly by 2? Write the day and date for each one.

Calculator

Use a calculator to subtract threes. First turn the calculator on and push the ⟨2⟩ key and the ⟨7⟩ key. Then push the ⟨−⟩ key and the ⟨3⟩ key. Now push the ⟨=⟩ key. Every time you push the ⟨=⟩ key 3 will be subtracted from the number on the screen.

Use a calculator to complete the chart.

⟨=⟩ Key Pushes	1	2	3	4	5	6	7	8	9
Number on Screen	24	21	■	■	■	■	■	■	■

Use MEASUREMENT and a CALCULATOR to divide by twos and threes.

LOOKING BACK
Reviewing and Testing Chapter 11

In Chapter 11 you formulated problems about shopping. Look at pages 140 and 141.

1. Write a sentence telling about the things you could buy at a pet store.

You learned something new about dividing by twos. To review what you learned, study the sample problem on page 142. Then use the new skill to find each quotient for examples 2 to 14.

2. $6 \div 2$ 3. $10 \div 2$ 4. $14 \div 2$ 5. $12 \div 2$ 6. $8 \div 2$

7. $2 \overline{) 16}$ 8. $2 \overline{) 4}$ 9. $2 \overline{) 18}$ 10. $2 \overline{) 10}$ 11. $2 \overline{) 6}$ 12. $2 \overline{) 12}$

13. Steve has 12 books and 2 shelves to put them on. He puts the same number of books on each shelf. How many books are on each shelf?

14. Kathy has 16 books and 2 boxes to put them in. She puts the same number of books in each box. How many books will she put in each box?

You learned something new about dividing by threes. To review what you learned, look at pages 146 and 147. Then use the new skill to find each quotient for examples 15 to 27.

15. $6 \div 3$ 16. $24 \div 3$ 17. $12 \div 3$ 18. $21 \div 3$ 19. $15 \div 3$

20. $3 \overline{) 21}$ 21. $3 \overline{) 9}$ 22. $3 \overline{) 27}$ 23. $3 \overline{) 18}$ 24. $3 \overline{) 12}$ 25. $3 \overline{) 24}$

26. Shirley has 15 turtles and 3 bowls to put them in. She puts the same number of turtles in each bowl. How many turtles are in each bowl?

27. Ralph has 27 fish and 3 tanks to put them in. He puts the same number of fish in each tank. How many fish are in each tank?

FOCUS   Review and test skills learned and practiced.

150

LOOKING AHEAD
Preparing for New Skills for Chapter 12

In the next chapter you will focus on

- formulating problems.
- dividing by fours.
- a problem-solving strategy.

- dividing by fives.
- using patterns and functions.
- how math is used with maps.

New division skills will be easier to learn if you brush up on division skills you already know.

Study the model. Then complete the PRACTICE exercises. Check your work with the model.

Model

There are 20 tulips. How many groups of 5 tulips are there?

There are 4 groups of 5 tulips.

PRACTICE

Answer the questions. Review the model.

1. There are 12 lilies. How many groups of 4 lilies are there?

2. There are 15 roses. How many groups of 5 roses are there?

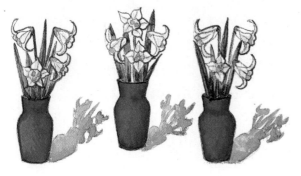   

Review NUMBER skills in preparation for learning a new skill.

12

Division Facts: 4 and 5 as Divisors

Event	Class trip
Place	National Air and Space Museum
Hours	10 A.M.–5:30 P.M.
Cost	No charge

Things to see

Kitty Hawk Flyer (1903 plane)

Moon-landing spacecraft

First solo-flight planes

Puppet shows

Model of "Star Trek" *Enterprise*

Astronauts' spacesuits

Planetarium

A museum is an interesting place to visit. Some museums are filled with paintings and sculptures. Others show objects from human history, such as pottery or armor. There are also science museums. They display objects made by different types of scientists. They also offer information about how these discoveries were made.

Joanna's class is learning about the American space program. Today they are going on a class trip to the National Air and Space Museum. This museum has exciting exhibits showing the history of space exploration. Some of the actual spacecraft used are on display!

Decide what problems had to be solved before the class went on the trip. Is there anything missing from the data that they needed to know?

DIVISION
Dividing by Fours

Look at the picture. How many beads are there?

There are 24 beads in all. How many groups of 4 are there?

Divide to find how many groups of 4 there are. Divide the number of beads in all by the number of beads in each group.

24 beads in all   4 in each group   6 groups

$$24 \div 4 = 6$$

Twenty-four **divided by** four **is equal to** six.

There are 6 groups of 4 beads.

$$24 \div 4 = 6 \qquad 4\overline{)24} = 6$$

GUIDED PRACTICE

Divide to show how many groups there are.

1.

How many 4s
are in 8?

$$8 \div 4 = 2$$

2.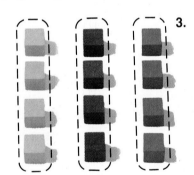

How many 4s
are in 12?

$$12 \div 4 = \blacksquare$$

3.

How many 4s
are in 16?

$$16 \div 4 = \blacksquare$$

4. $4\overline{)4}$ **5.** $4\overline{)20}$ **6.** $4\overline{)28}$ **7.** $4\overline{)32}$ **8.** $4\overline{)24}$ **9.** $4\overline{)36}$

FOCUS | Use NUMBER skills to divide by fours.

154

PRACTICE

Divide.

10. $12 \div 4$ **11.** $4 \div 4$ **12.** $16 \div 4$ **13.** $8 \div 4$ **14.** $20 \div 4$

15. $32 \div 4$ **16.** $24 \div 4$ **17.** $36 \div 4$ **18.** $28 \div 4$ **19.** $4 \div 4$

20. $4\overline{)8}$ **21.** $4\overline{)16}$ **22.** $4\overline{)28}$ **23.** $4\overline{)36}$ **24.** $4\overline{)4}$ **25.** $4\overline{)32}$

26. $4\overline{)28}$ **27.** $4\overline{)12}$ **28.** $4\overline{)16}$ **29.** $4\overline{)24}$ **30.** $4\overline{)20}$ **31.** $4\overline{)36}$

Solve each problem.

32. Rena is making 4 necklaces, with the same number of beads on each necklace. She has 28 beads. How many beads should Rena put on each necklace?

33. Luther is painting 20 stripes on 4 tables. Each table will have the same number of stripes. How many stripes does Luther paint on each table?

MIXED PRACTICE
Maintaining and Reviewing Skills

Add, subtract, multiply or divide.

34. $32 \div 4$ **35.** $4\overline{)20}$ **36.** $27 \div 3$ **37.** 4×7 **38.** 3×6

39.

40.

CHALLENGE

41. Jason is making 3 puppets. He will sew 6 buttons on each puppet. He has 20 buttons. How many buttons will Jason have left over?

42. Marjorie is making 4 dolls. She will sew 4 buttons on each doll. She has 17 buttons. How many buttons will she have left over?

DIVISION
Dividing by Fours

Ray spends 32¢ for 4 balloons. How much does each balloon cost?

Use division to find the cost of each balloon.

Divide the money Ray spends by the number of balloons he buys. Then write ¢ in the answer.

$$32¢ \div 4 = 8¢ \qquad 4\overline{)\,32¢}\;\overset{8¢}{}$$

Each balloon costs 8¢.

PRACTICE

Divide. Remember the ¢.

1. $12¢ \div 4$ 2. $4¢ \div 4$ 3. $20¢ \div 4$ 4. $8¢ \div 4$ 5. $16¢ \div 4$

6. $32 \div 4$ 7. $24 \div 4$ 8. $4 \div 4$ 9. $28 \div 4$ 10. $36 \div 4$

11. $4\overline{)\,16¢}$ 12. $4\overline{)\,32¢}$ 13. $4\overline{)\,8¢}$ 14. $4\overline{)\,36¢}$ 15. $4\overline{)\,12¢}$ 16. $4\overline{)\,24¢}$

17. $4\overline{)\,20}$ 18. $4\overline{)\,4}$ 19. $4\overline{)\,12}$ 20. $4\overline{)\,20}$ 21. $4\overline{)\,28}$ 22. $4\overline{)\,36}$

MIXED PRACTICE
Maintaining and Reviewing Skills

Add, subtract, multiply, or divide.

23. $8 \div 4$ 24. $4\overline{)\,32¢}$ 25. $27 \div 3$ 26. 6×2 27. 7×3

28. $\begin{array}{r} 4 \\ \times 8 \\ \hline \end{array}$
29. $\begin{array}{r} 18 \\ +12 \\ \hline \end{array}$
30. $\begin{array}{r} 97 \\ -62 \\ \hline \end{array}$
31. $\begin{array}{r} 3 \\ \times 6 \\ \hline \end{array}$
32. $\begin{array}{r} 542 \\ +361 \\ \hline \end{array}$
33. $\begin{array}{r} \overset{2}{8}35 \\ -207 \\ \hline 628 \end{array}$

| FOCUS | Use MEASUREMENT and NUMBER skills to divide by fours. |

156

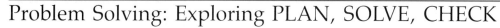

Problem Solving: Exploring PLAN, SOLVE, CHECK

Remember to READ, KNOW, PLAN, SOLVE, and CHECK all problems. See the Five-Step Plan on page 425 in the Data Bank.

There are 365 days in a year. A **leap year,** which happens once every 4 years, has 366 days. The extra day in a leap year is February 29.

Follow the steps to find out if a year is a leap year.

> Step 1: Write the last 2 digits of the year.
> Step 2: Divide this number by 4.
> Step 3: If the number can be divided by 4 evenly, it is a leap year.

Which of the following years are leap years?

34. 1820: 20 ÷ 4 = 5
1820 is a leap year.

35. 1909: 9 cannot be divided by 4 evenly. 1909 is not a leap year.

36. 1936 $36 \div 4 = 9$

37. 1824

38. 2004 $04 \div 4 = 1$

39. 1917

40. 1832 $\div 4$

41. 2012

42. 2027 $\div 27$

43. 1934

44. 1916

45. 1808

46. 1830

47. 2020

48. 2021

49. 1930

50. The year 1984 was a leap year. Write the 9 leap years that follow 1984.

Explore the PLAN, SOLVE, and CHECK steps of the Five-Step PROBLEM-SOLVING Plan.

DIVISION
Dividing by Fives

How many puzzle pieces are in this picture?

There are 25 puzzle pieces. How many groups of 5 pieces are there?

Divide to find how many groups of 5 there are. Divide the number of pieces in all by the number of pieces in each group.

25 pieces in all   5 in each group   5 groups

$$25 \div 5 = 5$$

Twenty-five **divided by** five **is equal to** five.

There are 5 groups of 5 puzzle pieces.

$$25 \div 5 = 5 \qquad 5\overline{)25} \;=\; 5$$

GUIDED PRACTICE

Divide to show how many groups there are.

1.

How many 5s
are in 10?

$$10 \div 5 = 2$$

2.

How many 5s
are in 5?

$$5 \div 5 = \blacksquare$$

3.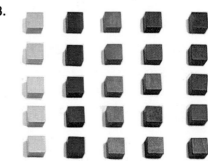

How many 5s
are in 25?

$$25 \div 5 = \blacksquare$$

4. $5\overline{)15}$ **5.** $5\overline{)25}$ **6.** $5\overline{)40}$ **7.** $5\overline{)20}$ **8.** $5\overline{)45}$ **9.** $5\overline{)35}$

| FOCUS | Use NUMBER skills to divide by fives. |

158

PRACTICE

Divide.

10. $5 \div 5$ **11.** $15 \div 5$ **12.** $25 \div 5$ **13.** $10 \div 5$ **14.** $20 \div 5$

15. $40 \div 5$ **16.** $30 \div 5$ **17.** $5 \div 5$ **18.** $35 \div 5$ **19.** $45 \div 5$

20. $5\overline{)10}$ **21.** $5\overline{)40}$ **22.** $5\overline{)20}$ **23.** $5\overline{)25}$ **24.** $5\overline{)5}$ **25.** $5\overline{)15}$

26. $5\overline{)45}$ **27.** $5\overline{)35}$ **28.** $5\overline{)15}$ **29.** $5\overline{)30}$ **30.** $5\overline{)40}$ **31.** $5\overline{)25}$

Solve each problem.

32. Write a word problem that could be solved by dividing 20 by 5. Then solve the problem.

33. Write a word problem that could be solved by dividing 45 by 5. Then solve the problem.

MIXED PRACTICE
Maintaining and Reviewing Skills

Add, subtract, multiply, or divide.

34. $15 \div 5$ **35.** $5\overline{)40}$ **36.** $16 \div 4$ **37.** $3\overline{)21}$ **38.** $18 \div 2$

39. 3×8 **40.** $15 - 7$ **41.** $18 + 8$ **42.** 2×6 **43.** 4×9

44. $\begin{array}{r} 27 \\ + 9 \\ \hline \end{array}$ **45.** $\begin{array}{r} 4 \\ \times 4 \\ \hline \end{array}$ **46.** $\begin{array}{r} 96 \\ - 7 \\ \hline \end{array}$ **47.** $\begin{array}{r} 2 \\ \times 7 \\ \hline \end{array}$ **48.** $\begin{array}{r} 62 \\ + 35 \\ \hline \end{array}$ **49.** $\begin{array}{r} 78 \\ - 59 \\ \hline \end{array}$

CHALLENGE

50. Sue has 3 apples. Each apple is cut into 4 pieces. Two people are going to eat the apples. How many pieces will each person eat?

51. Lee has 5 pizzas. Each is cut into 4 pieces. Five people are going to eat the pizzas. How many pieces will each person eat?

DIVISION
Dividing by Twos, Threes, Fours, and Fives

David has 16 doves. He has 4 cages. He wants to put the same number of doves in each cage.

Divide to find how many doves David will put in each cage.

$$16 \div 4 = 4 \quad \text{or} \quad 4\overline{)16}^{\;4}$$

David will put 4 doves in each cage.

PRACTICE

How many birds will David put in each cage?

1. He has 2 cages.   **2.** He has 5 cages.   **3.** He has 3 cages.

Divide.

4. $10 \div 5$ **5.** $12 \div 2$ **6.** $24 \div 4$ **7.** $3 \div 3$ **8.** $16 \div 2$

9. $3\overline{)21}$ **10.** $5\overline{)25}$ **11.** $4\overline{)4}$ **12.** $2\overline{)18}$ **13.** $4\overline{)36}$ **14.** $5\overline{)45}$

MIXED PRACTICE
Maintaining and Reviewing Skills

Add, subtract, multiply, or divide.

15. $27 \div 3$ **16.** $10 \div 2$ **17.** $5\overline{)35}$ **18.** $4\overline{)28}$ **19.** 7×3

20. $\begin{array}{r} 4 \\ \times 9 \\ \hline \end{array}$ **21.** $\begin{array}{r} 2 \\ \times 8 \\ \hline \end{array}$ **22.** $\begin{array}{r} 34 \\ -12 \\ \hline \end{array}$ **23.** $\begin{array}{r} 45 \\ +22 \\ \hline \end{array}$ **24.** $\begin{array}{r} 56 \\ +38 \\ \hline \end{array}$ **25.** $\begin{array}{r} 73 \\ -29 \\ \hline \end{array}$

FOCUS | Use NUMBER skills to divide by twos, threes, fours, and fives.

APPLICATION

Using Patterns and Functions

Use the number line to count backward by 2. Start with 18. What number do you end on?

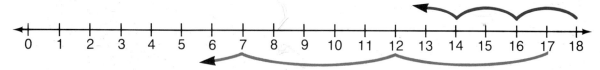

Now count backward by 5. Start with 17. What number do you end on?

When you count backward, you are subtracting.

When you count backward by 2, you are subtracting 2 from each number. When you count backward by 5, you are subtracting 5 from each number.

Count backward by 2 to complete each pattern.

26. 10, 8, 6, ▦, ▦
27. 14, 12, 10, ▦, ▦
28. 32, 30, 28, ▦, ▦

29. 15, 13, 11, ▦, ▦
30. 17, 15, 13, ▦, ▦
31. 29, 27, 25, ▦, ▦

Count backward by 5 to complete each pattern.

32. 25, 20, 15, ▦, ▦
33. 40, 35, 30, ▦, ▦
34. 85, 80, 75, ▦, ▦

35. 27, 22, 17, ▦, ▦
36. 33, 28, 23, ▦, ▦
37. 61, 56, 51, ▦, ▦

Mental Arithmetic

Any **even number** can be divided by 2.

Any number that ends in 0 or 5 can be divided by 5.

Can the numbers be divided by 2, 5, or both?

38. 15   **39.** 12   **40.** 44   **41.** 65   **42.** 20   **43.** 95   **44.** 60   **45.** 100

Use NUMBER skills and PATTERNS AND FUNCTIONS to count and divide by twos and fives.

Distance

Today, the city called Rome is the capital of Italy. But once it was the capital of a giant empire.

The rulers in Rome had to send messengers and soldiers all over the empire. They built many roads to make traveling easier. But there was a problem.

When the Romans first built these roads, they did not have maps. They just had to remember where the roads were. They needed to know where roads went and how far apart places were from each other. So they invented the road map.

This is how they did it. First they measured the roads. They put up a stone to mark each mile. They called them "milestones." The Roman mile was measured as 5,000 feet. Today, a land mile is measured as 5,280 feet.

The Romans counted the milestones to figure out distances between cities. Then they put these distances on a map with pictures of the roads.

They used Roman numerals that look like this: I, V, X (1, 5, 10). Mile markers are still used on highways today.

Road maps are still used today, too. They show distance as the Roman maps did, with numerals beside the road to tell the distance between cities. To figure out the distance from one place to another, add up all the numbers in between.

CRITICAL THINKING

1. How can road maps be helpful when making travel plans?

2. How else can a road map be helpful?

3. How many feet would you travel if you went 3 Roman miles? Is this more or less distance than 3 modern miles?

4. Compare Roman and modern mile markers. Which do you think are easier to use? Why?

FOCUS | Use MEASUREMENT and LOGIC to understand distance.

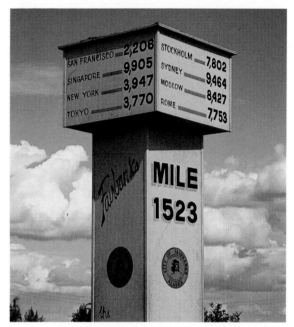

This ancient Roman milepost still stands.

This mile marker is on the Alaskan Highway.

This Third Century map of Rome was used by medieval travelers.

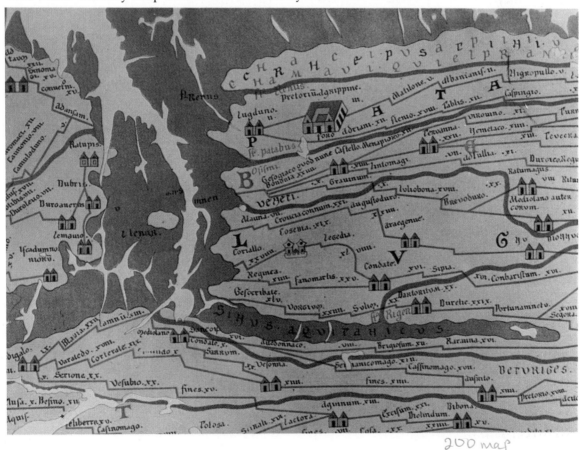

200 map

LOOKING BACK
Reviewing and Testing Chapter 12

In Chapter 12 you formulated problems about museums. Look at pages 152 and 153.

1. Write a sentence telling what you might see in a history museum.

You learned something new about dividing fours. To review what you learned, study the sample on page 154. Then use the new skill to find each quotient for examples 2 to 14.

2. $8 \div 4$ **3.** $16 \div 4$ **4.** $32 \div 4$ **5.** $20 \div 4$ **6.** $36 \div 4$

7. $4\overline{)28}$ **8.** $4\overline{)12}$ **9.** $4\overline{)36}$ **10.** $4\overline{)24}$ **11.** $4\overline{)16}$ **12.** $4\overline{)32}$

13. Ruth has 20 bananas. She puts 4 in each bowl. How many bowls does she use?

14. Write a word problem that you could solve by dividing 32 by 4. Then solve the problem.

You learned something new about dividing fives. To review, look at pages 158 and 159. Use the new skill to find each quotient for examples 15 to 27.

15. $35 \div 5$ **16.** $10 \div 5$ **17.** $40 \div 5$ **18.** $30 \div 5$ **19.** $45 \div 5$

20. $5\overline{)30}$ **21.** $5\overline{)15}$ **22.** $5\overline{)45}$ **23.** $5\overline{)25}$ **24.** $5\overline{)20}$ **25.** $5\overline{)40}$

26. Joe has 10 pieces of fruit. He puts 5 in each bag. How many bags does Joe use?

27. Write a word problem that you could solve by dividing 35 by 5. Then solve the problem.

You learned about road maps. Look at page 162 to review what you learned.

28. Why did the Romans invent the road map?

FOCUS | Review and test skills learned and practiced.

164

LOOKING AHEAD

Preparing for New Skills for Chapter 13

In the next chapter you will focus on

- formulating problems.
- understanding inverse operations.
- multiplying and dividing by one.
- using logic.
- a problem-solving strategy.
- multiplying three factors.
- multiplying by zero.

Learning new multiplication and division skills will be easier if you brush up on the skills you already know. Study the model.

Then complete the PRACTICE exercises. Check your work with the model.

Model

There are 3 bowls. Each bowl has 4 oranges. How many oranges are there in all?

There are 12 oranges in bowls. Each bowl has 4 oranges. How many bowls are there?

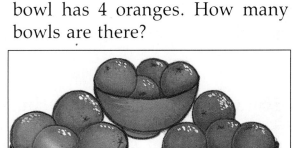

There are 12 oranges in all because $3 \times 4 = 12$.

There are 3 bowls because $12 \div 4 = 3$.

PRACTICE

Multiply or divide. Review the model.

1. 4×5
2. 7×2
3. 9×3
4. 6×4
5. 8×5

6. $20 \div 5$
7. $14 \div 2$
8. $27 \div 3$
9. $24 \div 4$
10. $40 \div 5$

Review NUMBER skills in preparation for learning a new skill.

FOCUS   Formulate problems using picture cues, text, and data.

CHAPTER 13

Multiplication and Division

DATA

Pet owner   Ben Davis

Type of pet

  Gerbil

    Moves most during day
    Cage not too big
    Very clean animal
    Can be tamed

  Rabbit

    Moves most during
      night
    Big cage
    Easy to tame a baby
      rabbit
    May shed fur a few
      times each year

As you can see from the picture, a pet needs to be cared for. A dog or a cat needs a corner to sleep in. Fish need a tank. A hamster needs a cage. Pets need water, the right food, and room in which to play and exercise. Some pets can be touched. Others can be watched through glass. You must think carefully before you choose a pet.

Can you think of some questions to ask about a type of pet? For example, what kind of food does it eat? Does it like to be held by its owner?

What will Ben need to keep in mind when he chooses a pet? What problems might come up? Using the data, decide which pet would be best for Ben. Give your reasons.

MULTIPLICATION AND DIVISION
Inverse Operations

Sue sees 4 rows of pumpkins. She sees 2 pumpkins in each row. How many pumpkins does Sue see?

Multiply to solve. $4 \times 2 = 8$

Sue sees 8 pumpkins.

Will sees 8 pumpkins. He sees 2 pumpkins in each row. How many rows of pumpkins does Will see?

Use the multiplication fact to solve the division fact.

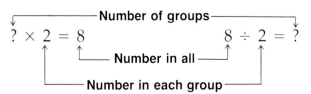

$4 \times 2 = 8$ so $8 \div 2 = 4$ Will sees 4 rows of pumpkins.

GUIDED PRACTICE

Use the picture to find the missing numbers.

1.

$3 \times 5 = 15$ $15 \div 5 = 3$

2.

$\blacksquare \times 3 = 6$ $6 \div 3 = \blacksquare$

3.

$\blacksquare \times 4 = 20$ $20 \div 4 = \blacksquare$

4.

$\blacksquare \times 5 = 20$ $20 \div 5 = \blacksquare$

PRACTICE

Complete.

5. $6 \times 3 = 18$
$18 \div 3 = 6$

6. $5 \times 5 = 25$
$25 \div 5 = 5$

7. $8 \times 2 = 16$
$16 \div 2 = 8$

8. $6 \times 4 = 24$
$24 \div 4 = 6$

9. $\blacksquare \times 4 = 32$
$32 \div 4 = \blacksquare$

10. $\blacksquare \times 3 = 24$
$24 \div 3 = \blacksquare$

11. $\blacksquare \times 5 = 30$
$30 \div 5 = 6$

12. $\blacksquare \times 2 = 18$
$18 \div 2 = 9$

Write the fact that does not belong.

13. $4 \times 3 = 12$	**14.** $10 \div 2 = 5$	**15.** $4 \times 2 = 8$	**16.** $15 \div 5 = 3$
$12 \div 3 = 4$	$10 - 2 = 8$ ✗	$2 \times 4 = 8$	$3 \times 5 = 15$
$12 \div 4 = 3$	$5 \times 2 = 10$	$8 \times 1 = 8$ ✗	$5 \times 3 = 15$
$3 \times 4 = 12$	$10 \div 5 = 2$	$8 \div 2 = 4$	$15 \div 3 = 5$
$12 \div 6 = 2$ ✗	$2 \times 5 = 10$	$8 \div 4 = 2$	$5 + 3 = 8$ ✗

Multiply or divide.

17. $35 \div 5$ **18.** 7×2 **19.** $21 \div 3$ **20.** 8×5 **21.** $36 \div 4$

MIXED PRACTICE
Maintaining and Reviewing Skills

Add, subtract, multiply, or divide.

22. $\blacksquare \times 3 = 27$
$27 \div 3 = \blacksquare$

23. $\blacksquare \times 5 = 40$
$40 \div 5 = \blacksquare$

24. $\begin{array}{r} 7 \\ \times 3 \\ \hline \end{array}$

25. $\begin{array}{r} 168 \\ + 107 \\ \hline \end{array}$

26. $\begin{array}{r} 394 \\ - 285 \\ \hline \end{array}$

CHALLENGE

Use each group of 3 numbers to write a multiplication sentence and a division sentence.

27. 4, 8, 32   **28.** 2, 16, 8   **29.** 5, 3, 15   **30.** 27, 9, 3   **31.** 3, 12, 4

MULTIPLICATION AND DIVISION
Multiplying and Dividing by One

Yoko has 3 vases. She puts 1 flower in each vase. How many flowers does Yoko have?

$$3 \times 1 = 3$$

Yoko has 3 flowers.

Luis has 3 flowers in all. He puts 1 flower in each vase. How many vases does Luis have?

$$3 \div 1 = 3$$

Luis has 3 vases.

> When a number is multiplied by 1, the answer is that number.

> When a number is divided by 1, the answer is that number.

PRACTICE

Multiply or divide.

1. $4 \div 1$ 2. 5×1 3. 4×1 4. 1×1 5. $2 \div 1$

6. 6×1 7. $8 \div 1$ 8. $9 \div 1$ 9. 7×1 10. $5 \div 1$

11. $1\overline{)7}$ 12. $\begin{array}{r} 1 \\ \times 9 \\ \hline \end{array}$ 13. $1\overline{)6}$ 14. $\begin{array}{r} 1 \\ \times 8 \\ \hline \end{array}$ 15. $1\overline{)3}$ 16. $\begin{array}{r} 1 \\ \times 2 \\ \hline \end{array}$

17. Arthur has 5 seeds in all. He puts 1 seed in each hole. How many holes did Arthur dig?

18. Cindy has 7 pots. She puts 1 plant in each pot. How many plants does Cindy have?

MIXED PRACTICE
Maintaining and Reviewing Skills

Add, subtract, multiply, or divide.

19. $\begin{array}{r} 1 \\ \times 9 \\ \hline \end{array}$ 20. $1\overline{)8}$ 21. $\begin{array}{r} 33 \\ + 66 \\ \hline \end{array}$ 22. $\begin{array}{r} 77 \\ - 58 \\ \hline \end{array}$ 23. $\begin{array}{r} 458 \\ - 37 \\ \hline \end{array}$ 24. $\begin{array}{r} 655 \\ + 39 \\ \hline \end{array}$

FOCUS   Use NUMBER skills to multiply and divide by ones.

APPLICATION
Using Logic

If today is Monday, **then** tomorrow will be Tuesday.

Sentences like this are called **if/then statements.**

Here is another if/then statement.

> **If** 2 times 3 equals 6, **then** 6 divided by 3 equals 2.
> **If** $2 \times 3 = 6$, **then** $6 \div 3 = 2$.

Complete each if/then statement.

25. If today is Friday, then tomorrow will be ■.

26. If this month is May, then next month will be ■.

27. If it is Fall in Maine, then the leaves change ■.

28. If a number is multiplied by 1, then the product is ■.

29. If $6 \times 3 = 18$, then $18 \div 3 = $ ■

30. If $5 \times 2 = 10$, then $10 \div 2 = $ ■

31. If $21 \div 3 = 7$, then $7 \times 3 = $ ■

32. If $36 \div 4 = 9$, then $9 \times 4 = $ ■

33. If $6 \times 4 = 24$, then ■ $\div$ ■ $=$ ■

34. If $40 \div 5 = 8$, then ■ $\times$ ■ $=$ ■

35. If $35 \div 5 = 7$, then ■ $\times$ ■ $=$ ■

36. If $7 \times 6 = 42$, then ■ $\div$ ■ $=$ ■

37. If $9 \times 2 = 18$, then ■ $\div$ ■ $=$ ■

38. If $24 \div 3 = 8$, then ■ $\times$ ■ $=$ ■

Mental Arithmetic

Read each fact. Then write the answer as quickly as you can.

39. 5×1

40. $1 \overline{)3}$

41. 1×1

42. $1 \overline{)6}$

43. 8×1

44. $1 \overline{)2}$

45. 6×1

46. $1 \overline{)4}$

47. 9×1

48. $1 \overline{)7}$

49. 4×1

50. $1 \overline{)9}$

51. 7×1

52. $1 \overline{)8}$

53. 2×1

Use LOGIC and MENTAL ARITHMETIC to solve problems.

PROBLEM SOLVING
Selecting a Strategy: Using a Diagram

Selecting a strategy is part of the PLAN step. Using a diagram is a strategy you can choose. A **diagram** is a drawing that shows the information you are given. Use a diagram to help you KNOW what the problem is and to help you PLAN and SOLVE the problem. Sometimes a diagram is given. Sometimes you will need to draw your own diagram.

1. READ   Debbie is making a window with colored glass. How many pieces of glass have only 3 sides?

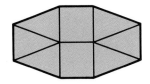

2. KNOW   Ask yourself: What am I being asked to find? How many pieces of glass have 3 sides? What **key facts** do I need? Triangles have 3 sides.

3. PLAN   Select a strategy: try using a diagram. Look at each piece of glass in the diagram and count the triangles.

4. SOLVE   There are 6 pieces of glass with 3 sides.

5. CHECK   Ask yourself: Why is my answer reasonable? There are 8 pieces of glass in all. The number of pieces with 3 sides is less than 8, so 6 is a reasonable answer.

| FOCUS | Evaluate information as part of the Five-Step PROBLEM-SOLVING Plan. |

PRACTICE

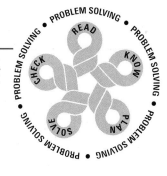

Use the diagram to solve Problems 1–3. The area of each square is one square unit.

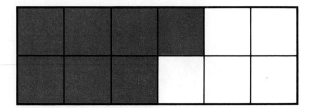

1. What is the area of the red part of the figure?

2. What is the area of the white part of the figure?

3. What is the area of the whole rectangle?

Draw a diagram to help you solve Problems 4 and 5.

4. A figure has an area of 9 square units. Each square unit is red or blue. If 4 square units are red, what is the area of the blue part of the figure?

5. A rectangle has an area of 10 square units. Each square unit is green, orange, or purple. If 6 square units are green, what could the areas of the orange and purple parts be?

Class Project

Work with a partner. Draw a rectangle with an area of 12 square units so that there are 4 square units across and 3 square units down. Using 3 different color crayons, color each square unit so that none of the square units with the same color touch each other.

MULTIPLICATION
Multiplying Three Factors

How many seashells are there?

Here is one way to find the total number of seashells.

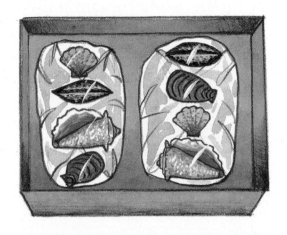

NUMBER OF BOXES	SHELLS IN EACH BOX	
	Packs in each box	Shells in each pack
↓	↓	↓
2 ×	2 ×	4
2 ×	8	= 16

Here is another way to find the number of shells in all.

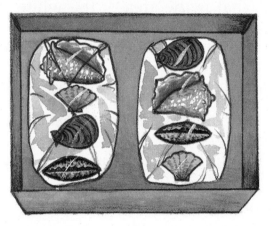

NUMBER OF PACKS		SHELLS IN EACH PACK
Number of boxes	Packs in each box	
↓	↓	↓
2 ×	2 ×	4
4	· ×	4 = 16

The grouping of the factors does not matter.
The product will stay the same.

There are 16 seashells in all.

GUIDED PRACTICE

Multiply.

1. 1 × 4 × 5 = ■

4 × 5 = ■

2. 4 × 1 × 5 = ■

4 × ■ = ■

3. 5 × 1 × 4 = ■

■ × ■ = ■

PRACTICE

Multiply.

4. $2 \times 1 \times 4$ **5.** $5 \times 1 \times 3$ **6.** $2 \times 4 \times 2$ **7.** $1 \times 3 \times 3$

8. $1 \times 5 \times 5$ **9.** $2 \times 3 \times 2$ **10.** $1 \times 1 \times 1$ **11.** $5 \times 1 \times 2$

12. $2 \times 2 \times 2$ **13.** $4 \times 4 \times 1$ **14.** $3 \times 2 \times 4$ **15.** $2 \times 3 \times 3$

Multiply. Then use another grouping
and multiply.

16. $5 \times 2 \times 1$ **17.** $2 \times 2 \times 3$ **18.** $4 \times 1 \times 4$ **19.** $4 \times 2 \times 3$

Solve each problem.

20. Sara has 2 boxes of rings.
There are 3 packs in each box.
There is 1 ring in each pack.
How many rings are there
in all?

21. Mark has 1 box of pins.
There are 4 packs in each box.
There are 5 pins in each pack.
How many pins are there in all?

MIXED PRACTICE
Maintaining and Reviewing Skills

Add, subtract, multiply, or divide.

22. $4 \times 1 \times 2$ **23.** $2 \times 1 \times 3$ **24.** $24 \div 3$ **25.** $18 \div 2$

26. $\begin{array}{r} 25 \\ +13 \end{array}$ **27.** $\begin{array}{r} 37 \\ -21 \end{array}$ **28.** $\begin{array}{r} 5 \\ \times 7 \end{array}$ **29.** $\begin{array}{r} 9 \\ \times 1 \end{array}$ **30.** $\begin{array}{r} 438 \\ +249 \end{array}$ **31.** $\begin{array}{r} 387 \\ -158 \end{array}$

CHALLENGE

32. There are 2 brown houses. Each house has 3 bedrooms. Each bedroom has 2 beds. How many beds are there in all?

33. Draw a picture to answer the question in exercise 32.

MULTIPLICATION
Multiplying by Zero

Edgar has 2 fish tanks. Each fish tank is empty. How many fish does Edgar have?

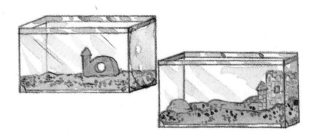

$$2 \times 0 = 0$$

Edgar has 0 fish.

When a number is multiplied by 0, the product is 0.

PRACTICE

Fill in the boxes. Then find the product.

1.

There are ■ cages.
There are ■ birds in each cage.
$$3 \times 0 = ■$$

2.

There are ■ nests.
There are ■ birds in each nest.
$$4 \times 0 = ■$$

Multiply.

3. 5×0 **4.** 8×0 **5.** 1×0 **6.** 7×0 **7.** 3×0

8. $\begin{array}{r} 0 \\ \times 7 \\ \hline \end{array}$ **9.** $\begin{array}{r} 0 \\ \times 2 \\ \hline \end{array}$ **10.** $\begin{array}{r} 0 \\ \times 6 \\ \hline \end{array}$ **11.** $\begin{array}{r} 0 \\ \times 4 \\ \hline \end{array}$ **12.** $\begin{array}{r} 0 \\ \times 9 \\ \hline \end{array}$ **13.** $\begin{array}{r} 0 \\ \times 0 \\ \hline \end{array}$

MIXED PRACTICE
Maintaining and Reviewing Skills

Multiply or divide.

14. $\begin{array}{r} 0 \\ \times 6 \\ \hline \end{array}$ **15.** $\begin{array}{r} 0 \\ \times 0 \\ \hline \end{array}$ **16.** $\begin{array}{r} 1 \\ \times 8 \\ \hline \end{array}$ **17.** $\begin{array}{r} 1 \\ \times 3 \\ \hline \end{array}$ **18.** $1\overline{)7}$ **19.** $1\overline{)9}$

FOCUS   Use NUMBER skills to multiply by zero.

APPLICATION
Problem Solving: Using a Diagram

Remember to READ, KNOW, PLAN, SOLVE, and CHECK all problems. See the Five-Step Plan on page 425 in the Data Bank.

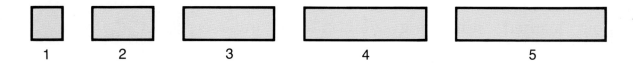

| 1 | 2 | 3 | 4 | 5 |

Trace the shapes, placing them side by side, to show each multiplication sentence. Is each pair the same length? Multiply. Does each pair have the same product?

20. 1×4
4×1

21. 2×3
3×2

22. 1×2
2×1

23. 2×4
4×2

24. 4×5
5×4

25. 1×3
3×1

26. 3×5
5×3

27. 3×4
4×3

28. 4×1
1×4

29. 2×5
5×2

30. 1×5
5×1

Draw a diagram to solve the problem.

31. Glynn has three boxes. Two boxes have one doll. One box has three dolls. How many dolls does Glynn have?

Use a diagram and apply the Five-Step PROBLEM-SOLVING Plan.

LOOKING BACK
Reviewing and Testing Chapter 13

In Chapter 13 you formulated problems about owning a pet. Look at pages 166 and 167.

1. Write a sentence telling how to care for a pet.

You learned something new about inverse operations. To review what you learned, study the sample problem on page 168. Then use the new skill to find each answer for examples 2 to 9.

2. ■ × 4 = 12
   12 ÷ 4 = ■

3. ■ × 2 = 10
   10 ÷ 2 = ■

4. ■ × 3 = 9
   9 ÷ 3 = ■

5. ■ × 5 = 40
   40 ÷ 5 = ■

6. ■ × 2 = 8
   8 ÷ 2 = ■

7. ■ × 4 = 36
   36 ÷ 4 = ■

8. ■ × 5 = 25
   25 ÷ 5 = ■

9. ■ × 3 = 21
   21 ÷ 3 = ■

You learned how to use a diagram to help you solve problems. To review, look at pages 172 and 173. Use the diagram to solve problems 10 and 11.

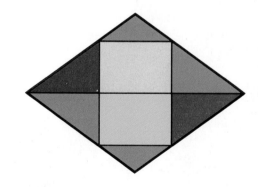

10. The stained glass picture has different pieces of colored glass. How many pieces have four sides?

11. How many blue pieces of glass with three sides are in the picture?

You learned something new about multiplying three factors. To review, look at page 174. Use the new skill to find each product for examples 12 to 19.

12. 3 × 2 × 2

13. 2 × 2 × 1

14. 5 × 2 × 1

15. 2 × 3 × 2

16. 2 × 2 × 2

17. 3 × 3 × 2

18. 4 × 4 × 1

19. 5 × 1 × 5

| FOCUS | Review and test skills learned and practiced. |

LOOKING AHEAD

Preparing for New Skills for Chapter 14

In the next chapter you will focus on

- formulating problems.
- telling time to the minute.
- understanding elapsed time.
- statistics and probability.
- reading Celsius temperature.
- graphing Celsius temperature.
- a problem-solving strategy.
- math in social studies.

New time-telling skills will be easier to learn if you review the time-telling skills you already know. Study Models A and B. Do the PRACTICE exercises. Check your work with the models.

Model A—Time on the hour.

1 o'clock   6 o'clock
1:00   6:00

Model B—Time on the half hour.

30 minutes   30 minutes
after 1   after 6
1:30   6:30

PRACTICE

1. Which clock shows that it is 8 o'clock?

A.    B.    C.

2. Which clock shows that it is 30 minutes after 2?

A.    B.    C.

Review MEASUREMENT in preparation for learning new skills.

FOCUS   Formulate problems using picture cues, text, and data.

14

Time and Temperature

DATA

Store	Ricky's Rink Shop
Skaters	Holly Katie
Customer	Katie
Katie's shoe size	5
Spending money	$35.00

Ice skates for sale

Single-blade boot (stays same size)	$29.95
Color	White
Sizes	5 and up
Double-blade attaches to shoe (expands to change size)	$12.95
Color	White
Size	5 and up

Ice-skating is an exciting sport! A skater may glide around the rim of a frozen pond. He or she may spin in circles on the smooth surface of an ice-skating rink. In any case, a skater must have a pair of skates that fits properly. Ice skates must fit snugly and securely on the feet to help a skater balance.

Katie is learning how to skate. Her sister Holly is an expert skater. Holly is teaching Katie at a local rink. She is also going to help Katie choose her skates. Using the picture and the data, think about the things a skater must know in order to buy a pair of skates. What problems must be solved before Katie gets a new pair of skates?

TIME

Reading a Clock

The minute hand is the long hand. As this minute hand moves from 12 to 3, 15 minutes pass.

As the minute hand moves from one number to the next, 5 minutes pass.

There are 60 minutes in one hour.

As the hour hand moves from one number to the next, 1 hour passes.

5:15
Hour Minutes

Look at these clocks.

Read: 10 minutes after 11 OR 11:10

Read: 30 minutes after 2 OR 2:30

Read: 37 minutes after 4 OR 4:37

GUIDED PRACTICE

Write the time shown on each clock in two ways.

1.

5:45

2.

9:■

3.

■:■

PRACTICE

Write the time shown on each clock in two ways.

4.  **5.**  **6.**  **7.**

8.  **9.**  **10.**  **11.**

12.  **13.**  **14.**  **15.**

16.  **17.**  **18.**  **19.**

MIXED PRACTICE
Maintaining and Reviewing Skills

Add, subtract, or multiply.

20. $18 - 12$ **21.** 5×7 **22.** $23 + 46$ **23.** 9×5 **24.** $11 + 21$

CHALLENGE

25. How many 5-minute periods are in 1 hour?

TIME

Using A.M. and P.M.

The hour hand goes around a clock twice each day, covering 24 hours. Twelve o'clock noon and twelve o'clock midnight divide the day.

A.M. is from midnight to noon. From 6:30 A.M. to 6:52 A.M. 22 minutes pass.

P.M. is from noon to midnight. From 6:30 P.M. to 9:46 P.M. 3 hours and 16 minutes pass.

$$\begin{array}{r} 6\text{:}52 \text{ A.M.} \\ -\,6\text{:}30 \text{ A.M.} \\ \hline 22 \text{ minutes} \end{array}$$

$$\begin{array}{r} 9\text{:}46 \text{ P.M.} \\ -\,6\text{:}30 \text{ P.M.} \\ \hline 3 \text{ h } 16 \text{ min} \end{array}$$

PRACTICE

Mr. Andrews and Mr. Sanchez work nights at a post office. Complete the chart to show how they spend their time.

Post Office Job	Time In	Working Time	Time Out
1. Pick up letters	10:00 P.M.	45 minutes	■
2. Empty mailboxes	11:10 P.M.	1 hour	■
3. Lunch break	12:05 A.M.	35 minutes	■
4. Sort out letters	1:15 A.M.	40 minutes	■
5. Pick up packages	2:00 A.M.	■	3:25 A.M.
6. Pack truck with mail	2:15 A.M.	■	3:45 A.M.
7. Fill stamp machines	■	20 minutes	3:45 A.M.
8. Clean post office	4:00 A.M.	45 minutes	■

MIXED PRACTICE

Maintaining and Reviewing Skills

Add, subtract, or multiply.

9. 5×4 **10.** $72 + 15$ **11.** $86 - 32$ **12.** 2×9 **13.** $48 - 36$

FOCUS | Use MEASUREMENT to explore A.M. and P.M. and elapsed time, and to complete a time schedule.

184

APPLICATION
Using Statistics and Probability

The Booneville Rapid Transit Company is proud of its on-time record. The chart below shows the daily morning timetable of trains and stops.

Station	Arrival Time
Oak Street	7:33 A.M.
First Avenue	7:46 A.M.
Kings Highway	8:01 A.M.
Main Street	8:15 A.M.
Fifth Avenue	8:28 A.M.
Court Street	8:42 A.M.

Use the timetable to solve each problem.

14. How long does it take to go from Oak Street to First Avenue?

15. How long does it take to go from Kings Highway to Court Street?

16. Does the train stop at Main Street or Court Street first?

17. Mr. Larson catches the train at 8:01 A.M. Where does he get on?

18. Bad weather one day caused the train to arrive 15 minutes late at the Kings Highway station. What time did it get there?

19. Mrs. Murphy gets to the Fifth Avenue station at 8:20 A.M. How long must she wait for the train?

20. Mr. Baron gets on the train at 7:46 A.M. He gets off the train at 8:42 A.M. At which station does he get on? At which station does he get off?

21. Ms. Dennis got on the train at Oak Street and off at Court Street. What time did she get on? What time did she get off? How long was she on the train?

Use MEASUREMENT and STATISTICS AND PROBABILITY to read and interpret a timetable.

185

TEMPERATURE
Reading a Celsius Thermometer

We use a thermometer to find the temperature of things. Temperature is measured in **degrees**. A **Celsius thermometer** shows the temperature in degrees Celsius (°C). The thermometer on the right is a Celsius thermometer.

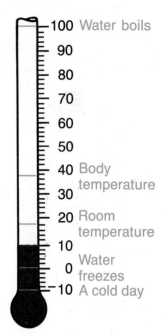

The distance between each mark is 2°.

The temperature on the thermometer reads 10°C or ten degrees Celsius.

When the temperature drops below zero to −10°C, we say "10 degrees below zero."

GUIDED PRACTICE

Read each thermometer and write the temperature.
Remember to write °C after each temperature.

1.
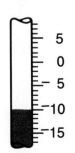

2.
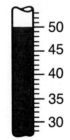

3.
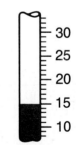

4.
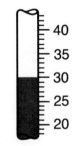

5.
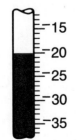

6.
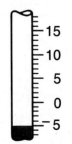

FOCUS Use MEASUREMENT to read a thermometer and determine temperature differences.

186

PRACTICE

Write each temperature in degrees Celsius.

7. 70 60 50 40 30

8. 20 10 0 -10 -20

9. 80 70 60 50 40

10. 60 50 40 30 20

11. 100 90 80 70 60

12. 20 10 0 -10 -20

13. 50 40 30 20 10

14. 10 0 -10 -20 -30

Use the thermometer on page 186 to solve each problem.

15. What is 25 degrees above room temperature?

$20° + 25° = $ ▨

16. What is 30 degrees below boiling?

$100° - 30° = $ ▨

17. What is 15 degrees above freezing?

▨ $+$ ▨ $=$ ▨

MIXED PRACTICE

Maintaining and Reviewing Skills

Add, subtract, or multiply.

18. 9×5 **19.** $382 - 146$ **20.** $156 + 318$ **21.** 2×8 **22.** $64 + 13$

CHALLENGE

23. At 7 A.M. the temperature outside was 4°C. By 2 P.M. that day the temperature had dropped 10 degrees. What was the temperature at 2 P.M.?

TEMPERATURE

Graphing Celsius Temperatures

Class 3A in the Central City School kept track of outdoor temperatures for 7 days. Then they drew a bar graph using the data they collected.

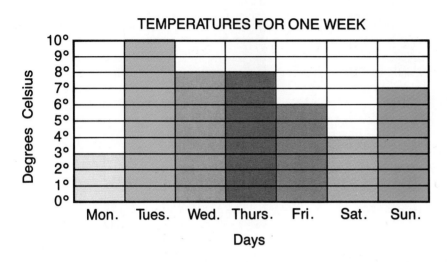

TEMPERATURES FOR ONE WEEK

PRACTICE

Use the bar graph to answer the questions.

1. Which day was the coldest?

2. Which day was the warmest?

3. What was the temperature on Thursday?

4. What was the temperature on Sunday?

5. Between which two days did the temperature rise the most?

6. How did the temperature change from Saturday to Sunday?

MIXED PRACTICE

Maintaining and Reviewing Skills

Add, subtract, or multiply.

7. 218
   −157

8. 376
   +241

9.   8
   ×4

10. 67
    −38

11. 74
    +28

FOCUS | Use STATISTICS AND PROBABILITY to read and interpret a bar graph.

APPLICATION

Problem Solving: Using a Diagram

Remember to READ, KNOW, PLAN, SOLVE, and CHECK all problems. See the Five-Step Plan on page 425 in the Data Bank.

The diagram below is a Celsius thermometer. Look at the thermometer and write the letter of the temperature that matches each statement.

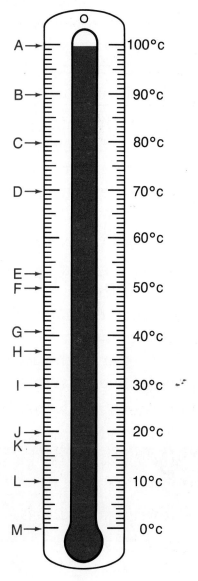

12. Water boils at 100° C.

13. The average normal body temperature is 37° C.

14. Butter melts at 30° C.

15. Some germs can live at 70° C.

16. Water freezes at 0° C.

17. A comfortable room temperature is 20° C.

18. The body temperature of a sparrow is 41° C.

19. The highest temperature in Arizona was 53° C.

20. Most house plants like the temperature to be at least 18°C.

21. The temperature of a day in autumn is 10°C.

Use a diagram and apply the Five-Step PROBLEM-SOLVING Plan

Streets and Roads

Roads and highways help us get where we are going. Cars, buses, trucks, and bicycles use roads.

The early Americans had dirt roads. The first hard-topped road was built in Pennsylvania in 1795. The first concrete road was built in Detroit, Michigan, in 1908.

Now we have many big roads called highways. They connect big cities to each other. Some also connect the states. These are called interstate highways.

As more roads were built in America, a way was needed to keep track of them. A Wisconsin highway engineer named A. R. Hirst made up a system of numbering the highways. Each highway is given a number. It is in a shield that looks like this:

Interstate Highway Signs

5 **95**

The number tells something about the highway. Even numbers go east to west. Odd numbers go north to south.

The north–south numbers start on the West Coast. Interstate 5 is the farthest west. Interstate 95 is the farthest east.

The east–west numbers start in the South. Interstate 4 is the farthest south. Interstates 90 and 94 are the farthest north.

CRITICAL THINKING

1. Which numbers do north–south highways end with?

2. Which numbers do east–west highways end with?

3. Which is farther east, Interstate 55 or 57?

4. Which is farther south, Interstate 64 or 30?

5. In which states does Interstate 25 run?

6. In which states does Interstate 8 run?

FOCUS | Use LOGIC to understand and analyze maps.

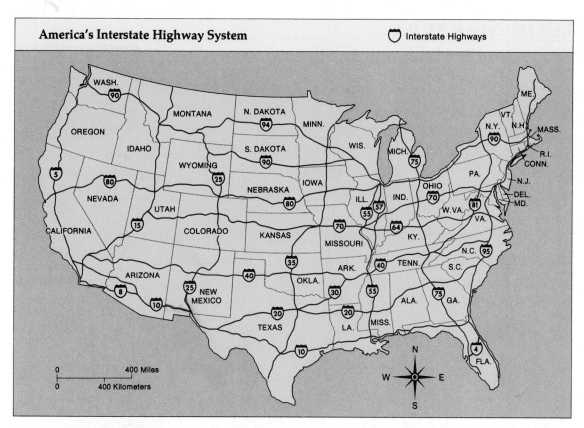

America's Interstate Highway System

⬡ Interstate Highways

The Hollywood freeway has interstate and intrastate highways.

LOOKING BACK

Reviewing and Testing Chapter 14

In Chapter 14 you formulated problems about ice skating. Look at pages 180 and 181.

1. Write a sentence telling why it is important to have ice skates that fit properly.

You learned something new about reading a clock. To review what you learned, study the sample problem on page 182. Use the new skill to write the time shown in two ways for examples 2 to 5.

2.

3.

4.

5.

You learned something new about reading a Celsius thermometer. To review, look at pages 186 and 187. Then use the new skill to write the correct temperature for examples 6 to 9.

6.
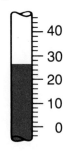

7.

8.
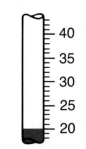

9.

You learned about streets and roads. Look at page 190 to review the numbering of interstate highways.

10. What does the number of an interstate highway tell you?

FOCUS | Review and test skills learned and practiced.

LOOKING AHEAD

Preparing for New Skills for Chapter 15

In the next chapter you will focus on

- **formulating problems.**
- **multiplying sixes.**
- **using geometry.**
- **multiplying sevens.**
- **multiplying money.**
- **using measurement.**

New multiplication skills will be easier to learn if you brush up on the addition skills you already know. Study the model. Then complete the PRACTICE exercises. Check your work with the model.

Model
There are 5 bird feeders. Each feeder has 7 birds. How many birds are there in all?

$$7 \;+\; 7 \;+\; 7 \;+\; 7 \;+\; 7 \;=\; 35$$

There are 35 birds in all because 5 sevens equal 35.

PRACTICE

Complete. Review the model if you need to.

1.

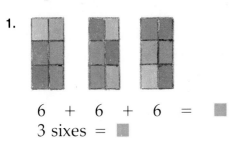

$6 + 6 + 6 =$ ▪
3 sixes = ▪

2.

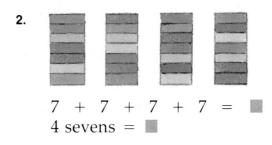

$7 + 7 + 7 + 7 =$ ▪
4 sevens = ▪

Review NUMBER skills in preparation for learning a new skill.

QUARTERLY REVIEW/TEST

Write the letter of the correct answer.

How many faces does each solid figure have?

1.
   A. 4
   B. 5
   C. 6
   D. 8

2.
   E. 2
   F. 3
   G. 4
   H. 6

Multiply.

3. $\begin{array}{r} 4 \\ \times 3 \end{array}$
   A. 12 B. 32
   C. 16 D. 9

4. $\begin{array}{r} 2 \\ \times 8 \end{array}$
   E. 10 F. 12
   G. 14 H. 16

5. $\begin{array}{r} 3 \\ \times 7 \end{array}$
   A. 27 B. 12
   C. 21 D. 14

6. $\begin{array}{r} 5 \\ \times 4 \end{array}$
   E. 25 F. 24
   G. 9   H. 20

7. $\begin{array}{r} 4 \\ \times 6 \end{array}$
   A. 24 B. 18
   C. 30 D. 36

8. $\begin{array}{r} 5 \\ \times 9 \end{array}$
   E. 54 F. 30
   G. 45 H. 35

Divide.

9. $5 \overline{)35}$
   A. 8   B. 6
   C. 7   D. 9

10. $2 \overline{)18}$
    E. 8   F. 3
    G. 5   H. 9

11. $4 \overline{)28}$
    A. 6   B. 7
    C. 8   D. 5

12. $3 \overline{)24}$
    E. 8   F. 9
    G. 7   H. 6

13. $5 \overline{)30}$
    A. 7   B. 6
    C. 4   D. 8

14. $4 \overline{)36}$
    E. 9   F. 8
    G. 4   H. 6

Solve each problem.

15. Ellie spent 21¢ for 3 pins. How much did she spend on each pin if each one cost the same?

    A. 8¢   B. 24¢
    C. 18¢   D. 7¢

16. Roy bought 8 blocks. He paid 4¢ for each block. How much did Roy spend?

    E. 2¢   F. 32¢
    G. 36¢   H. 4¢

FOCUS | Review concepts and skills taught in Chapters 8 to 14.

Complete. Choose one answer.

17. $5 \times 2 = \blacksquare$ **A.** 5   **B.** 2
    $\blacksquare \div 2 = 5$ **C.** 10   **D.** 15

18. $8 \times \blacksquare = 24$ **E.** 24   **F.** 3
    $24 \div \blacksquare = 8$ **G.** 8   **H.** 4

19. $\blacksquare \times 5 = 25$ **A.** 4   **B.** 5
    $25 \div 5 = \blacksquare$ **C.** 25   **D.** 6

20. $9 \times 4 = \blacksquare$ **E.** 9   **F.** 32
    $\blacksquare \div 4 = 9$ **G.** 36   **H.** 4

Multiply. Choose one answer.

21. $6 \times 2 = \blacksquare$ **A.** 3   **B.** 6
    $2 \times 6 = \blacksquare$ **C.** 18   **D.** 12

22. $5 \times 4 = \blacksquare$ **E.** 25   **F.** 20
    $4 \times 5 = \blacksquare$ **G.** 5   **H.** 4

23. $1 \times 2 \times 3 = \blacksquare$
    A. 1   **B.** 3   **C.** 6   **D.** 12

24. $2 \times 3 \times 4 = \blacksquare$
    E. 12   **F.** 6   **G.** 24   **H.** 8

What is the time?

25.    **A.** 10:00
    B. 1:00
    C. 2:00
    D. 11:00

26.    **E.** 8:20
    F. 5:45
    G. 6:45
    H. 9:30

What is the time?

27.    **A.** 8:12
    B. 7:47
    C. 7:52
    D. 10:48

What is the temperature?

28.   **E.** 8°C
    F. 12°C
    G. 7°C
    H. 9°C

29.   **A.** 26°C
    B. 29°C
    C. 34°C
    D. 25°C

Solve each problem.

30. Sasha slept for 8 hours on Monday night and 7 hours on Tuesday night. How many hours did she sleep in the two nights?

    E. 1 hour   **F.** 40 hours
    G. 15 hours   **H.** 25 hours

31. Alex began studying at 2:00 P.M. He stopped studying at 5:00 P.M. How many hours did Alex study?

    A. 7 hours   **B.** 3 hours
    C. 2 hours   **D.** 10 hours

FOCUS   Formulate several problems using picture cues, text, and data.

196

DATA

Grades in school
  Kindergarten to fifth grade

Number of classes per grade
  5

Number of students per grade
  100

Number of students per class
  20

Number of teachers per class
  Kindergarten to
    second grade   2
  Third grade to
    fifth grade   1

Total number of students
  600

Total number of teachers
  45

Principals   1
Assistant principals   2
Secretaries   3
Librarians   2
Cafeteria workers   10
Custodians   2

CHAPTER **15**

Multiplication Facts for Sixes and Sevens

The population of a place is the number of people who live there. Cities, states, and countries have populations.

A census is a count of a population. It can also include other information, such as the different jobs people do. The picture shows a census taker asking someone a set of questions.

A third-grade class at the Lincoln School did a census of their school. They found out how many students and teachers there are. They also found out how many other people work in the school.

How do you think the class went about doing the census? What problems did they have to solve? Did they always give exact numbers in their data? What data numbers might have been rounded?

197

MULTIPLICATION
Multiplying Sixes

Bob buys 7 cartons of eggs. Each carton has 6 eggs.

Multiply to find the total number of eggs Bob buys.

7 sixes are 42:

number → $7 \times 6 = 42$
of cartons ↑
eggs in each carton

$$\begin{array}{r} 6 \\ \times 7 \\ \hline 42 \end{array}$$

Bob buys 42 eggs in all.

Here are some facts you have seen before.

1	6	2	6	3	6	4	6	5	6
×6	×1	×6	×2	×6	×3	×6	×4	×6	×5
6	6	12	12	18	18	24	24	30	30

These are the new facts for sixes.

6	6	6	6
×6	×7	×8	×9
36	42	48	54

GUIDED PRACTICE

1. Count by 6s to 54. 6, 12, 18, ▮, ▮, ▮, ▮, ▮, ▮

Multiply.

2. 4×6 3. 1×6 4. 3×6 5. 5×6 6. 2×6

7. $\begin{array}{r} 6 \\ \times 5 \end{array}$ 8. $\begin{array}{r} 6 \\ \times 6 \end{array}$ 9. $\begin{array}{r} 6 \\ \times 9 \end{array}$ 10. $\begin{array}{r} 6 \\ \times 1 \end{array}$ 11. $\begin{array}{r} 6 \\ \times 7 \end{array}$ 12. $\begin{array}{r} 6 \\ \times 8 \end{array}$

FOCUS Use NUMBER skills to multiply sixes.

198

PRACTICE

Multiply.

13. 1×6 **14.** 3×6 **15.** 5×6 **16.** 2×6 **17.** 4×6

18. 7×6 **19.** 6×6 **20.** 9×6 **21.** 8×6 **22.** 0×6

23. $\begin{array}{r} 6 \\ \times 6 \\ \hline \end{array}$ **24.** $\begin{array}{r} 6 \\ \times 1 \\ \hline \end{array}$ **25.** $\begin{array}{r} 7 \\ \times 6 \\ \hline \end{array}$ **26.** $\begin{array}{r} 6 \\ \times 2 \\ \hline \end{array}$ **27.** $\begin{array}{r} 5 \\ \times 6 \\ \hline \end{array}$ **28.** $\begin{array}{r} 6 \\ \times 4 \\ \hline \end{array}$

29. $\begin{array}{r} 6 \\ \times 0 \\ \hline \end{array}$ **30.** $\begin{array}{r} 8 \\ \times 6 \\ \hline \end{array}$ **31.** $\begin{array}{r} 6 \\ \times 3 \\ \hline \end{array}$ **32.** $\begin{array}{r} 9 \\ \times 6 \\ \hline \end{array}$ **33.** $\begin{array}{r} 6 \\ \times 7 \\ \hline \end{array}$ **34.** $\begin{array}{r} 6 \\ \times 5 \\ \hline \end{array}$

35. There are 9 oranges in each basket. There are 6 baskets. How many oranges are there altogether?

36. There are 7 glasses on each table. There are 6 tables. How many glasses are there in all?

MIXED PRACTICE
Maintaining and Reviewing Skills

Add, subtract, multiply, or divide.

37. 6×6 **38.** 6×4 **39.** 5×6 **40.** 4×8 **41.** 3×9

42. $12 - 4$ **43.** $17 + 6$ **44.** $4\overline{)36}$ **45.** $3\overline{)21}$ **46.** $5\overline{)40}$

47.

48.

CHALLENGE

49. Write the pairs of exercises that have the same product.

$\begin{array}{r} 6 \\ \times 5 \\ \hline \end{array}$ $\begin{array}{r} 9 \\ \times 6 \\ \hline 54 \end{array}$ $\begin{array}{r} 4 \\ \times 6 \\ \hline \end{array}$ $\begin{array}{r} 3 \\ \times 6 \\ \hline \end{array}$ $\begin{array}{r} 5 \\ \times 6 \\ \hline \end{array}$ $\begin{array}{r} 1 \\ \times 6 \\ \hline \end{array}$ $\begin{array}{r} 6 \\ \times 9 \\ \hline 54 \end{array}$ $\begin{array}{r} 6 \\ \times 3 \\ \hline \end{array}$ $\begin{array}{r} 6 \\ \times 7 \\ \hline 42 \end{array}$

MULTIPLICATION
Multiplying Sixes

Kerry buys 8 crayons. She pays 6¢ for each crayon. How much does Kerry spend?

Use multiplication to find how much Kerry spends.

Multiply the cost of each crayon by the number of crayons.
Then write ¢ in the product.

$$8 \times 6¢ = 48¢ \qquad \begin{array}{r} 6¢ \\ \times 8 \\ \hline 48¢ \end{array}$$

Kerry spends 48¢.

6¢ each

PRACTICE

Multiply. Remember the ¢.

1. $3 \times 6¢$ 2. $1 \times 6¢$ 3. $4 \times 6¢$ 4. $5 \times 6¢$ 5. $2 \times 6¢$

6. 7×6 7. 9×6 8. 6×6 9. 0×6 10. 8×6

11. $\begin{array}{r} 6¢ \\ \times 4 \\ \hline \end{array}$ 12. $\begin{array}{r} 6¢ \\ \times 8 \\ \hline \end{array}$ 13. $\begin{array}{r} 6¢ \\ \times 1 \\ \hline \end{array}$ 14. $\begin{array}{r} 6 \\ \times 9 \\ \hline \end{array}$ 15. $\begin{array}{r} 6 \\ \times 7 \\ \hline \end{array}$ 16. $\begin{array}{r} 6 \\ \times 0 \\ \hline \end{array}$

MIXED PRACTICE
Maintaining and Reviewing Skills

Add, subtract, multiply, or divide.

17. $3 \times 6¢$ 18. $6 \times 6¢$ 19. 9×6 20. $28 \div 4$ 21. $5 \overline{)45}$

22. $\begin{array}{r} 18¢ \\ + 12¢ \\ \hline \end{array}$ 23. $\begin{array}{r} 4 \\ \times 7 \\ \hline \end{array}$ 24. $\begin{array}{r} 25¢ \\ - 16¢ \\ \hline \end{array}$ 25. $\begin{array}{r} 5 \\ \times 0 \\ \hline \end{array}$ 26. $\begin{array}{r} 824 \\ - 605 \\ \hline \end{array}$ 27. $\begin{array}{r} 428 \\ + 390 \\ \hline \end{array}$

FOCUS   Use MEASUREMENT and NUMBER skills to multiply sixes.

APPLICATION
Using Geometry

Look at the shapes. Count the number of sides each shape has.

28.

Rectangles have ▧ sides.

29.

Pentagons have ▧ sides.

30.

Hexagons have ▧ sides.

Multiply to find the number of sides in all.

31.

$2 \times 4 = $ ▧

32.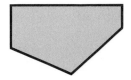

$2 \times 5 = $ ▧

Write the name of each shape. Write the number of sides each shape has. Write a multiplication sentence to find the number of sides in all.

33.

34.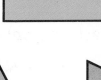

35.

Use GEOMETRY and NUMBER skills to multiply fours, fives, and sixes.

201

MULTIPLICATION
Multiplying Sevens

Susan has 8 fish tanks. Each tank has 7 fish.

Multiply to find the total number of fish Susan has.

8 sevens are 56:

number → 8 × 7 = 56
of tanks   ↑
      fish in each tank

$$\begin{array}{r} 7 \\ \times 8 \\ \hline 56 \end{array}$$

Susan has 56 fish in all.

Here are some facts you have seen before.

1	7	2	7	3	7	4	7	5	7	6	7
×7	×1	×7	×2	×7	×3	×7	×4	×7	×5	×7	×6
7	7	14	14	21	21	28	28	35	35	42	42

These are the new facts for sevens.

7	7	7
×7	×8	×9
49	56	63

GUIDED PRACTICE

1. Count by 7s to 63. 7, 14, 21, ■, ■, ■, ■, ■, ■

Multiply.

2. 2 × 7   **3.** 5 × 7   **4.** 1 × 7   **5.** 3 × 7   **6.** 4 × 7

7. $\begin{array}{r} 7 \\ \times 8 \\ \hline \end{array}$ **8.** $\begin{array}{r} 7 \\ \times 1 \\ \hline \end{array}$ **9.** $\begin{array}{r} 7 \\ \times 6 \\ \hline \end{array}$ **10.** $\begin{array}{r} 7 \\ \times 5 \\ \hline \end{array}$ **11.** $\begin{array}{r} 7 \\ \times 7 \\ \hline \end{array}$ **12.** $\begin{array}{r} 7 \\ \times 9 \\ \hline \end{array}$

FOCUS | Use NUMBER skills to multiply sevens.

PRACTICE

Multiply.

13. 3×7 **14.** 5×7 **15.** 1×7 **16.** 4×7 **17.** 2×7

18. 7×7 **19.** 0×7 **20.** 6×7 **21.** 9×7 **22.** 8×7

23. $\begin{array}{r} 1 \\ \times 7 \\ \hline \end{array}$ **24.** $\begin{array}{r} 7 \\ \times 5 \\ \hline \end{array}$ **25.** $\begin{array}{r} 7 \\ \times 3 \\ \hline \end{array}$ **26.** $\begin{array}{r} 9 \\ \times 7 \\ \hline \end{array}$ **27.** $\begin{array}{r} 7 \\ \times 0 \\ \hline \end{array}$ **28.** $\begin{array}{r} 7 \\ \times 7 \\ \hline \end{array}$

29. $\begin{array}{r} 7 \\ \times 6 \\ \hline \end{array}$ **30.** $\begin{array}{r} 0 \\ \times 7 \\ \hline \end{array}$ **31.** $\begin{array}{r} 7 \\ \times 7 \\ \hline \end{array}$ **32.** $\begin{array}{r} 7 \\ \times 2 \\ \hline \end{array}$ **33.** $\begin{array}{r} 7 \\ \times 8 \\ \hline \end{array}$ **34.** $\begin{array}{r} 4 \\ \times 7 \\ \hline \end{array}$

Solve each problem.

35. Teresa has 9 bowls. She has 7 turtles in each bowl. How many turtles does Teresa have?

36. Murray has 6 fish tanks. He bought 7 rocks for each tank. How many rocks did he buy?

MIXED PRACTICE
Maintaining and Reviewing Skills

Add, subtract, multiply, or divide.

37. 7×7 **38.** 5×7 **39.** 3×6 **40.** $5 \overline{)40}$ **41.** $17 - 9$

42. $7 + 8$ **43.** $4 \overline{)32}$ **44.** $3 \overline{)21}$ **45.** 9×4 **46.** 6×6

47. + +

48. −

CHALLENGE

Solve these riddles.

49. What number is 7 times as great as 3 times 3?

50. Multiply me by myself. The product is 1 less than 50. What number am I?

MULTIPLICATION
Multiplying Sevens

Alex buys 9 cherries. He pays 7¢ for each cherry. How much does Alex spend?

Use multiplication to find how much Alex spends.

Multiply the cost of each cherry by the number of cherries.
Then write ¢ in the product.

$$9 \times 7¢ = 63¢ \qquad \begin{array}{r} 7¢ \\ \times 9 \\ \hline 63¢ \end{array}$$

Alex spends 63¢.

7¢ each

PRACTICE

Multiply. Remember the ¢.

1. $2 \times 7¢$ **2.** $4 \times 7¢$ **3.** $1 \times 7¢$ **4.** $3 \times 7¢$ **5.** $5 \times 7¢$

6. 7×7 **7.** 0×7 **8.** 6×7 **9.** 9×7 **10.** 8×7

11. $\begin{array}{r} 7¢ \\ \times 8 \\ \hline \end{array}$ **12.** $\begin{array}{r} 7¢ \\ \times 4 \\ \hline \end{array}$ **13.** $\begin{array}{r} 7¢ \\ \times 6 \\ \hline \end{array}$ **14.** $\begin{array}{r} 7 \\ \times 9 \\ \hline \end{array}$ **15.** $\begin{array}{r} 7 \\ \times 0 \\ \hline \end{array}$ **16.** $\begin{array}{r} 7 \\ \times 7 \\ \hline \end{array}$

MIXED PRACTICE
Maintaining and Reviewing Skills

Add, subtract, multiply, or divide.

17. $5 \times 7¢$ **18.** $8 \times 7¢$ **19.** 6×7 **20.** $30 \div 5$ **21.** $4\overline{)36}$

22. $\begin{array}{r} 26¢ \\ +13¢ \\ \hline \end{array}$ **23.** $\begin{array}{r} 59¢ \\ -37¢ \\ \hline \end{array}$ **24.** $\begin{array}{r} 7 \\ \times 3 \\ \hline \end{array}$ **25.** $\begin{array}{r} 637 \\ +191 \\ \hline \end{array}$ **26.** $\begin{array}{r} 6 \\ \times 8 \\ \hline \end{array}$ **27.** $\begin{array}{r} 798 \\ -679 \\ \hline \end{array}$

FOCUS │ Use MEASUREMENT and NUMBER skills to multiply sevens.

204

Using Measurement

			MAY			
Sunday	Monday	Tuesday	Wednesday	Thursday	Friday	Saturday
1	2	3	4	5	6	7
8	9	10	11	12	13	14
15	16	17	18	19	20	21
22	23	24	25	26	27	28
29	30	31				

Use the calendar to solve.

28. How many days are in the month of May?

29. The date of the first Saturday is May 7. What is the date of the third Saturday in May?

30. May 21 is on a Saturday. What day of the week is May 28?

31. A week is 7 days. There are 4 full weeks in May. How many days are left over?

Write a multiplication sentence for each question.

32. How many days are in 3 weeks?   **33.** How many days are in 7 weeks?

34. How many days are in 6 weeks?   **35.** How many days are in 9 weeks?

36. How many days are in the 4 full weeks in May?

37. How many days are in the first 2 weeks in May?

Use MEASUREMENT to explore a calendar.

LOOKING BACK
Reviewing and Testing Chapter 15

In Chapter 15 you formulated problems about taking a census. Look at pages 196 and 197.

1. Write a sentence telling how a census might be used.

You learned something new about multiplying sixes. To review what you learned, study the sample problem on page 198. Then use the new skill to find each product for examples 2 to 19.

2. 6 ×8	**3.** 6 ×4	**4.** 6 ×2	**5.** 6 ×9	**6.** 6 ×6	**7.** 6 ×1

8. 0×6 **9.** 5×6 **10.** 3×6 **11.** 8×6 **12.** 9×6

13. $6 \times 6¢$ **14.** $2 \times 6¢$ **15.** $4 \times 6¢$ **16.** $1 \times 6¢$ **17.** $7 \times 6¢$

18. There are 5 books on each shelf. There are 6 shelves. How many books are there?

19. There are 4 buttons on each shirt. There are 6 shirts. How many buttons are there?

You learned something new about multiplying sevens. To review, look at page 202. Use the new skill to find each product for examples 20 to 37.

20. 7 ×7	**21.** 7 ×4	**22.** 7 ×8	**23.** 7 ×2	**24.** 7 ×1	**25.** 7 ×9

26. 3×7 **27.** 5×7 **28.** 0×7 **29.** 4×7 **30.** 8×7

31. $1 \times 7¢$ **32.** $9 \times 7¢$ **33.** $2 \times 7¢$ **34.** $7 \times 7¢$ **35.** $6 \times 7¢$

36. Jill has 9 envelopes. She put 7 stamps in each envelope. How many stamps does she have?

37. Seth wrote 3 letters. Each letter was 7 pages long. How many pages did Seth write?

FOCUS   Review and test skills learned and practiced.

LOOKING AHEAD
Preparing for New Skills for Chapter 16

In the next chapter you will focus on

- formulating problems.
- dividing by sixes.
- using patterns and functions.
- dividing by sevens.
- a problem-solving strategy.
- math in technology.

New division skills will be easier to learn if you know how to find equal parts of a group. Study the model. Then complete the PRACTICE exercises. Check your work with the model.

Model

There are 21 cherries in 3 equal groups. How many cherries are in each group?

There are 7 cherries in each group.

PRACTICE

Complete. Review the model if you need to.

1. Count and copy the triangles. Then ring 5 equal groups of triangles.

2. How many triangles are there in all?

3. How many triangles are in each group?

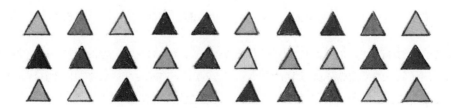

Review NUMBER skills in preparation for learning a new skill.

16

Division Facts for Sixes and Sevens

DATA

Event	Camping trip
Campers	Mr. Glenn
	Mrs. Glenn
	Gary Glenn
	Katie Glenn
	Hector Paz

Campgrounds

Big Pond Park	150 campsites
	Lake
	Swimming pool
	Restaurant
	"Movie night"
Bear Hollow	75 campsites
	Lake
	Nature hikes
	Snack bar

If you have ever gone camping, you know the adventure of having a tent over your head instead of a roof. Camping brings you closer to the outdoors and to nature.

A camping trip does not appeal to everyone. But those who enjoy camping learn to plan ahead to make the trip as much fun as possible. They also try to learn from their experiences.

Look at the data. It shows some choices that the campers may make. Using the picture and the data, think about what kind of camping experience they may desire. Which of the two campgrounds do you think the campers will choose? Which would you choose? Give your reasons. List three problems that the Glenn family and their friend Hector might have to solve.

DIVISION
Dividing by Sixes

There are 18 people going on a trip. If 6 people ride in each car, how many cars will they need?

Divide to find the number of cars that the people will need. Divide the number of people in all by the number of people that will ride in each car.

people in all		people in each car		cars
18	÷	6	=	3

$18 \div 6 = 3$ can be written as $6\overline{)18}$ with quotient 3.

The people will need 3 cars.

GUIDED PRACTICE

Divide to show how many groups there are.

1.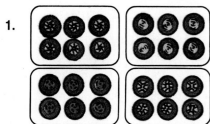

How many 6s are in 24?

$24 \div 6 = 4$

2.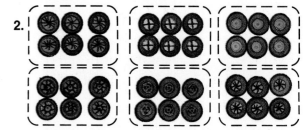

How many 6s are in 36?

$36 \div 6 = $ ▦

3. $6\overline{)30}$ 4. $6\overline{)6}$ 5. $6\overline{)48}$ 6. $6\overline{)12}$ 7. $6\overline{)42}$ 8. $6\overline{)54}$

| FOCUS | Use NUMBER skills to divide by sixes. |

PRACTICE

Divide.

9. $6 \div 6$ **10.** $24 \div 6$ **11.** $12 \div 6$ **12.** $30 \div 6$ **13.** $18 \div 6$

14. $48 \div 6$ **15.** $36 \div 6$ **16.** $54 \div 6$ **17.** $42 \div 6$ **18.** $24 \div 6$

19. $6\overline{)18}$ **20.** $6\overline{)30}$ **21.** $6\overline{)42}$ **22.** $6\overline{)6}$ **23.** $6\overline{)48}$ **24.** $6\overline{)54}$

25. $6\overline{)12}$ **26.** $6\overline{)54}$ **27.** $6\overline{)36}$ **28.** $6\overline{)42}$ **29.** $6\overline{)24}$ **30.** $6\overline{)6}$

Solve each problem.

31. There are 6 trucks in the garage. Mr. Ruez will load 42 crates. How many crates will he put on each truck if he puts the same number on each one?

32. Six small airplanes are at the airport. There are 54 people waiting to fly. If each plane carries the same number of passengers, how many people will board each airplane?

MIXED PRACTICE
Maintaining and Reviewing Skills

Add, subtract, multiply, or divide.

33. $42 \div 6$ **34.** $6\overline{)36}$ **35.** 7×5 **36.** 8×6 **37.** $5\overline{)45}$

38.

39.

CHALLENGE

40. Ian has 8 full bags of apples. Each bag holds 6 apples. If 6 people gave Ian an equal number, how many apples did each person give him?

DIVISION
Dividing by Sixes

Lenore spends 42¢ for 6 tickets. How much does each ticket cost?

Use division to find the cost of each ticket.

Divide the money Lenore spends by the number of tickets she buys. Then write ¢ in the answer.

$$42¢ \div 6 = 7¢ \qquad 6 \overline{)\, 42¢}^{\,7¢}$$

Each ticket costs 7¢.

PRACTICE

Divide. Remember the ¢.

1. 18¢ ÷ 6   2. 6¢ ÷ 6   3. 30¢ ÷ 6   4. 12¢ ÷ 6   5. 24¢ ÷ 6

6. 36 ÷ 6   7. 24 ÷ 6   8. 42 ÷ 6   9. 54 ÷ 6   10. 48 ÷ 6

11. $6 \overline{)\, 30¢}$ 12. $6 \overline{)\, 42¢}$ 13. $6 \overline{)\, 12¢}$ 14. $6 \overline{)\, 6¢}$ 15. $6 \overline{)\, 18¢}$ 16. $6 \overline{)\, 54¢}$

17. $6 \overline{)\, 48}$ 18. $6 \overline{)\, 12}$ 19. $6 \overline{)\, 36}$ 20. $6 \overline{)\, 24}$ 21. $6 \overline{)\, 54}$ 22. $6 \overline{)\, 30}$

MIXED PRACTICE
Maintaining and Reviewing Skills

Add, subtract, multiply, or divide.

23. 36 ÷ 6   24. $6 \overline{)\, 48¢}$ 25. 45 ÷ 5   26. 7 × 6   27. 8 × 7

28.   4
    ×9

29.   37
    −19

30.   56
    +27

31.   5
    ×6

32.   984
    −169

33.   421
    +395

FOCUS | Use MEASUREMENT and NUMBER skills to divide by sixes.

212

APPLICATION

Using Patterns and Functions

Carmen buys 24 cans of orange juice. The cans come in packages of 6. How many six-packs of orange juice does Carmen buy?

cans in all	cans in each package	six-packs
24	÷ 6	= 4

Carmen buys 4 six-packs of orange juice.

Use the pictures to answer the questions.

34.

How many cans in all?
How many in each package?
How many six-packs of cans?

35.

How many cans in all?
How many in each package?
How many six-packs of cans?

Draw the correct number of six-packs.

36. There are 42 batteries in packages. There are 6 batteries in each package. How many six-packs are there in all?

37. There are 36 rolls in packages. There are 6 rolls in each package. How many six-packs are there in all?

38. There are 54 boxes of raisins in packages. There are 6 boxes in each package. How many six-packs are there in all?

39. There are 48 cans of juice in packages. There are 6 cans in each package. How many six-packs are there in all?

Use PATTERNS AND FUNCTIONS to divide by sixes.

DIVISION
Dividing by Sevens

There are 35 dogs in the pet show. There are 7 of each type of dog. How many different types of dogs are in the pet show?

Divide to find the number of different types of dogs at the pet show. Divide the number of dogs in all by the number of each type of dog.

dogs in all		dogs of each type		types of dogs
35	÷	7	=	5

$35 \div 7 = 5$ or $7\overline{)35}$ with quotient 5

There are 5 different types of dogs at the pet show.

GUIDED PRACTICE

Divide to show how many groups there are.

1.

How many 7s are in 28?

$28 \div 7 = 4$

2.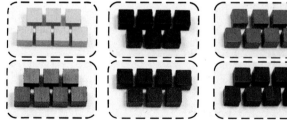

How many 7s are in 42?

$42 \div 7 = \blacksquare$

3. $7\overline{)21}$ **4.** $7\overline{)7}$ **5.** $7\overline{)56}$ **6.** $7\overline{)14}$ **7.** $7\overline{)49}$ **8.** $7\overline{)63}$

PRACTICE

Divide.

9. $21 \div 7$ **10.** $7 \div 7$ **11.** $35 \div 7$ **12.** $14 \div 7$ **13.** $28 \div 7$

14. $42 \div 7$ **15.** $56 \div 7$ **16.** $49 \div 7$ **17.** $63 \div 7$ **18.** $35 \div 7$

19. $7\overline{)14}$ **20.** $7\overline{)21}$ **21.** $7\overline{)42}$ **22.** $7\overline{)7}$ **23.** $7\overline{)28}$ **24.** $7\overline{)56}$

25. $7\overline{)35}$ **26.** $7\overline{)56}$ **27.** $7\overline{)21}$ **28.** $7\overline{)49}$ **29.** $7\overline{)63}$ **30.** $7\overline{)42}$

Solve each problem.

31. The zoo has 49 monkeys. There are 7 monkeys in each cage. How many cages at the zoo have monkeys?

32. Gena sees 35 baby birds. She sees 7 baby birds in each nest. How many nests does Gena see?

MIXED PRACTICE
Maintaining and Reviewing Skills

Add, subtract, multiply, or divide.

33. $49 \div 7$ **34.** $7\overline{)63}$ **35.** 9×6 **36.** 8×7 **37.** $5\overline{)40}$

38. + +

39.  −

CHALLENGE

Read the clues to find the numbers.

40. Divide this number by 7. Then add 4 to the answer. The sum will be 12.

41. Divide this number by 7. Then add 6 to the answer. The sum will be 9.

DIVISION
Dividing by Sevens

Dwane spends 63¢ for 7 sticks of chalk. If each stick costs the same, how much does each one cost?

Use division to find the cost of each stick of chalk.

Divide the money he spends by the number of sticks of chalk he buys. Then write ¢ in the answer.

$$63¢ \div 7 = 9¢ \qquad 7\overline{)63¢}$$

Each stick of chalk costs 9¢.

PRACTICE

Divide. Remember the ¢.

1. 14¢ ÷ 7   2. 28¢ ÷ 7   3. 7¢ ÷ 7   4. 21¢ ÷ 7   5. 35¢ ÷ 7

6. 56 ÷ 7   7. 42 ÷ 7   8. 63 ÷ 7   9. 49 ÷ 7   10. 28 ÷ 7

11. $7\overline{)28¢}$ 12. $7\overline{)14¢}$ 13. $7\overline{)35¢}$ 14. $7\overline{)56¢}$ 15. $7\overline{)7¢}$ 16. $7\overline{)21¢}$

17. $7\overline{)56}$ 18. $7\overline{)7}$ 19. $7\overline{)21}$ 20. $7\overline{)49}$ 21. $7\overline{)63}$ 22. $7\overline{)35}$

MIXED PRACTICE
Maintaining and Reviewing Skills

Add, subtract, multiply, or divide.

23. 49¢ ÷ 7   24. $7\overline{)63}$ 25. 48 ÷ 6   26. 9 × 6   27. 8 × 4

28. 7
    ×8

29. 39
    −18

30. 5
    ×6

31. 42
    +28

32. 372
    +191

33. 568
    −380

FOCUS | Use MEASUREMENT and NUMBER skills to divide by sevens.

APPLICATION
Problem Solving: Exploring PLAN, SOLVE, CHECK

Remember to READ, KNOW, PLAN, SOLVE, and CHECK all problems. See the Five-Step Plan on page 425 in the Data Bank.

Write a number sentence to PLAN. SOLVE each problem. Then CHECK by multiplying.

34. Thirty-five students sit at 7 tables. How many are at each table if the tables have the same number of students?

35. Seven squirrels share 49 acorns equally. How many acorns does each squirrel get?

36. Sixty-three raisins are put into 7 bags. The same number of raisins are put in each bag. How many raisins are in 1 bag?

37. Twenty-eight races were run by 4 students. Each student ran the same number of races. How many races did each student run?

38. Fifty-six flowers are put into bunches that are the same size. There are 7 bunches. How many flowers are in each bunch?

39. Forty-two grapes are in a bag. Seven children share them equally. How many grapes does each child get?

40. You have to read fourteen poems in 7 days for a class at school. If you read the same number of poems every day, how many poems do you read a day?

Explore the PLAN, SOLVE, and CHECK steps of the Five-Step PROBLEM-SOLVING Plan.

Computer Graphics

Did you ever draw a picture by connecting dots? A computer makes pictures on the screen by turning on very small lights. We call computer drawings **graphics.**

The computer can only make graphics if it is told where to light up the screen. An ordered pair of numbers tells the computer where to light up one small square, called a **pixel.** The first number of the ordered pair tells the computer how many spaces to move across the screen from left to right. The second number tells the computer how many spaces to move up the screen counting from the bottom. Finding the pixel at a point is like following directions on a map.

The streets on the computer screen begin in the lower left hand corner. Look at the third position across and the first position up in the picture on this page. To light up a pixel here, use the ordered pair (3, 1). To light up the screen at the point found at 4 across and 1 up, use the ordered pair (4, 1).

Making computer graphics is as easy as connecting all the pixels.

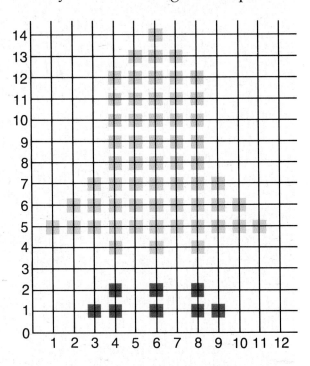

CRITICAL THINKING

1. What is the ordered pair for the highest tip of the rocket?

2. Would the point at (20, 35) be visible on our screen?

3. Is the point found at 3 across and 3 up part of the rocket?

4. What shape do the ordered pairs (2, 1), (2, 2), and (2, 3) make?

FOCUS   Use NUMBER skills and LOGIC to understand and appreciate computer graphics.

218

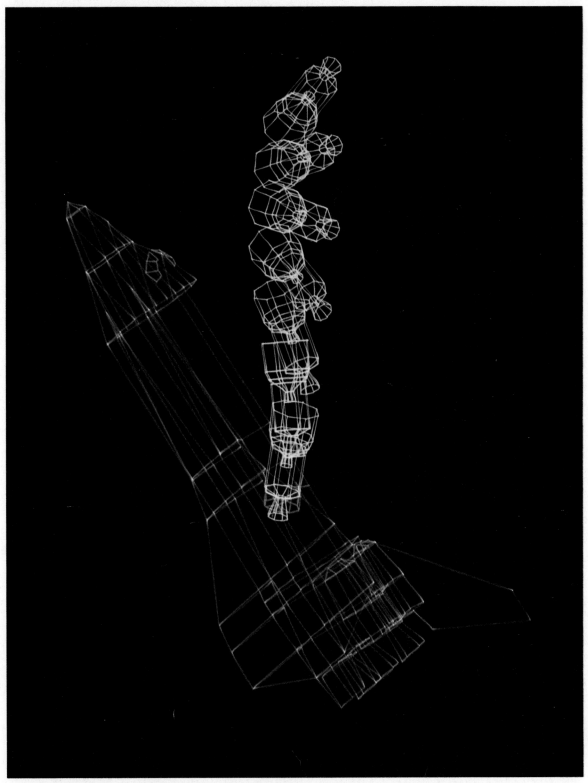

A computer graphic satellite is launched from a shuttle.

LOOKING BACK
Reviewing and Testing Chapter 16

In Chapter 16 you formulated problems about camping. Look at pages 208 and 209.

1. Write a sentence telling what you would bring on a camping trip.

You learned something new about dividing by sixes. To review, look at page 210. Then use the new skill to find each quotient for examples 2 to 14.

2. $12 \div 6$ 3. $30 \div 6$ 4. $18 \div 6$ 5. $54 \div 6$ 6. $36 \div 6$

7. $6\overline{)24}$ 8. $6\overline{)6}$ 9. $6\overline{)42}$ 10. $6\overline{)30}$ 11. $6\overline{)48}$ 12. $6\overline{)54}$

13. There are 36 students in class. There are 6 rows, each with the same number of students. How many students are in each row?

14. There are 48 birds in 6 trees. Each tree has the same number of birds. How many birds are in each tree?

You learned something new about dividing by sevens. To review, look at page 214. Use the new skill to find each quotient for examples 15 to 27.

15. $21 \div 7$ 16. $7 \div 7$ 17. $42 \div 7$ 18. $14 \div 7$ 19. $63 \div 7$

20. $7\overline{)28}$ 21. $7\overline{)63}$ 22. $7\overline{)56}$ 23. $7\overline{)21}$ 24. $7\overline{)7}$ 25. $7\overline{)49}$

26. Write a word problem that you could solve by dividing 35 by 7. Then solve the problem.

27. Write a word problem that you could solve by dividing 56 by 7. Then solve the problem.

You learned about computer graphics. Look at page 218 to review what you have learned.

28. What tells the computer where to light up a pixel?

| FOCUS | Review and test skills learned and practiced. |

LOOKING AHEAD

Preparing for New Skills for Chapter 17

In the next chapter you will focus on

- formulating problems.
- multiplying eights.
- a problem-solving strategy.
- multiplying nines.
- using a multiplication table.
- using algebra.

New multiplication skills will be easier to learn if you brush up on the addition skills you already know. Study the model. Then complete the PRACTICE exercises. Check your work with the model.

Model

There are 8 cheese pies. Each pie has 9 pieces. How many pieces are there in all?

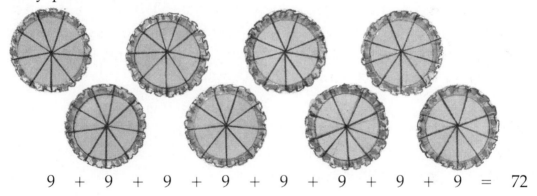

$$9 + 9 + 9 + 9 + 9 + 9 + 9 + 9 = 72$$

There are 72 pieces in all because 8 nines equal 72.

PRACTICE

Complete. Review the model if you need to.

1.
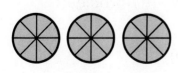

$8 + 8 + 8 = \blacksquare$
3 eights = $\blacksquare$

2.
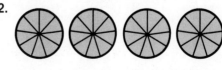

$9 + 9 + 9 + 9 = \blacksquare$
4 nines = $\blacksquare$

Review NUMBER skills in preparation for learning a new skill.

FOCUS   Formulate problems using picture cues, text, and data.

CHAPTER 17

Multiplication Facts for Eights and Nines

DATA

Event   Grade 3
             Spelling Bee

Place   Johnson School

Team 3-A

   Students competing   24
   Students out   20
   Students left   4

Team 3-B

   Students competing   25
   Students out   16
   Students left   9

Round of bee   6

Word to be
   spelled
    now   *mystery*

Time given   2 minutes

A spelling bee is a challenge. During the bee, a teacher reads a word aloud. A student tries to spell it. The winner of the bee is the person who spells all of the words without making a mistake. Some of the words on the list are hard, and some are easy. But a student must be ready to spell them all.

To remember all of the words on the list, a student must study a long time. But being in a spelling bee means more than knowing how to spell. It also means knowing how to stay calm as the audience watches.

Using the data, decide what is going through the minds of the students on the teams. What did they have to do to prepare? What kinds of problems do the teams face? What problems does each student on a team face?

MULTIPLICATION
Multiplying Eights

There are 9 octopuses in the sea. Each octopus has 8 arms.

Multiply to find the total number of arms.

9 eights are 72 $9 \times 8 = 72$

$$\begin{array}{r} 8 \\ \times 9 \\ \hline 72 \end{array}$$

The 9 octopuses have 72 arms altogether.

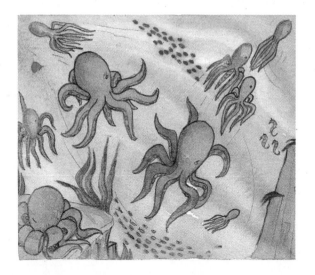

Here are some facts you have seen before.

$$\begin{array}{r} 8 \\ \times 1 \\ \hline 8 \end{array} \quad \begin{array}{r} 8 \\ \times 2 \\ \hline 16 \end{array} \quad \begin{array}{r} 8 \\ \times 3 \\ \hline 24 \end{array} \quad \begin{array}{r} 8 \\ \times 4 \\ \hline 32 \end{array} \quad \begin{array}{r} 8 \\ \times 5 \\ \hline 40 \end{array} \quad \begin{array}{r} 8 \\ \times 6 \\ \hline 48 \end{array} \quad \begin{array}{r} 8 \\ \times 7 \\ \hline 56 \end{array}$$

These are the new facts for eights.

$$\begin{array}{r} 8 \\ \times 8 \\ \hline 64 \end{array} \quad \begin{array}{r} 8 \\ \times 9 \\ \hline 72 \end{array}$$

GUIDED PRACTICE

1. Count by 8s to 72. 8, 16, 24, ▪, ▪, ▪, ▪, ▪, ▪

Multiply.

2. 5×8 3. 2×8 4. 4×8 5. 3×8 6. 7×8

7. $\begin{array}{r} 8 \\ \times 1 \\ \hline \end{array}$ 8. $\begin{array}{r} 8 \\ \times 7 \\ \hline \end{array}$ 9. $\begin{array}{r} 8 \\ \times 4 \\ \hline \end{array}$ 10. $\begin{array}{r} 8 \\ \times 9 \\ \hline \end{array}$ 11. $\begin{array}{r} 8 \\ \times 6 \\ \hline \end{array}$ 12. $\begin{array}{r} 8 \\ \times 8 \\ \hline \end{array}$

FOCUS   Use NUMBER skills to multiply eights.

PRACTICE

Multiply.

13. 2×8 **14.** 4×8 **15.** 1×8 **16.** 3×8 **17.** 5×8

18. 8×8 **19.** 6×8 **20.** 0×8 **21.** 7×8 **22.** 9×8

23. $\begin{array}{r} 8 \\ \times 5 \\ \hline \end{array}$ **24.** $\begin{array}{r} 8 \\ \times 1 \\ \hline \end{array}$ **25.** $\begin{array}{r} 3 \\ \times 8 \\ \hline \end{array}$ **26.** $\begin{array}{r} 8 \\ \times 0 \\ \hline \end{array}$ **27.** $\begin{array}{r} 8 \\ \times 4 \\ \hline \end{array}$ **28.** $\begin{array}{r} 7 \\ \times 8 \\ \hline \end{array}$

29. $\begin{array}{r} 8 \\ \times 8 \\ \hline \end{array}$ **30.** $\begin{array}{r} 2 \\ \times 8 \\ \hline \end{array}$ **31.** $\begin{array}{r} 8 \\ \times 6 \\ \hline \end{array}$ **32.** $\begin{array}{r} 8 \\ \times 7 \\ \hline \end{array}$ **33.** $\begin{array}{r} 3 \\ \times 8 \\ \hline \end{array}$ **34.** $\begin{array}{r} 8 \\ \times 9 \\ \hline \end{array}$

Solve each problem.

35. Steve sees 8 rocks. He sees 6 turtles on each rock. How many turtles does Steve see?

36. Jo sees 8 puddles. She sees 8 frogs in each puddle. How many frogs does Jo see?

MIXED PRACTICE
Maintaining and Reviewing Skills

Add, subtract, multiply, or divide.

37. 5×8 **38.** 9×8 **39.** 7×7 **40.** 8×6 **41.** 9×7

42. $58 - 32$ **43.** $16 + 13$ **44.** $7 \overline{)56}$ **45.** $5 \overline{)45}$ **46.** $6 \overline{)42}$

47. + +   **48.**  −

CHALLENGE

49. Mr. Tanner's classroom has 8 rows of desks. Each row has 4 desks. There are 28 children in his class. How many extra desks are in the classroom?

MULTIPLICATION
Multiplying Eights

Sara buys 8 balls. She pays 8¢ for each ball. How much does Sara spend?

Use multiplication to find how much Sara spends.

Multiply the cost of each ball by the number of balls.
Then write ¢ in the product.

$$8 \times 8¢ = 64¢$$

$$
\begin{array}{r}
8¢ \\
\times 8 \\
\hline
64¢
\end{array}
$$

Sara spends 64¢.

8¢
each

PRACTICE

Multiply. Remember the ¢.

1. $3 \times 8¢$ **2.** $8 \times 6¢$ **3.** $1 \times 8¢$ **4.** $8 \times 8¢$ **5.** $8 \times 4¢$

6. 8×5 **7.** 0×8 **8.** 8×7 **9.** 2×8 **10.** 8×9

11.
$$
\begin{array}{r}
8¢ \\
\times 5 \\
\hline
\end{array}
$$
12.
$$
\begin{array}{r}
8¢ \\
\times 7 \\
\hline
\end{array}
$$
13.
$$
\begin{array}{r}
8¢ \\
\times 3 \\
\hline
\end{array}
$$
14.
$$
\begin{array}{r}
8 \\
\times 8 \\
\hline
\end{array}
$$
15.
$$
\begin{array}{r}
0 \\
\times 8 \\
\hline
\end{array}
$$
16.
$$
\begin{array}{r}
8 \\
\times 9 \\
\hline
\end{array}
$$

MIXED PRACTICE
Maintaining and Reviewing Skills

Add, subtract, multiply, or divide.

17. $6 \times 8¢$ **18.** $9 \times 8¢$ **19.** 5×8 **20.** $7 \overline{)49}$ **21.** $6 \overline{)24}$

22.
$$
\begin{array}{r}
17¢ \\
+15¢ \\
\hline
\end{array}
$$
23.
$$
\begin{array}{r}
36¢ \\
-18¢ \\
\hline
\end{array}
$$
24.
$$
\begin{array}{r}
7 \\
\times 9 \\
\hline
\end{array}
$$
25.
$$
\begin{array}{r}
333 \\
-118 \\
\hline
\end{array}
$$
26.
$$
\begin{array}{r}
6 \\
\times 0 \\
\hline
\end{array}
$$
27.
$$
\begin{array}{r}
968 \\
+\ 23 \\
\hline
\end{array}
$$

FOCUS	Use MEASUREMENT and NUMBER skills to multiply eights.

APPLICATION

Problem Solving: Using a Diagram

Remember to READ, KNOW, PLAN, SOLVE, and CHECK all problems. See the Five-Step Plan on page 425 in the Data Bank.

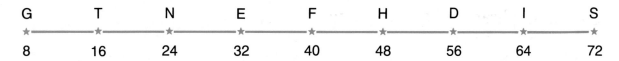

G	T	N	E	F	H	D	I	S
★	★	★	★	★	★	★	★	★
8	16	24	32	40	48	56	64	72

Solve each problem. Copy the exercise numbers in the order shown at the bottom of the page. Find the letter that matches your answer at the top of the page. Then write the letter below the exercise number it matches. Read the name of this activity.

28. One octopus has eight legs. Eight octopuses have ■ legs.

29. A spider has eight legs. Two spiders have ■ legs.

30. A group of eight singers is an octet. Five octets have ■ singers.

31. An octave has eight notes. There are ■ notes in three octaves.

32. An octagon has eight sides. Six octagons have ■ sides.

33. A group of four swimming octopuses have ■ legs.

34. Six octopuses have ■ legs.

35. Two octets have ■ singers.

36. Eight spiders have ■ legs.

37. ■ sides could form one octagon.

38. Seven octets have ■ singers.

39. Nine octopuses have ■ legs.

40. One singer sings four octaves. ■ notes are sung.

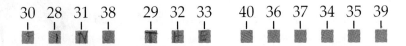

30 28 31 38   29 32 33   40 36 37 34 35 39

Use a diagram and apply the Five-Step PROBLEM-SOLVING Plan.

PROBLEM SOLVING
Selecting a Strategy: Finding a Pattern

Finding a pattern is a strategy you can use when you PLAN and SOLVE a problem. Finding a rule helps you find a pattern. A rule tells you how the items in a pattern relate to each other.

1. READ   What is the next number in this number pattern?
1, 3, 5, 7, 9, ■

2. KNOW   Ask yourself: What am I being asked to find? What number comes after 9? What **key facts** do I need? The numbers in the pattern become greater from left to right.

3. PLAN   Select a strategy: try finding a pattern. Study the pattern. Look for the rule. Add or multiply to make numbers larger. Try addition first.

4. SOLVE $1 + 2 = 3,$ $3 + 2 = 5,$ $5 + 2 = 7,$ $7 + 2 = 9$

The second number is 2 more than the first number. The third number is 2 more than the second number. The same pattern works for the next two numbers.
Rule: Add 2 to get the next number.
The next number in the pattern is 11.

5. CHECK   The answer is reasonable. It follows the rule. 11 is 2 more than 9.

FOCUS | Evaluate information as part of the Five-Step PROBLEM-SOLVING Plan.

PRACTICE

Copy and complete each pattern.

1.

2.

3.

Copy and complete each number pattern.

4. 2, 4, 6, 8, ▧, ▧

5. 25, 35, 45, 55, ▧, ▧

6. 900, 800, 700, 600, ▧, ▧

7. 606, 505, 404, 303, ▧, ▧

8. 11, 9, 7, 5, ▧, ▧

9. 7, 14, 21, 28, ▧, ▧

10. 4, 8, 12, 16, ▧, ▧

11. 300, 250, 200, 150, ▧, ▧

12. 50, 45, 40, 35, ▧, ▧

13. 42, 48, 54, 60, ▧, ▧

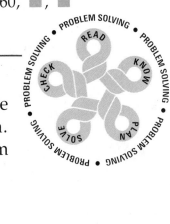

Class Project

Form a group with several classmates. Write three number patterns with 5 numbers in each pattern. Then trade lists with another group, and have them write the next 2 numbers in each pattern.

MULTIPLICATION
Multiplying Nines

There are 9 kickball teams.
Each team has 9 players.

Multiply to find the total number of players.

9 nines are 81 $9 \times 9 = 81$ $\begin{array}{r} 9 \\ \times 9 \\ \hline 81 \end{array}$

There are 81 players altogether.

GUIDED PRACTICE

1. Count by 9s to 81. 9, 18, 27, ■, ■, ■, ■, ■, ■

Multiply.

2. 5×9 **3.** 8×9 **4.** 1×9 **5.** 4×9 **6.** 3×9

7. $\begin{array}{r} 9 \\ \times 4 \\ \hline \end{array}$ **8.** $\begin{array}{r} 9 \\ \times 6 \\ \hline \end{array}$ **9.** $\begin{array}{r} 9 \\ \times 2 \\ \hline \end{array}$ **10.** $\begin{array}{r} 9 \\ \times 7 \\ \hline \end{array}$ **11.** $\begin{array}{r} 9 \\ \times 9 \\ \hline \end{array}$ **12.** $\begin{array}{r} 9 \\ \times 8 \\ \hline \end{array}$

FOCUS   Use NUMBER skills to multiply nines.

230

PRACTICE

Multiply.

13. 2×9 **14.** 4×9 **15.** 1×9 **16.** 3×9 **17.** 5×9

18. 7×9 **19.** 9×9 **20.** 6×9 **21.** 8×9 **22.** 0×9

23. $\begin{array}{r} 2 \\ \times 9 \\ \hline \end{array}$ **24.** $\begin{array}{r} 9 \\ \times 5 \\ \hline \end{array}$ **25.** $\begin{array}{r} 9 \\ \times 1 \\ \hline \end{array}$ **26.** $\begin{array}{r} 6 \\ \times 9 \\ \hline \end{array}$ **27.** $\begin{array}{r} 9 \\ \times 4 \\ \hline \end{array}$ **28.** $\begin{array}{r} 9 \\ \times 7 \\ \hline \end{array}$

29. $\begin{array}{r} 9 \\ \times 9 \\ \hline \end{array}$ **30.** $\begin{array}{r} 3 \\ \times 9 \\ \hline \end{array}$ **31.** $\begin{array}{r} 9 \\ \times 0 \\ \hline \end{array}$ **32.** $\begin{array}{r} 8 \\ \times 9 \\ \hline \end{array}$ **33.** $\begin{array}{r} 9 \\ \times 6 \\ \hline \end{array}$ **34.** $\begin{array}{r} 9 \\ \times 9 \\ \hline \end{array}$

Solve each problem.

35. Write a word problem that could be solved by multiplying 7 and 9. Then solve the problem.

36. Write a word problem that could be solved by multiplying 9 and 8. Then solve the problem.

MIXED PRACTICE
Maintaining and Reviewing Skills

Add, subtract, multiply, or divide.

37. 6×9 **38.** 0×9 **39.** 7×8 **40.** $3 \overline{)27}$ **41.** $8 \overline{)48}$

42. $18 - 7$ **43.** $12 + 13$ **44.** $6 \overline{)42}$ **45.** $7 \overline{)49}$ **46.** 8×5

47. $\begin{array}{r} 23 \\ +18 \\ \hline \end{array}$ **48.** $\begin{array}{r} 7 \\ \times 6 \\ \hline \end{array}$ **49.** $\begin{array}{r} 59 \\ -38 \\ \hline \end{array}$ **50.** $\begin{array}{r} 9 \\ \times 4 \\ \hline \end{array}$ **51.** $\begin{array}{r} 560 \\ -248 \\ \hline \end{array}$ **52.** $\begin{array}{r} 675 \\ +132 \\ \hline \end{array}$

CHALLENGE

53. Yesterday, each baseball cap cost eleven dollars. Today, each cap is on sale for two dollars less. If Mark buys 5 caps, how much does he spend?

MULTIPLICATION
Multiplying Through Nines

   This **multiplication table** shows all the multiplication facts you have learned.

Find the product of 7 and 6.

Step 1: Find 7 in the top row.
Step 2: Find 6 in the left column.
Step 3: Follow the 7 column down until it meets with the 6 row.

$7 \times 6 = 42$

x	0	1	2	3	4	5	6	7	8	9
0	0	0	0	0	0	0	0	0	0	0
1	0	1	2	3	4	5	6	7	8	9
2	0	2	4	6	8	10	12	14	16	18
3	0	3	6	9	12	15	18	21	24	27
4	0	4	8	12	16	20	24	28	32	36
5	0	5	10	15	20	25	30	35	40	45
6	0	6	12	18	24	30	36	42	48	54
7	0	7	14	21	28	35	42	49	56	63
8	0	8	16	24	32	40	48	56	64	72
9	0	9	18	27	36	45	54	63	72	81

PRACTICE

Use the multiplication table to find the product.

1. 7×6 2. 8×3 3. 9×7 4. 5×4 5. 3×7

6. $\begin{array}{r} 7 \\ \times 7 \\ \hline \end{array}$ 7. $\begin{array}{r} 9 \\ \times 4 \\ \hline \end{array}$ 8. $\begin{array}{r} 6 \\ \times 3 \\ \hline \end{array}$ 9. $\begin{array}{r} 1 \\ \times 9 \\ \hline \end{array}$ 10. $\begin{array}{r} 2 \\ \times 8 \\ \hline \end{array}$ 11. $\begin{array}{r} 8 \\ \times 7 \\ \hline \end{array}$

12. $\begin{array}{r} 0 \\ \times 4 \\ \hline \end{array}$ 13. $\begin{array}{r} 2 \\ \times 9 \\ \hline \end{array}$ 14. $\begin{array}{r} 9 \\ \times 9 \\ \hline \end{array}$ 15. $\begin{array}{r} 9 \\ \times 6 \\ \hline \end{array}$ 16. $\begin{array}{r} 7 \\ \times 5 \\ \hline \end{array}$ 17. $\begin{array}{r} 8 \\ \times 9 \\ \hline \end{array}$

MIXED PRACTICE
Maintaining and Reviewing Skills

Multiply or divide.

18. 6×9 19. 0×8 20. $1 \overline{)8}$ 21. $7 \overline{)56}$ 22. $8 \overline{)64}$

FOCUS | Use NUMBER skills to multiply through nines.

APPLICATION

Using Algebra

Eliot has 9 boxes of 5 trucks. Susie has 9 boxes of 6 trucks. Do Eliot and Susie have the same number of trucks?

Multiply to find out:

$9 \times 5 = 45 \qquad 9 \times 6 = 54$

9×5 **is not equal to** 9×6
$$9 \times 5 \neq 9 \times 6$$
$$45 \neq 54$$

No, Eliot and Susie do not have the same number of trucks.

Write = or ≠.

23. $3 \times 9 \blacksquare 9 \times 3$ **24.** $9 \times 8 \blacksquare 8 \times 9$ **25.** $0 \times 9 \blacksquare 9 \times 1$

26. $9 \times 7 \blacksquare 6 \times 9$ **27.** $4 \times 9 \blacksquare 9 \times 4$ **28.** $2 \times 9 \blacksquare 1 \times 9$

29. $6 \times 6 \blacksquare 9 \times 4$ **30.** $3 \times 3 \blacksquare 1 \times 9$ **31.** $9 \times 6 \blacksquare 7 \times 8$

Solve each problem.

32. Peg has 9 jars of 4 stones. Ray has 4 jars of 9 stones. Do Peg and Ray have the same number of stones?

33. Franklyn has 2 bags of 9 balls. Francine has 3 bags of 7 balls. Do Franklyn and Francine have the same number of balls?

Mental Arithmetic

Write whether the product is odd or even.

34. 3×5 **35.** 2×4 **36.** 9×3 **37.** 9×4 **38.** 7×8

39. $\begin{array}{r} 9 \\ \times 6 \\ \hline \end{array}$ **40.** $\begin{array}{r} 8 \\ \times 3 \\ \hline \end{array}$ **41.** $\begin{array}{r} 5 \\ \times 6 \\ \hline \end{array}$ **42.** $\begin{array}{r} 9 \\ \times 7 \\ \hline \end{array}$ **43.** $\begin{array}{r} 3 \\ \times 4 \\ \hline \end{array}$ **44.** $\begin{array}{r} 5 \\ \times 7 \\ \hline \end{array}$

Use ALGEBRA to explore the symbol ≠ and MENTAL ARITHMETIC to distinguish between odd and even products.

LOOKING BACK
Reviewing and Testing Chapter 17

In Chapter 17 you formulated problems about a spelling bee. Look at pages 222 and 223.

1. Write a sentence telling why you would, or would not, want to be in a spelling bee.

You learned something new about multiplying eights. To review what you learned, study the sample problem on page 224. Then use the new skill to find each product for examples 2 to 12.

2. 8 ×3	3. 8 ×5	4. 8 ×7	5. 8 ×8	6. 8 ×1	7. 8 ×9

8. 4 × 8   9. 6 × 8   10. 2 × 8   11. 5 × 8   12. 7 × 8

You learned how to find a pattern. To review what you learned, look at pages 228 and 229. Copy and complete each number pattern.

13. 101, 202, 303, ▪, ▪   14. 25, 20, 15, ▪, ▪

You learned something new about multiplying nines. To review, look at pages 230 and 231. Use the new skill to find each product for examples 15 to 27.

15. 9 ×2	16. 9 ×9	17. 9 ×6	18. 9 ×4	19. 9 ×8	20. 9 ×1

21. 3 × 9   22. 5 × 9   23. 7 × 9   24. 2 × 9   25. 6 × 9

26. There are 6 bags of potatoes. Each bag has 9 potatoes. How many are there altogether?

27. Write a word problem that you could solve by multiplying 9 and 8. Then solve the problem.

FOCUS	Review and test skills learned and practiced.

LOOKING AHEAD

Preparing for New Skills for Chapter 18

In the next chapter you will focus on

- formulating problems.
- dividing by eights.
- using algebra.
- dividing by nines.
- using patterns and functions.
- how math is used with maps.

New division skills will be easier to learn if you know how to find equal parts of a group. Study the model. Then complete the PRACTICE exercises. Check your work with the model.

Model

There are 24 jacks. How many groups of 8 jacks are there?

There are 3 groups of 8 jacks.

PRACTICE

Complete. Review the model if you need to.

1. Count and copy the rectangles. Then ring groups of 9 rectangles.

2. How many rectangles are there in all?

3. How many groups of 9 rectangles are there?

☐ ☐ ☐ ☐ ☐ ☐ ☐ ☐ ☐

☐ ☐ ☐ ☐ ☐ ☐ ☐ ☐ ☐

☐ ☐ ☐ ☐ ☐ ☐ ☐ ☐ ☐

Review NUMBER skills in preparation for learning a new skill.

Formulate problems using picture cues, text, and data.

18

Division Facts for Eights and Nines

DATA

Activity	Snowshoeing
Number of people	4
Leader of group	Betsy
Distance	10 miles
Time	Day trip (7 A.M.–5 P.M.)
Snow	6–10 inches
Travel kit	Map Compass Flashlight Snowshoe repair kit
Clothing	Snowshoes Wool pants Wool shirt Jacket Moccasins Hat

People can travel on snow using skis or a sled. Or they can use snowshoes. Snowshoes were first used in North America about 6,000 years ago. They helped hunters walk easily through the heavy snows.

Today, snowshoes are still important to hunters. But many other people use snowshoes for fun. Wearing snowshoes, you can enjoy the quiet of the woods in winter.

But before you pull on your snowshoes, you must do some thinking. Look at the photograph and the data. You can see that snowshoes are one of the most important items on this trip. What other items are important? What would you need to do before leaving on a snowshoeing trip? What problems might you have to solve on the trip?

DIVISION
Dividing by Eights

Charlie has 56 keys. If he puts 8 keys on a key ring, how many key rings will Charlie need?

Divide to find the number of key rings that Charlie will need. Divide the number of keys in all by the number of keys that he will put on each key ring.

keys in all		keys on each ring		key rings
56	÷	8	=	7

$56 \div 8 = 7$ can be written as $8\overline{)56}$ with quotient 7.

Charlie will need 7 key rings.

GUIDED PRACTICE

Divide to show how many groups there are.

1.

How many 8s are in 48?

$48 \div 8 = 6$

2.

How many 8s are in 32?

$32 \div 8 = \blacksquare$

3. $8\overline{)24}$ **4.** $8\overline{)8}$ **5.** $8\overline{)40}$ **6.** $8\overline{)16}$ **7.** $8\overline{)72}$ **8.** $8\overline{)64}$

FOCUS | Use NUMBER skills to divide by eights.

238

PRACTICE

Divide.

9. $40 \div 8$ **10.** $8 \div 8$ **11.** $32 \div 8$ **12.** $16 \div 8$ **13.** $24 \div 8$

14. $56 \div 8$ **15.** $48 \div 8$ **16.** $24 \div 8$ **17.** $64 \div 8$ **18.** $72 \div 8$

19. $8\overline{)16}$ **20.** $8\overline{)40}$ **21.** $8\overline{)8}$ **22.** $8\overline{)56}$ **23.** $8\overline{)48}$ **24.** $8\overline{)72}$

25. $8\overline{)32}$ **26.** $8\overline{)24}$ **27.** $8\overline{)72}$ **28.** $8\overline{)64}$ **29.** $8\overline{)40}$ **30.** $8\overline{)48}$

Solve each problem.

31. Trudy has 48 light bulbs and 8 ceiling lamps. If each ceiling lamp uses the same number of light bulbs, how many will she put in each ceiling lamp?

32. There are 64 tires in all and 8 trucks. Each truck needs the same number of tires. How many tires will be put on each truck?

MIXED PRACTICE
Maintaining and Reviewing Skills

Add, subtract, multiply, or divide.

33. $32 \div 8$ **34.** $8\overline{)56}$ **35.** 9×8 **36.** 7×6 **37.** $6\overline{)54}$

38.

39.

CHALLENGE

40. Fifty-two people bought tickets for a ride on the train. Then 20 more people bought tickets. Each train car holds 8 people. How many train cars are needed for everyone?

$$\begin{array}{r} 5\overset{1}{2} \\ +20 \\ \hline 72 \end{array}$$

$72 \div 8 = 9$ train cars

239

DIVISION

Dividing by Eights

Emily spends 72¢ for 8 tops. If each top costs the same, how much does each one cost?

Use division to find the cost of each top.

Divide the money Emily spends by the number of tops she buys. Then write ¢ in the answer.

$$72¢ \div 8 = 9¢ \qquad 8\overline{)72¢}^{\,9¢}$$

Each top costs 9¢.

PRACTICE

Divide. Remember the ¢.

1. 8¢ ÷ 8   2. 32¢ ÷ 8   3. 16¢ ÷ 8   4. 40¢ ÷ 8   5. 24¢ ÷ 8

6. 64 ÷ 8   7. 48 ÷ 8   8. 72 ÷ 8   9. 56 ÷ 8   10. 32 ÷ 8

11. $8\overline{)16¢}$ 12. $8\overline{)40¢}$ 13. $8\overline{)64¢}$ 14. $8\overline{)48¢}$ 15. $8\overline{)8¢}$ 16. $8\overline{)72¢}$

17. $8\overline{)56}$ 18. $8\overline{)8}$ 19. $8\overline{)32}$ 20. $8\overline{)72}$ 21. $8\overline{)64}$ 22. $8\overline{)48}$

MIXED PRACTICE

Maintaining and Reviewing Skills

Add, subtract, multiply, or divide.

23. 64¢ ÷ 8   24. $8\overline{)56}$ 25. 49 ÷ 7   26. 8 × 8   27. 9 × 6

28. 7   29. 47   30. 90   31.   8   32. 233   33. 598
    ×9   +23   −12   ×6   +129   −179

APPLICATION

Using Algebra

Rhonda is buying some boxes of crayons. Each box has 8 crayons. How many boxes will Rhonda buy to get 48 crayons in all?

One way to solve the problem is to find the missing factor.

$$\blacksquare \quad \times \quad 8 \quad = \quad 48$$

Number of boxes	Crayons in each box	Crayons in all

Divide to find the missing factor.

$$48 \quad \div \quad 8 \quad = \quad 6$$

Crayons in all	Crayons in each box	Number of boxes

Six is the missing factor.

$6 \times 8 = 48$

Rhonda will buy 6 boxes of crayons.

Divide to find each missing factor.

34. $4 \times \blacksquare = 24$ **35.** $7 \times \blacksquare = 21$ **36.** $6 \times \blacksquare = 30$ **37.** $2 \times \blacksquare = 12$

38. $\blacksquare \times 3 = 27$ **39.** $\blacksquare \times 8 = 24$ **40.** $\blacksquare \times 5 = 45$ **41.** $\blacksquare \times 8 = 64$

42.
$$\begin{array}{r} 1 \\ \times\, \blacksquare \\ \hline 8 \end{array}$$

43.
$$\begin{array}{r} 7 \\ \times\, \blacksquare \\ \hline 49 \end{array}$$

44.
$$\begin{array}{r} 4 \\ \times\, \blacksquare \\ \hline 32 \end{array}$$

45.
$$\begin{array}{r} \blacksquare \\ \times\, 8 \\ \hline 16 \end{array}$$

46.
$$\begin{array}{r} \blacksquare \\ \times\, 6 \\ \hline 42 \end{array}$$

47.
$$\begin{array}{r} 3 \\ \times\, \blacksquare \\ \hline 27 \end{array}$$

48.
$$\begin{array}{r} 2 \\ \times\, \blacksquare \\ \hline 18 \end{array}$$

49.
$$\begin{array}{r} \blacksquare \\ \times\, 8 \\ \hline 40 \end{array}$$

50.
$$\begin{array}{r} 3 \\ \times\, \blacksquare \\ \hline 9 \end{array}$$

51.
$$\begin{array}{r} 5 \\ \times\, \blacksquare \\ \hline 20 \end{array}$$

52.
$$\begin{array}{r} \blacksquare \\ \times\, 9 \\ \hline 36 \end{array}$$

53.
$$\begin{array}{r} \blacksquare \\ \times\, 7 \\ \hline 28 \end{array}$$

Use ALGEBRA to find missing factors.

DIVISION
Dividing by Nines

Mrs. Mark ordered 63 books. There are 9 books in each box. How many boxes of books did Mrs. Mark order?

Divide to find the number of boxes of books that Mrs. Mark ordered. Divide the number of books in all by the number of books in each box.

63 books in all   9 books in each box   7 boxes
   63 **divided by**   9   **is equal to** 7

$$63 \div 9 = 7 \text{ can be written as } 9\overline{)63}^{\,7}$$

Mrs. Mark ordered 7 boxes of books.

GUIDED PRACTICE

Divide to show how many groups there are.

1.

How many 9s
are in 27?

$$27 \div 9 = 3$$

2.

How many 9s
are in 36?

$$36 \div 9 = \blacksquare$$

3. $9\overline{)45}$ **4.** $9\overline{)18}$ **5.** $9\overline{)9}$ **6.** $9\overline{)54}$ **7.** $9\overline{)81}$ **8.** $9\overline{)72}$

FOCUS   Use NUMBER skills to divide by nines.

PRACTICE

Divide.

9. $18 \div 9$ **10.** $36 \div 9$ **11.** $9 \div 9$ **12.** $27 \div 9$ **13.** $45 \div 9$

14. $72 \div 9$ **15.** $54 \div 9$ **16.** $81 \div 9$ **17.** $63 \div 9$ **18.** $36 \div 9$

19. $9\overline{)45}$ **20.** $9\overline{)18}$ **21.** $9\overline{)72}$ **22.** $9\overline{)36}$ **23.** $9\overline{)63}$ **24.** $9\overline{)81}$

25. $9\overline{)27}$ **26.** $9\overline{)9}$ **27.** $9\overline{)54}$ **28.** $9\overline{)81}$ **29.** $9\overline{)45}$ **30.** $9\overline{)72}$

Solve each problem.

31. Write a word problem that could be solved by dividing 36 by 9. Then solve the problem.

32. Write a word problem that could be solved by dividing 72 by 9. Then solve the problem.

MIXED PRACTICE
Maintaining and Reviewing Skills

Add, subtract, multiply, or divide.

33. $36 \div 9$ **34.** $9\overline{)81}$ **35.** 7×9 **36.** 4×8 **37.** $8\overline{)64}$

38. $12 + 15$ **39.** $30 - 15$ **40.** $72 \div 9$ **41.** $6\overline{)36}$ **42.** 9×8

43. $\begin{array}{r} 9 \\ \times 5 \\ \hline \end{array}$ **44.** $\begin{array}{r} 78 \\ -35 \\ \hline \end{array}$ **45.** $\begin{array}{r} 45 \\ +41 \\ \hline \end{array}$ **46.** $\begin{array}{r} 8 \\ \times 8 \\ \hline \end{array}$ **47.** $\begin{array}{r} 578 \\ +419 \\ \hline \end{array}$ **48.** $\begin{array}{r} 692 \\ -489 \\ \hline \end{array}$

CHALLENGE

Complete the number sentences.

49. $\blacksquare \times 9 = 81 \rightarrow 81 \div \blacksquare = 9$ **50.** $54 \div \blacksquare = 6 \rightarrow 6 \times 9 = \blacksquare$

51. $\blacksquare \div 9 = 7 \rightarrow 7 \times \blacksquare = 63$ **52.** $8 \times \blacksquare = 72 \rightarrow 72 \div \blacksquare = 8$

DIVISION
Dividing Through Nines

Ron has 54 buttons. He puts 9 buttons in each pile. How many piles of buttons does Ron have?

Divide to solve. $54 \div 9 = 6$

Ron has 6 piles of buttons.

PRACTICE

Divide.

1. $12 \div 3$ 2. $9 \div 1$ 3. $25 \div 5$ 4. $2 \div 2$ 5. $28 \div 4$

6. $8 \div 2$ 7. $15 \div 5$ 8. $1 \div 1$ 9. $6 \div 3$ 10. $4 \div 4$

11. $6\overline{)18}$ 12. $4\overline{)36}$ 13. $7\overline{)42}$ 14. $2\overline{)4}$ 15. $5\overline{)20}$ 16. $6\overline{)36}$

17. $7\overline{)35}$ 18. $1\overline{)8}$ 19. $8\overline{)64}$ 20. $3\overline{)9}$ 21. $6\overline{)48}$ 22. $9\overline{)63}$

23. $8\overline{)40}$ 24. $9\overline{)72}$ 25. $7\overline{)49}$ 26. $9\overline{)81}$ 27. $8\overline{)56}$ 28. $9\overline{)54}$

MIXED PRACTICE
Maintaining and Reviewing Skills

Add, subtract, multiply, or divide.

29. $21 \div 7$ 30. $18 \div 6$ 31. $8\overline{)64}$ 32. 7×6 33. 9×5

34. $\begin{array}{r} 6 \\ \times 9 \\ \hline \end{array}$ 35. $\begin{array}{r} 7 \\ \times 5 \\ \hline \end{array}$ 36. $\begin{array}{r} 43 \\ -25 \\ \hline \end{array}$ 37. $\begin{array}{r} 54 \\ +37 \\ \hline \end{array}$ 38. $\begin{array}{r} 67 \\ -59 \\ \hline \end{array}$ 39. $\begin{array}{r} 37 \\ +35 \\ \hline \end{array}$

| FOCUS | Use NUMBER skills to divide through nines. |

244

APPLICATION

Using Patterns and Functions

Use the multiplication table to divide.

Find $48 \div 8$.

Step 1: Find 8 in the left column.

Step 2: Follow the 8 across to 48.

Step 3: Follow the 48 up to 6.

$$48 \div 8 = 6$$

X	1	2	3	4	5	6	7	8	9
1	1	2	3	4	5	6	7	8	9
2	2	4	6	8	10	12	14	16	18
3	3	6	9	12	15	18	21	24	27
4	4	8	12	16	20	24	28	32	36
5	5	10	15	20	25	30	35	40	45
6	6	12	18	24	30	36	42	48	54
7	7	14	21	28	35	42	49	56	63
8	8	16	24	32	40	48	56	64	72
9	9	18	27	36	45	54	63	72	81

Use the multiplication table to divide.

40. $12 \div 2$ **41.** $7 \div 1$ **42.** $10 \div 5$ **43.** $3 \div 3$ **44.** $20 \div 4$

45. $35 \div 5$ **46.** $48 \div 6$ **47.** $2 \div 1$ **48.** $24 \div 8$ **49.** $63 \div 7$

50. $4 \div 4$ **51.** $16 \div 2$ **52.** $21 \div 7$ **53.** $24 \div 6$ **54.** $18 \div 3$

55. $8\overline{)40}$ **56.** $1\overline{)5}$ **57.** $5\overline{)15}$ **58.** $4\overline{)16}$ **59.** $7\overline{)14}$ **60.** $9\overline{)54}$

61. $3\overline{)24}$ **62.** $8\overline{)64}$ **63.** $7\overline{)49}$ **64.** $2\overline{)18}$ **65.** $9\overline{)36}$ **66.** $5\overline{)25}$

67. $4\overline{)28}$ **68.** $6\overline{)36}$ **69.** $1\overline{)8}$ **70.** $8\overline{)56}$ **71.** $3\overline{)6}$ **72.** $9\overline{)9}$

73. $9\overline{)27}$ **74.** $2\overline{)8}$ **75.** $8\overline{)72}$ **76.** $6\overline{)6}$ **77.** $7\overline{)42}$ **78.** $9\overline{)81}$

Use PATTERNS AND FUNCTIONS to divide using a multiplication table.

Direction

The four directions, north, south, east, and west, have always been important in geography.

Six continents are named for these directions. North and South America are two examples. Antarctica, the continent near the South Pole, gets its name because it is opposite the North Pole. In Greek, *ant(i)* means opposite and *arktikos* means northern, so Antarctica means opposite northern. The name Australia comes from the Latin word *auster* meaning south. The names Europe and Asia also come from directions. The word Europe comes from a word *Ereb* meaning west. Asia comes from a word *Assu* meaning east.

Africa was named for the Libyan mythological figure Afer, who was similar to Hercules.

North, south, east, and west are called the four cardinal (main) points. It is important to know the cardinal points when reading a map.

Almost all modern maps are drawn with north at the top. This was started by Claudius Ptolemy, a scientist who lived in Egypt about 1,800 years ago. Most of the world that he knew about was in the north, so he put north at the top of his maps.

On a map, you can see what direction is on top by looking at the compass "rose" which looks like this:

CRITICAL THINKING

1. How many continents are there?

2. How did they get their names?

3. Why is north at the top of the maps?

4. How many cardinal points are there? What are their names?

FOCUS Use LOGIC to understand and analyze direction points on maps.

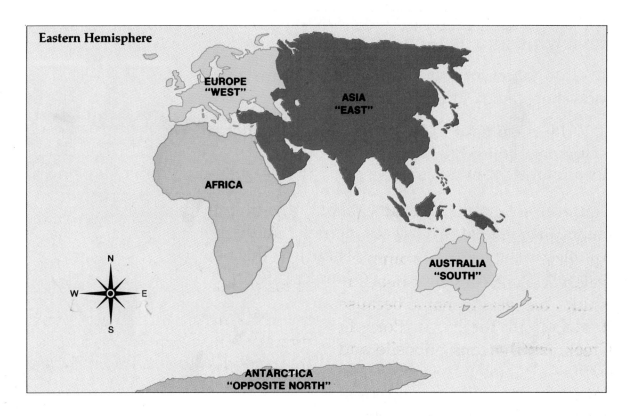

Eastern Hemisphere

EUROPE "WEST"

ASIA "EAST"

AFRICA

AUSTRALIA "SOUTH"

ANTARCTICA "OPPOSITE NORTH"

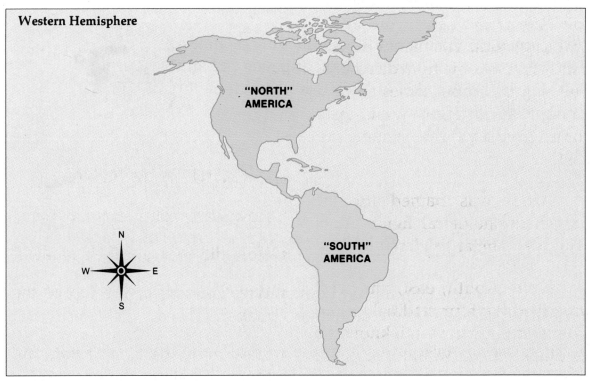

Western Hemisphere

"NORTH" AMERICA

"SOUTH" AMERICA

LOOKING BACK
Reviewing and Testing Chapter 18

In Chapter 18 you formulated problems about snowshoes. Look at pages 236 and 237.

1. Write a sentence telling some things you might see on a snowshoeing trip.

You learned something new about dividing by eights. To review what you learned, study the sample problem on page 238. Then use the new skill to find each quotient for examples 2 to 18.

2. $32 \div 8$ 3. $16 \div 8$ 4. $56 \div 8$ 5. $8 \div 8$ 6. $40 \div 8$

7. $8 \overline{) 48}$ 8. $8 \overline{) 8}$ 9. $8 \overline{) 64}$ 10. $8 \overline{) 24}$ 11. $8 \overline{) 72}$ 12. $8 \overline{) 56}$

13. $8 \overline{) 40}$ 14. $8 \overline{) 24}$ 15. $8 \overline{) 32}$ 16. $8 \overline{) 16}$ 17. $8 \overline{) 64}$ 18. $8 \overline{) 48}$

You learned something new about dividing by nines. To review what you learned, look at pages 242 and 243. Use the new skill to find each quotient for examples 19 to 35.

19. $9 \div 9$ 20. $45 \div 9$ 21. $63 \div 9$ 22. $18 \div 9$ 23. $72 \div 9$

24. $9 \overline{) 27}$ 25. $9 \overline{) 72}$ 26. $9 \overline{) 9}$ 27. $9 \overline{) 54}$ 28. $9 \overline{) 81}$ 29. $9 \overline{) 36}$

30. $9 \overline{) 54}$ 31. $9 \overline{) 18}$ 32. $9 \overline{) 81}$ 33. $9 \overline{) 27}$ 34. $9 \overline{) 63}$ 35. $9 \overline{) 45}$

You learned about geography. Look at page 246 to review the names of the continents.

36. There are seven continents in the world. Write the name of each continent.

FOCUS | Review and test skills learned and practiced.

LOOKING AHEAD

Preparing for New Skills for Chapter 19

In the next chapter you will focus on

- formulating problems.
- place value to 9,999.
- rounding 4-digit numbers.

- comparing and ordering 4-digit numbers.
- statistics and probability.

Learning about a new place value will be easier if you review what you already know about place value. Study the place-value chart. Then complete the PRACTICE exercises. Use the chart for help.

Model

Hundreds	Tens	Ones
4	5	8

⟶ 458

PRACTICE

Read the place-value chart. Then write the number.

1.
Hundreds	Tens	Ones
6	9	4

→ 694

2.
Hundreds	Tens	Ones
9	0	3

→ 903

3.
Hundreds	Tens	Ones
8	6	0

→ 860

4.
Hundreds	Tens	Ones
9	8	7

→ 987

5.
Hundreds	Tens	Ones
1	0	9

→ 109

6.
Hundreds	Tens	Ones
3	2	0

→ 320

Review NUMBER skills in preparation for learning a new skill.

FORMULATING PROBLEMS

CHAPTER **19**

Place Value

DATA

Activity	Relay race
Place	Treetop Park
Day	Saturday
Time	Noon
Players	
Star Team	Tammy
	Tim
	Sara
Rabbit Team	Lonnie
	Ronald
	Shari
Win/loss record	
Star Team	1 win/
	4 losses
Rabbit Team	4 wins/1 loss
Object for passing	Stick

A relay race is a contest between two or more teams of runners. Each player runs to a goal line and back, holding something that he or she passes to the next runner on the team. A stick works well, since it can be held and passed easily by a runner.

A runner must go as fast as he or she can to help the team win. Several things can affect the outcome of a relay race. Can you think of any?

Use the picture and the data to think about which team has a better chance of winning the race. What might happen as a player tries to pass the stick? What might happen to a runner who is moving very fast? What problems might each team have during the relay race?

PLACE VALUE
Writing Four-Digit Numbers

How many cubes are in the picture?

The cubes are grouped by thousands:
10 hundreds equal 1 thousand.

2 thousands   3 hundreds   1 ten   5 ones

Thousands	Hundreds	Tens	Ones
2	3	1	5

$\longrightarrow$ 2,315

There are two thousand three hundred fifteen cubes in the picture.

GUIDED PRACTICE

Copy and complete the place value chart. Then write the number.

1.

Thousands	Hundreds	Tens	Ones

FOCUS | Use NUMBER skills to identify the place value of four-digit numbers.

PRACTICE

Write the number.

2. 5 thousands   6 hundreds   2 tens   3 ones

3. 7 thousands   9 hundreds   0 tens   9 ones

4. 1 thousand   5 hundreds   8 tens   0 ones

5. 9 thousands   0 hundreds   1 ten   7 ones

6. 0 thousands   8 hundreds   0 tens   1 one

Write the place value of the underlined digit.

7. 5,7<u>6</u>4   **8.** <u>3</u>99   **9.** 5<u>7</u>   **10.** <u>9</u>,010   **11.** <u>7</u>,562

12. 22<u>2</u>   **13.** <u>1</u>,168   **14.** 60<u>3</u>   **15.** 8,43<u>5</u>   **16.** <u>3</u>,910

17. <u>4</u>,809   **18.** <u>7</u>5   **19.** 2,<u>1</u>98   **20.** 1<u>6</u>2   **21.** <u>5</u>,484

MIXED PRACTICE
Maintaining and Reviewing Skills

Write the number.

22. 8 thousands   2 hundreds   3 tens   6 ones

23. 4 thousands   0 hundreds   7 tens   0 ones

24. 6 hundreds   3 tens   9 ones   **25.** 9 hundreds   0 tens   4 ones

CHALLENGE

Write each number.

26. 10 more than 1,865   **27.** 100 more than 5,498   **28.** 1,000 more than 7,970

PLACE VALUE
Writing Four-Digit Numbers

Jay eats 1,095 meals in a year.

What is the place value of the digit 1?

The place value of the digit 1 is thousands.

Jay eats one thousand ninety-five meals in a year.

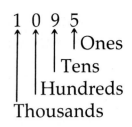

PRACTICE

Write the number.

1. four thousand six hundred twenty-five

2. nine thousand fifty-eight

3. two thousand seven hundred six

4. Jean sleeps about two thousand nine hundred twenty hours in a year.

5. Lauren goes to school about one thousand two hundred hours in a year.

What is the place value of the underlined digit?
Write **thousands, hundreds, tens,** or **ones.**

6. 6,47<u>8</u>   7. 4,<u>2</u>10   8. <u>7</u>64   9. 5<u>5</u>   10. <u>2</u>,853

11. 3<u>1</u>0   12. <u>8</u>3   13. 1,9<u>3</u>6   14. <u>9</u>,763   15. 7,0<u>2</u>9

MIXED PRACTICE
Maintaining and Reviewing Skills

Write the number.

16. seven thousand five hundred ninety-nine

17. three hundred forty-three   18. two hundred nine

FOCUS | Use NUMBER skills to identify the place value of four-digit numbers.

APPLICATION

Using Algebra

What is the greatest number and the least number that can be made using these four digits?

| 7 | 5 | 8 | 3 |

To find the greatest number, write the digits in order from greatest to least.

The greatest number that can be made is 8,753.

To find the least number, write the digits in order from least to greatest.

The least number that can be made is 3,578.

Write the greatest number and the least number using each group of four digits.

19. | 5 | 6 | 3 | 9 | 20. | 2 | 8 | 4 | 1 | 21. | 0 | 5 | 8 | 4 |

22. | 2 | 6 | 4 | 1 | 23. | 7 | 3 | 9 | 5 | 24. | 3 | 9 | 0 | 7 |

25. | 7 | 1 | 5 | 3 | 26. | 4 | 9 | 2 | 6 | 27. | 8 | 0 | 6 | 0 |

Mental Arithmetic

See how quickly you can finish each pattern.

28. 100, 200, 300, ■ , ■ , ■ , ■ , ■ , ■

29. 1,000, 2,000, 3,000, ■ , ■ , ■ , ■ , ■ , ■

30. 140, 240, 340, ■ , ■ , ■ , ■ , ■ , ■

31. 1,560, 2,560, 3,560, ■ , ■ , ■ , ■ , ■ , ■

Use ALGEBRA to identify the greatest and the least possible number made from 4 digits.
Use MENTAL ARITHMETIC to count by hundreds and thousands.

ESTIMATION
Rounding Four-Digit Numbers

Max's parking lot holds 1,624 cars. About how many cars does Max's parking lot hold?

Round to find *about* how many cars Max's parking lot holds.

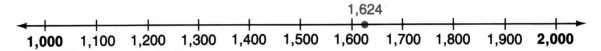

Round 1,624 to the nearest thousand:
- 1,624 is between 1,000 and 2,000
- 1,624 is closer to 2,000
- 1,624 rounds up to 2,000
- Max's parking lot holds *about* 2,000 cars.

GUIDED PRACTICE

Complete to round each number to the nearest thousand.

1. 1,300 is between ■ and ■.
   1,300 is closer to ■.
   1,300 rounds down to ■.

2. 2,800 is between ■ and ■.
   2,800 is closer to ■.
   2,800 rounds up to ■.

3. 4,500 is halfway between
   ■ and ■.
   4,500 rounds up to ■.

4. 7,100 is between ■ and ■.
   7,100 is closer to ■.
   7,100 rounds down to ■.

5. 1,238 is between ■ and ■.
   1,238 is closer to ■.
   1,238 rounds ■ to ■.

6. 1,963 is between ■ and ■.
   1,963 is closer to ■.
   1,963 rounds ■ to ■.

7. 3,098 is between ■ and ■.
   3,098 is closer to ■.
   3,098 rounds ■ to ■.

8. 5,500 is halfway between
   ■ and ■.
   5,500 rounds ■ to ■.

FOCUS | Use NUMBER skills to round four-digit numbers.

256

PRACTICE

Round to the nearest thousand.

9. 1,200   10. 3,500   11. 5,700   12. 6,300   13. 9,100

14. 5,900   15. 7,300   16. 8,400   17. 4,800   18. 5,500

19. 3,672   20. 9,234   21. 4,908   22. 6,372   23. 8,734

24. The Town Garage changed 1,839 tires over the past year. About how many tires did The Town Garage change?

25. Ronald and his cousin counted 2,315 cars. About how many cars did Ronald and his cousin count?

MIXED PRACTICE
Maintaining and Reviewing Skills

Round to the nearest thousand.

26. 1,400   27. 2,700   28. 7,986   29. 5,172   30. 3,623

31. 6,805   32. 9,382   33. 4,500   34. 1,096   35. 8,200

Round to the nearest hundred.

36. 764   37. 925   38. 582   39. 450   40. 215

41. 350   42. 838   43. 173   44. 694   45. 982

Round to the nearest ten.

46. 23   47. 88   48. 65   49. 91   50. 59   51. 16

52. 75   53. 39   54. 12   55. 47   56. 93   57. 61

CHALLENGE

58. Write three numbers that round up to 2,000.

59. Write three numbers that round down to 5,000.

PLACE VALUE
Comparing Four-Digit Numbers

The Knot Shop has 1,248 skeins of yarn. The Yarn Place has 1,256 skeins of yarn. Which store has more skeins of yarn?

	Th	H	T	O			Th	H	T	O
Compare	1	2	4	8	and		1	2	5	6 |.

- Compare the thousands. They are the same.
- Compare the hundreds. They are the same.
- Compare the tens: forty is less than fifty.

1,248 **is less than** 1,256   and   1,256 **is greater than** 1,248
    $1,248 < 1,256$ $1,256 > 1,248$

The Yarn Place has more skeins of yarn.

PRACTICE

Compare. Write $<$ or $>$.

1. 3,659 ■ 7,964
2. 8,567 ■ 9,339
3. 5,862 ■ 2,865

4. 8,461 ■ 8,416
5. 7,203 ■ 7,502
6. 4,191 ■ 4,193

Write the numbers in order from greatest to least.

7. 4,625, 8,796, 6,452, 9,730
8. 3,321, 5,312, 5,231, 3,213

9. 7,183, 9,009, 5,632, 2,541
10. 4,873, 1,989, 4,837, 1,998

MIXED PRACTICE
Maintaining and Reviewing Skills

Compare. Write $<$ or $>$.

11. 1,562 ■ 7,483   12. 4,715 ■ 4,751   13. 397 ■ 362   14. 529 ■ 527

FOCUS | Use NUMBER skills to compare and order four-digit numbers.

258

APPLICATION

Using Statistics and Probability

Population is the number of people who live in a place.

This table shows the population of some American cities.

City	State	Population
Ada	Minnesota	1,971
Barry	Illinois	1,487
Bethel	Alaska	3,576
Dora	Alabama	2,327
Cynthiana	Kentucky	5,929

15. In which state is the city of Dora?

16. Which has a smaller population, Barry or Ada?

17. Which has a larger population, Bethel or Cynthiana?

18. Which city has the largest population?

19. Write the population figures in order from least to greatest.

Estimation

The population of Barry, Illinois is 1,487. About how many people live in Barry, Illinois?

Round the population to the nearest thousand.
    1,487 rounds down to 1,000

About 1,000 people live in Barry, Illinois.

20. Make a table like the one at the right. Copy each city name and population figure from the table above. Then round each figure to the nearest thousand.

City	Population	Nearest Thousand
Barry	1,487	1,000

Use STATISTICS AND PROBABILITY to read and interpret a table.
Use NUMBER skills and ESTIMATION to round, compare, and order four-digit numbers.

LOOKING BACK
Reviewing and Testing Chapter 19

In Chapter 19 you formulated problems about a relay race. Look at pages 250 and 251.

1. Write a sentence telling what things can affect the outcome of the race.

You learned something new about writing four-digit numbers. To review what you learned, study the sample problem on page 252. Then use the new skill to write each number for examples 2 to 6.

2. 4 thousands 6 hundreds 5 tens 0 ones

3. 7 thousands 2 hundreds 8 tens 9 ones

4. 1 thousand 0 hundreds 2 tens 1 one

5. 3 thousands 4 hundreds 0 tens 7 ones

6. 6 thousands 2 hundreds 3 tens 5 ones

You learned something new about rounding four-digit numbers. To review, look at pages 256 and 257. Then use the new skill to round to the nearest thousand for examples 7 to 18.

7. 1,800   8. 2,200   9. 7,600   10. 8,900   11. 4,500

12. 5,378   13. 7,153   14. 8,150   15. 1,453   16. 3,607

17. Gary runs 1 236 km in a year. About how many kilometers does Gary run in a year?

18. Regina goes to school 1,087 hours in one year. About how many hours does she go to school in one year?

FOCUS | Review and test skills learned and practiced.

LOOKING AHEAD
Preparing for New Skills for Chapter 20

In the next chapter you will focus on

- formulating problems.
- adding four-digit numbers.
- estimating sums.
- using patterns and functions.

- subtracting four-digit numbers.
- estimating differences.
- how math is used in music.

New addition and subtraction skills will be easier to learn if you review the skills you already know.

Study the models. Complete the PRACTICE exercises.

Model A

Add the ones.
Regroup.

```
   H T O
     1
   2 6 5        5
 + 7 9        +9
       4       14
```

Add the tens.
Regroup.

```
   H T O
     1 1
   2 6 5       1 ten
 + 7 9         6 tens
     4 4      +7 tens
              14 tens
```

Add the hundreds.

```
   H T O
   1 1
   2 6 5
 + 7 9
   3 4 4
```

Model B

Regroup to get some tens.

```
   H  T  O
   2  10
   3  0  9
 -    4  8
```

Subtract.

```
   H  T  O
   2  10
   3  0  9
 -    4  8
   2  6  1
```

PRACTICE

Add or subtract. Review Model A or B.

1. $743 + 146$ 2. $359 - 249$ 3. $805 - 475$ 4. $694 + 26$ 5. $900 - 93$

Review NUMBER skills in preparation for learning a new skill.

20

Addition and Subtraction of Larger Numbers

DATA

Items in fish house

 Bookcase
 Cat
 Chair
 Coffee table
 Couch
 Dogs
 Planter
 Pogo stick
 Radiator
 Rocking chair
 TV
 Telephone
 Trumpet

Money already
 spent on
 fish $350

Cost of fish
 house About $75
      (fish not
      included)

   Clara loved fish. She spent hours watching her fish swim in their tanks. She had two fish tanks—a freshwater tank and a saltwater tank.

   Clara liked to go to pet stores to look for new fish. One day, when she was in a pet store, she saw something that caught her eye. It was a house for fish. It didn't look like the fish tanks she had. It was like a dollhouse for fish!

   Clara wanted the fish house very much. But she already had two tanks at home.

   What problems will Clara have to solve before she decides what to do?

ADDITION
Adding Four-Digit Numbers

The distance from New York to San Francisco is 2,541 miles. The distance from San Francisco to Honolulu is 2,353 miles.

Add to find the total distance between the cities.

Add the ones.	Add the tens.	Add the hundreds.	Add the thousands.

Th	H	T	O
2	5	4	1
+2	3	5	3
			4

Th	H	T	O
2	5	4	1
+2	3	5	3
		9	4

Th	H	T	O
2	5	4	1
+2	3	5	3
	8	9	4

Th	H	T	O
2	5	4	1
+2	3	5	3
4	8	9	4

The total distance between the cities is 4,894 miles.

The distance from New York to Dallas is 1,558 miles. The distance from Dallas to San Francisco is 1,751 miles.

Add to find the total distance between the cities.

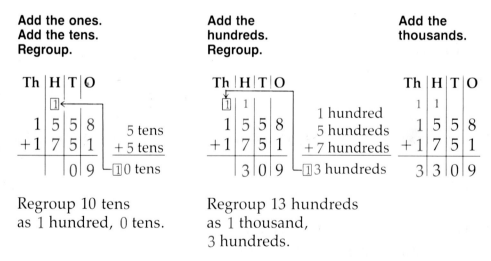

Add the ones. Add the tens. Regroup.	Add the hundreds. Regroup.	Add the thousands.

Regroup 10 tens as 1 hundred, 0 tens.

Regroup 13 hundreds as 1 thousand, 3 hundreds.

The total distance between the cities is 3,309 miles.

FOCUS   Use NUMBER skills to add four-digit numbers, with and without regrouping.

264

GUIDED PRACTICE

Add. Sometimes you will need to regroup.

1.
Th	H	T	O
5	2	1	6
+3	4	5	2
■	■	6	8

2.
Th	H	T	O
	1̲	□	
	5	2	5
+		8	9	4
■	■	1	9

3.
Th	H	T	O
	□	□	
6	8	2	7
+1	4	8	1
■	■	■	■

PRACTICE

Do you need to regroup? Write Y or N . Add.

4. 6,340
   +2,459

5. 7,229
   +1,620

6. 2,046
   +6,328

7. 5,671
   +3,158

8.   987
    +231

9. 1,550
   +8,438

10. 9,039
    + 862

11. 3,784
    +2,978

12. 2,397 + 3,404   13. 5,544 + 4,455   14. 7,662 + 1,289

15. Gerald traveled 1,278 miles last week. He will travel 1,965 miles this week. How many miles will Gerald travel in the two weeks?

MIXED PRACTICE
Maintaining and Reviewing Skills

Add or subtract.

16. 2,567 + 1,321   17. 3,698 + 3,540   18. 37 − 19   19. 741 + 26   20. 953 + 97

CHALLENGE

21. The hot air balloon was invented in 1783. The Wright brothers' airplane was invented 120 years later. When was the airplane invented?

ESTIMATION
Estimating Sums

A Denver Nuggets basketball player scored 2,326 points in one year. A Boston Celtics basketball player scored 1,867 points during the same year. About how many points did both players score?

Estimate to find *about* how many points both players scored during the year.

Step 1: Round each number to the nearest thousand.

$$
\begin{array}{rcr}
 & & \text{Estimate} \\
2,326 & \longrightarrow & 2,000 \\
1,867 & \longrightarrow & +\,2,000 \\
\hline
\end{array}
$$

Step 2: Add the rounded numbers. $\qquad$ 4,000

The two basketball players scored *about* 4,000 points during the year.

PRACTICE

Estimate each sum to the nearest thousand.

1. 4,268 ⟶ ■
   4,910 ⟶ + ■
   _____
   ■

2. 5,100 ⟶ ■
   3,500 ⟶ + ■
   _____
   ■

3. 1,965 ⟶ ■
   6,621 ⟶ + ■
   _____
   ■

4. 6,700 ⟶ ■
   1,300 ⟶ + ■
   _____
   ■

5. 2,299 ⟶ ■
   4,801 ⟶ + ■
   _____
   ■

6. 7,439 ⟶ ■
   2,394 ⟶ + ■
   _____
   ■

MIXED PRACTICE
Maintaining and Reviewing Skills

Estimate each sum to the nearest hundred.

7. 350 ⟶ ■
   540 ⟶ + ■
   _____
   ■

8. 723 ⟶ ■
   115 ⟶ + ■
   _____
   ■

9. 487 ⟶ ■
   236 ⟶ + ■
   _____
   ■

| FOCUS | Use NUMBER skills to estimate sums. |

APPLICATION
Using Patterns and Functions

4554 3333 1441 686 1001
343 787 3113 55 22 121

Look carefully at each number. Do you notice anything? Here's a hint. Read each number forward and backward. Each number is the same forward and backward. Numbers that read the same forward and backward are called **palindromes.**

You can make a palindrome using any number.

43 is not a palindrome.
To find the **palindrome,**
reverse the digits and add.

$$\begin{array}{r} 43 \\ +34 \longleftarrow \text{Reverse 43} \\ \hline 77 \end{array}$$

235 is not a palindrome.
Reverse the digits and add.
767 is a palindrome.

$$\begin{array}{r} 235 \\ +532 \longleftarrow \text{Reverse 235} \\ \hline 767 \end{array}$$

Sometimes you have to add more than once.

76 is not a palindrome.
Reverse the digits and add.
143 is not a palindrome.
Reverse the digits and add.
484 is a palindrome.

$$\begin{array}{r} 76 \\ +67 \longleftarrow \text{Reverse 76} \\ \hline 143 \\ +341 \longleftarrow \text{Reverse 143} \\ \hline 484 \end{array}$$

Use each number to make a palindrome. Remember, to make a palindrome, reverse the digits and add.

10. 25	**11.** 31	**12.** 63	**13.** 46	**14.** 38	**15.** 49
16. 134	**17.** 427	**18.** 146	**19.** 531	**20.** 369	**21.** 567
22. 1,321	**23.** 4,322	**24.** 6,412	**25.** 5,532	**26.** 3,631	**27.** 2,084

Use PATTERNS AND FUNCTIONS and NUMBER skills to make a palindrome from a given number.

SUBTRACTION
Subtracting Four-Digit Numbers

In 1974 there were 7,409 farms in New Jersey.
In 1978 there were 9,899 farms in New Jersey.

Subtract to find how many more farms there were in New Jersey in 1978 than in 1974.

Subtract the ones.	Subtract the tens.	Subtract the hundreds.	Subtract the thousands.

Th	H	T	O
9	8	9	9
−7	4	0	9
2	4	9	0

Th	H	T	O
9	8	9	9
−7	4	0	9
2	4	9	0

Th	H	T	O
9	8	9	9
−7	4	0	9
2	4	9	0

Th	H	T	O
9	8	9	9
−7	4	0	9
2	4	9	0

New Jersey had 2,490 more farms in 1978 than 1974.

In 1974 Arizona had 5,803 farms. In 1978 there were 7,660 farms in Arizona. What is the difference in the number of farms?

Subtract to find the difference in the number of farms.

Regroup. Subtract the ones and the tens.	Regroup. Subtract the hundreds.	Subtract the thousands.

Th	H	T	O
		5	10
7	6	6	0
−5	8	0	3
1	8	5	7

Th	H	T	O
6	16	5	10
7	6	6	0
−5	8	0	3
1	8	5	7

Th	H	T	O
6	16	5	10
7	6	6	0
−5	8	0	3
1	8	5	7

Regroup 6 tens, 0 ones as 5 tens, 10 ones.

Regroup 7 thousands, 6 hundreds as 6 thousands, 16 hundreds.

The difference in the number of farms is 1,857.

FOCUS | Use NUMBER skills to subtract four-digit numbers, with and without regrouping.

GUIDED PRACTICE

Subtract. Sometimes you will need to regroup.

1.
Th	H	T	O
7	6	9	3
− 4	2	7	0
∎	∎	∎	∎

2.
Th	H	T	O
	☐	☐	
		3	10
9	4̸	0̸	5
− 5	9	4	3
∎	∎	∎	∎

3.
Th	H	T	O
	☐	☐	
	☐	☐	
6̸	0̸	0̸	7
− 1	3	8	6
∎	∎	∎	∎

PRACTICE

Do you need to regroup? Write *Y* or *N*. Subtract.

4.   8,475
   − 3,261

5.   5,463
   − 2,239

6.   6,301
   − 4,181

7.   7,297
   − 6,128

8.   4,332
   − 1,820

9.   9,006
   − 7,689

10.   5,328
   − 2,986

11.   3,500
   − 1,375

12. 7,296 − 4,086   13. 4,135 − 2,933   14. 9,986 − 8,976   15. 2,004 − 1,263

MIXED PRACTICE
Maintaining and Reviewing Skills

Add or subtract.

16. 9,263 − 7,198   17. 372 − 58   18. 1,245 + 3,693   19. 487 + 96   20. 27 − 9

CHALLENGE

Write the missing digits.

21.   5,679
   − 1,3▮2
   ▮,32▮

22.   7,879
   − 3,▮▮6
   ▮,523

23.   9,432
   − ▮,345
   6,▮▮▮

24.   4,▮▮1
   − 1,234
   2,08▮

ESTIMATION
Estimating Differences

Walter Watts rode a unicycle for 4,550 miles across Canada. John Lees walked for 2,876 miles across the United States. About how much farther did Mr. Watts ride than Mr. Lees walked?

Estimate to find *about* how much farther Mr. Watts rode than Mr. Lees walked.

Step 1: Round each number to the nearest thousand.

$$
\begin{array}{rcr}
 & & \text{Estimate} \\
4,550 & \longrightarrow & 5,000 \\
2,876 & \longrightarrow & -\,3,000 \\
\hline
\end{array}
$$

Step 2: Subtract the rounded numbers.   2,000

Mr. Watts rode *about* 2,000 miles more.

PRACTICE

Estimate each difference to the nearest thousand.

1. 3,524 ⟶ ■
   2,874 ⟶ − ■
            ■

2. 5,398 ⟶ ■
   4,137 ⟶ − ■
            ■

3. 9,457 ⟶ ■
   6,978 ⟶ − ■
            ■

4. 7,625 ⟶ ■
   3,299 ⟶ − ■
            ■

5. 2,700 ⟶ ■
   1,463 ⟶ − ■
            ■

6. 8,093 ⟶ ■
   5,175 ⟶ − ■
            ■

MIXED PRACTICE
Maintaining and Reviewing Skills

Solve each problem.

7. Emma drove 3,932 miles. Holly flew 5,475 miles. About how much farther did Holly fly?

8. Sandy bicycled 150 miles. Mandy walked 79 miles. How much farther did Sandy bicycle?

FOCUS   Use NUMBER skills to estimate differences.

APPLICATION
Using Measurement

Michigan became a state in 1837. Henry Ford built the first American car in 1896.

Subtract the dates to find out how many years passed between the two events.

Henry Ford built his car:	1896
Michigan became a state:	− 1837
Years that have passed:	59

59 years passed between the two events.

Use the table to answer the questions.

State	Event	Date
California	Became a state First popular film made First explored by Spain	1850 1907 1542
Florida	Became a state City of St. Augustine founded First men sent to the moon	1845 1565 1969
Massachusetts	Became a state Pilgrims landed at Plymouth Rock Sewing machine invented	1788 1620 1845

9. How many years after California became a state was the first popular film made?

10. How many years before California became a state was it explored by Spain?

11. How many years after Florida became a state were the first men sent to the moon?

12. How many years before Florida became a state was the city of St. Augustine founded?

13. How many years before Massachusetts became a state did the Pilgrims land at Plymouth Rock?

Use MEASUREMENT and NUMBER skills to calculate the years between two dates.

Rhythm

Imagine the beat of the drums for the Buffalo Dance of the Plains Indians. The buffalo dancer enters. A big drum beats slowly. More dancers arrive. Other drums, tom-toms, beat faster. Everyone dances together. The first dances to a slow beat, the others to a fast beat. For every one boom of the big drum, the tom-tom beats one-two.

Counting and numbers are used to describe the **rhythm** of the music. Rhythm is about time. Counting helps the dancers and the players to stay together.

The **tempo** of music may be fast or slow. A tempo of 60 beats per minute is one beat every second, slower than a heart beats.

Composers (people who write music) may want some sounds to be short and others to be long. They write different **note values.** If a quarter note ♩ gets one beat, then a half note ♩ gets two beats, and a whole note o gets four beats.

A composer puts the beats in groups. Each group is called a

measure. The tune, or melody, must fit into the measure. Vertical bar lines (+) separate measures. So a measure is also called a **bar.**

Here are some measures written on music time lines.

(A)
♩ ♩	♩ ♩	♩
1 2	1 2	1 2

(B)
♩ ♩ ♩	♩ ♩ ♩	♩ ♩
1 2 3	1 2 3	1 2 3

(C)
♩ ♩ ♩ ♩	♩ ♩ ♩	o
1 2 3 4	1 2 3 4	1 2 3 4

Look at the music time lines A, B, and C, and answer the questions below.

CRITICAL THINKING

1. How many measures are on time line A? On line B? On line C?

2. How many beats are on time line A? On line B? On line C?

3. Which tempo is faster, 60 or 80 beats per minute?

FOCUS | Use NUMBER skills and LOGIC to understand rhythm.

272

The Buffalo Dance was painted by the American artist, George Catlin, in the 1830s. He visited over 40 different tribes, and painted nearly 500 pictures of North American Indians.

This painted hide drum was used by the Modoc tribe of Oklahoma. Players beat rhythms on it with their hands.

LOOKING BACK
Reviewing and Testing Chapter 20

In Chapter 20 you formulated problems about fish tanks. Look at pages 262 and 263.

1. Write a sentence telling what Clara might buy at a pet store for her fish.

You learned something new about adding four-digit numbers. To review what you learned, study the sample on page 264. Then use the new skill to find each sum for examples 2 to 11.

2.	3,621	3.	7,211	4.	5,231	5.	1,776
	+1,450		+2,314		+1,736		+1,492

6. 6,211 + 3,400   7. 3,333 + 2,121   8. 1,580 + 1,453

9. 4,437 + 2,631   10. 8,090 + 1,390   11. 3,241 + 5,839

You learned something new about subtracting four-digit numbers. To review, look at pages 268 and 269. Then use the new skill to find each difference for examples 12 to 21.

12.	5,748	13.	2,642	14.	7,843	15.	6,332
	−1,627		−1,540		−6,251		−5,331

16. 6,833 − 4,722   17. 4,563 − 2,346   18. 3,719 − 2,678

19. 8,975 − 7,865   20. 5,096 − 3,507   21. 9,304 − 4,193

You learned about rhythm in dancing. Look at page 272 to review what you learned.

22. Why are counting and numbers important to music?

FOCUS   Review and test skills learned and practiced.

274

LOOKING AHEAD

Preparing for New Skills for Chapter 21

In the next chapter you will focus on

- formulating problems.
- identifying parts of a whole.
- finding fractional parts of a group.
- a problem-solving strategy.

- finding equivalent fractions.
- comparing fractions.
- ordering fractions.
- statistics and probability.

Learning new skills about fractions will be easier if you review what you already know about fractions. Study the model. Then do the PRACTICE exercises. Check your work with the model.

Model

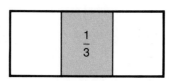
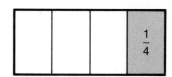

This rectangle has 2 equal parts. Each part is $\frac{1}{2}$.

This rectangle has 3 equal parts. Each part is $\frac{1}{3}$.

This rectangle has 4 equal parts. Each part is $\frac{1}{4}$.

PRACTICE

Copy the pictures. Write the numbers of the pictures that show $\frac{1}{4}$. Box the pictures that show $\frac{1}{2}$. Ring the pictures that show $\frac{1}{3}$.

1.

2.

3.

4.

5.

6.

Review NUMBER skills in preparation for learning a new skill.

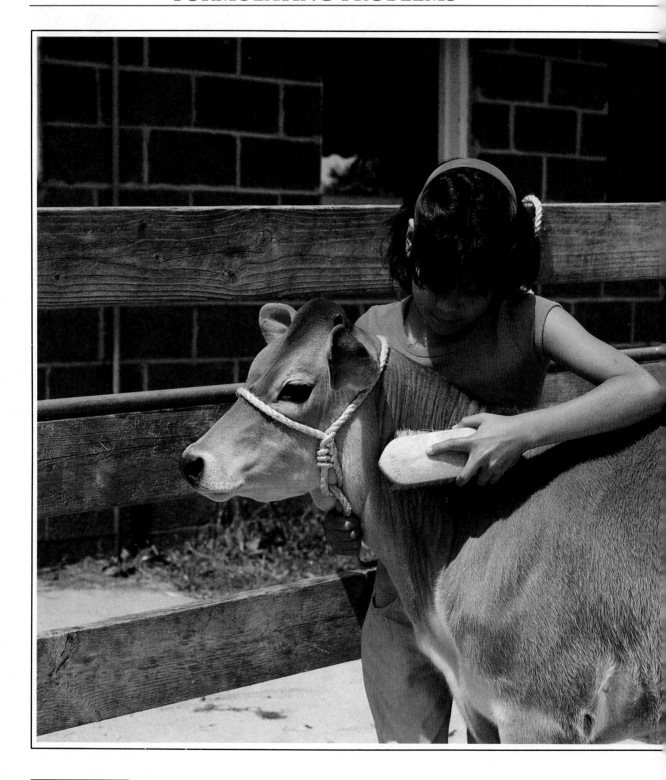

FOCUS Formulate problems using picture cues, text, and data.

21

Fractions

DATA

State Fair	September 24
Farm	Knox Hill
Name of calf	Amber
Breed	Jersey
Color	Gray brown
Height	4 feet
Weight	325 pounds
Coat	Smooth, short, and shiny
Date of birth	April 13
Sire (father)	Bart
Dam (mother)	Tess

Daily feed schedule
   15 pounds of corn
   10 pounds of red clover hay
   14 pounds of ground grain
   1 pound of cottonseed meal
   15 gallons of milk
Grooming and training
   Brush coat and trim hooves
Use halter to lead around
   yard 3 times daily

Young people all across the country join 4-H Clubs. Members of 4-H Clubs work on individual and community projects. One 4-H project might be raising a calf to show at the State Fair.

Petra Wagner has devoted much of her free time to raising her calf, Amber. Amber eats a lot of grain and hay. The calf also needs grooming and training to keep it healthy and free of insects.

Now Amber is being judged for a prize. The judges rate the calf's weight and color, the skin and hair on its body, and the way it stands.

Look at the data. What was Petra's goal? What problems did Petra meet every day as she cared for Amber?

FRACTIONS
Identifying Parts of a Whole

Ken is making a scarf with 5 rectangles. What part of the whole scarf is red?

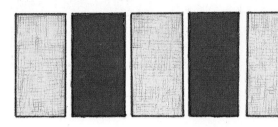

2 out of 5 are red. $\frac{2}{5}$ are red.

A **fraction** is a part of a whole.

This fraction shows what part of the whole scarf is red.

Numerator $\longrightarrow$ 2 $\longleftarrow$	Red rectangles
Denominator $\longrightarrow$ 5 $\longleftarrow$	Rectangles in the whole

$\frac{2}{5}$ can be written as two fifths.

Two fifths of Ken's scarf is red.

GUIDED PRACTICE

Complete to write each fraction.

1.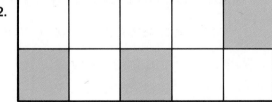

How many are blue? ▪
How many in all? ▪
What fraction is blue? $\frac{▪}{▪}$

2.

How many are green? ▪
How many in all? ▪
What fraction is green? $\frac{▪}{▪}$

PRACTICE

Write the fraction that tells what part of the figure
is red. Then ring the numerator.

3.

$\dfrac{1}{3}$ $\dfrac{2}{3}$ $\dfrac{3}{2}$

4.

$\dfrac{2}{5}$ $\dfrac{3}{5}$ $\dfrac{5}{3}$

5.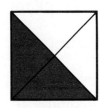

$\dfrac{1}{4}$ $\dfrac{2}{4}$ $\dfrac{4}{2}$

6.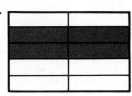

$\dfrac{10}{6}$ $\dfrac{6}{10}$ $\dfrac{4}{10}$

Write a fraction for the shaded part.

7.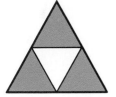

8.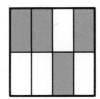

9.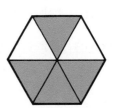

10.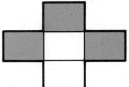

11.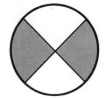

12.

13.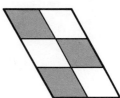

14.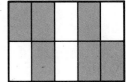

MIXED PRACTICE
Maintaining and Reviewing Skills

Add, subtract, multiply, or divide.

15. $5\overline{)35}$ 16. 9×5 17. 6×3 18. $\begin{array}{r} 1,245 \\ +3,248 \end{array}$ 19. $\begin{array}{r} 3,402 \\ -1,281 \end{array}$ 20. $\begin{array}{r} 7 \\ \times 3 \end{array}$

CHALLENGE

21. Draw a picture to show the fraction $\dfrac{3}{4}$.

FRACTIONS

Finding Fractional Parts of a Group of Objects

Fran bought 9 pears. She will cook $\frac{1}{3}$ of the pears. How many of the pears will Fran cook?

Fran will cook $\frac{1}{3}$ of the 9 pears.

To find the number of pears that Fran will cook, divide the number of pears in the whole group by the denominator.

$\frac{1}{3}$ of 9 = ■ becomes 9 ÷ 3 = ■. $\frac{1}{3}$ of 9 = 3.

Fran will cook 3 of the pears.

PRACTICE

1. Find $\frac{1}{2}$ of 8.   **2.** Find $\frac{1}{4}$ of 12.

$\frac{1}{2}$ of 8 becomes 8 ÷ 2 $\frac{1}{4}$ of 12 becomes 12 ÷ ■

$\frac{1}{2}$ of 8 = ■ $\frac{1}{4}$ of 12 = ■

Complete.

3. $\frac{1}{3}$ of 12 = ■   **4.** $\frac{1}{5}$ of 10 = ■   **5.** $\frac{1}{6}$ of 12 = ■

MIXED PRACTICE

Maintaining and Reviewing Skills

Multiply or divide.

6. 4)‾12   **7.** 6 × 3   **8.** 2 × 5   **9.** 8)‾32   **10.** 9 × 7

FOCUS | Use NUMBER skills to find a fractional part of a group of objects.

APPLICATION

Problem Solving: Finding a Pattern

Remember to READ, KNOW, PLAN, SOLVE, and CHECK all problems. See the Five-Step Plan on page 425 in the Data Bank.

11. Continue the pattern. Trace and shade $\frac{1}{2}$ of the last two figures.

12. Continue the pattern. Trace and shade $\frac{1}{4}$ of the last two figures.

13. Continue the pattern. Trace and shade $\frac{1}{3}$ of the last two figures.

14. Continue the pattern. Trace and shade $\frac{1}{6}$ of the last two figures.

$L \quad R$

15. Continue the pattern. Trace and shade $\frac{1}{8}$ of the last two figures.

Find a pattern and apply the Five-Step PROBLEM-SOLVING Plan.

PROBLEM SOLVING
Selecting a Strategy: Making a List

Making a list is a strategy you can use when you PLAN and SOLVE a problem.

1. READ Grand Canyon National Park in Arizona was established in 1919. The canyon is 5,800 feet deep at one point. That is more than one mile straight down. It was first visited by an explorer in 1540. It was discovered again in 1776. President Roosevelt visited it in 1903. What is the earliest date listed?

2. KNOW Ask yourself: What am I being asked to find? What is the earliest date listed? What **key facts** do I need? I need the date of each event.

3. PLAN Select a strategy: try making a list. Make a list of the events and the dates. Then compare the dates. The smallest number is the earliest date.

4. SOLVE
1919   The park is established
1540   First explorer sees it
1776   Discovered again
1903   Visited by President Roosevelt

The earliest date is 1540.

5. CHECK The smallest number is 1540, so that is the earliest date. It is a reasonable answer.

| FOCUS | Evaluate information as part of the Five-Step PROBLEM-SOLVING Plan. |

PRACTICE

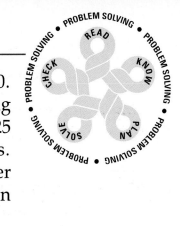

Yosemite National Park was established in 1890. About 78 species of mammals live here including bear and deer. There are 220 species of birds, 25 species of reptiles, and 9 species of amphibians. Indians lived in this area until 1851. The founder of the park first came to it in 1868. This man, John Muir, started the Sierra Club in 1892.

Make a list of the number and kind of each animal. Use this list to answer each question.

1. What kind of animal has less than 10 species?

2. What kind of animal has the largest number of species?

3. How many species of reptiles and amphibians are there altogether?

4. Which has more species that live in Yosemite, mammals or reptiles?

Make a list of the events and dates. Use this list to answer each question.

5. President Roosevelt visited this park in 1903. Was that before or after the Sierra Club was started?

6. What is the earliest event listed?

Class Project

Bear and deer are two species of mammals listed above. Work with some classmates. Make a list of other mammals. Try to get at least ten.

FRACTIONS
Finding Equivalent Fractions

Keena

Gina bought 2 large pizzas. One pizza was cut into halves. The other pizza was cut into fourths. Mushrooms were put on $\frac{1}{2}$ of one pizza. Mushrooms were put on $\frac{2}{4}$ of the other pizza. Which pizza has more mushrooms?

$\frac{1}{2}$ of this pizza has mushrooms. $\frac{2}{4}$ of this pizza has mushrooms.

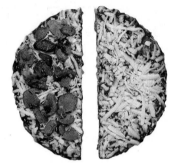

$$\frac{1}{2} \text{ is equivalent to } \frac{2}{4}$$
$$\frac{1}{2} = \frac{2}{4}$$

Equivalent fractions name the same number.

Each pizza has the same amount of mushrooms.

GUIDED PRACTICE

Complete the equivalent fraction.

1.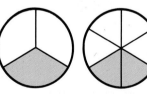

$$\frac{1}{3} = \frac{\blacksquare}{6}$$

2.

$$\frac{1}{4} = \frac{\blacksquare}{8}$$

3.

$$\frac{1}{6} = \frac{\blacksquare}{12}$$

| FOCUS | Use NUMBER skills to find equivalent fractions. |

PRACTICE

Complete the equivalent fraction.

 4.

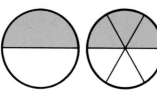 5.

 6.

$$\frac{1}{4} = \frac{\blacksquare}{12}$$

$$\frac{1}{2} = \frac{3}{\blacksquare}$$

$$\frac{1}{3} = \frac{\blacksquare}{12}$$

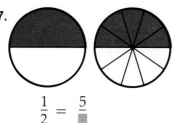 7.

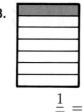 8.

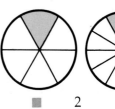 9.

$$\frac{1}{2} = \frac{5}{\blacksquare}$$

$$\frac{1}{\blacksquare} = \frac{2}{14}$$

$$\frac{\blacksquare}{6} = \frac{2}{12}$$

Write two equivalent fractions for each group of pictures.

 10.

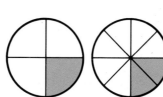 11.

  12.

MIXED PRACTICE
Maintaining and Reviewing Skills

Add or subtract.

13. $240 + 350$ **14.** $1,728 + 5,701$ **15.** $3,290 - 1,173$ **16.** $532 - 74$

CHALLENGE

17. Why isn't $\frac{1}{3}$ of the first shape the same size as $\frac{2}{6}$ of the second shape?

 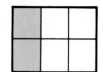

FRACTIONS

Comparing and Ordering Fractions

Paul ran $\frac{3}{10}$ of a mile. Noel ran $\frac{7}{10}$ of a mile.
Who ran the greater distance?

Compare $\frac{3}{10}$ and $\frac{7}{10}$.

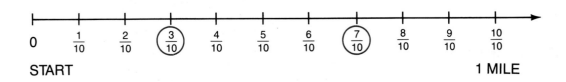

0   $\frac{1}{10}$ $\frac{2}{10}$ $\frac{3}{10}$ $\frac{4}{10}$ $\frac{5}{10}$ $\frac{6}{10}$ $\frac{7}{10}$ $\frac{8}{10}$ $\frac{9}{10}$ $\frac{10}{10}$

START   1 MILE

 $\frac{7}{10}$ **is greater than** $\frac{3}{10}$. $\frac{3}{10}$ **is less than** $\frac{7}{10}$.

$$\frac{7}{10} > \frac{3}{10}$$ $$\frac{3}{10} < \frac{7}{10}$$

Noel ran the greater distance.

PRACTICE

Write < or >. Draw a number line to help you.

1. $\frac{5}{10}$ $\frac{8}{10}$ **2.** $\frac{3}{4}$ ▪ $\frac{2}{4}$ **3.** $\frac{7}{8}$ ▪ $\frac{6}{8}$ **4.** $\frac{1}{5}$ ▪ $\frac{4}{5}$

Write the fractions in order from least to greatest.

5. $\frac{3}{4}, \frac{1}{4}, \frac{2}{4}$ **6.** $\frac{6}{10}, \frac{9}{10}, \frac{3}{10}$ **7.** $\frac{5}{6}, \frac{3}{6}, \frac{4}{6}$ **8.** $\frac{8}{9}, \frac{6}{9}, \frac{3}{9}$

MIXED PRACTICE

Maintaining and Reviewing Skills

Write < or >.

9. $\frac{2}{6}$ ▪ $\frac{4}{6}$ **10.** $\frac{7}{9}$ ▪ $\frac{6}{9}$ **11.** 324 ▪ 342   **12.** 5,679 ▪ 5,685

FOCUS   Use NUMBER skills to compare and order fractions.

APPLICATION

Using Statistics and Probability

This spinner has 3 colors. What is the chance of spinning each color?

The chance of spinning red is 1 out of 6 or $\frac{1}{6}$.

The chance of spinning blue is 2 out of 6 or $\frac{2}{6}$.

The chance of spinning yellow is 3 out of 6 or $\frac{3}{6}$.

Mei Ling put these 7 cubes in a paper bag.

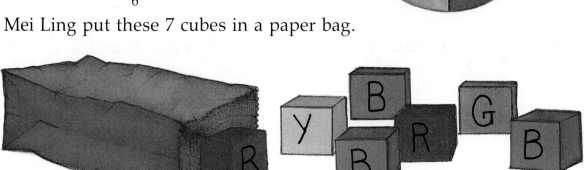

Complete the sentences below. Then write a fraction to show Mei Ling's chance of picking each color cube from the paper bag.

13. The chance of picking a yellow cube is ■ out of ■.

14. The chance of picking a blue cube is ■ out of ■.

15. The chance of picking a green cube is ■ out of ■.

16. The chance of picking a red cube is ■ out of ■.

Write a fraction to solve the problem.

17. Arlene has 5 colored shirts. She has 3 red shirts, 1 blue shirt, and 1 pink shirt. What is the chance that Arlene will choose a red shirt to wear?

Use STATISTICS AND PROBABILITY to introduce the concept of ratio.

LOOKING BACK
Reviewing and Testing Chapter 21

In Chapter 21 you formulated problems about showing calves. Look at pages 276 and 277.

1. Write a sentence telling how a calf might be judged.

You learned something new about identifying parts of a whole. To review, study the sample problem on page 278. Use the new skill to write a fraction for the shaded part for examples 2 to 5.

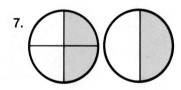

2.   3.   4.   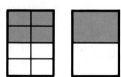   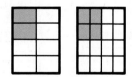   5.

You have learned how to make a list to solve problems. To review, look at pages 282 and 283.

6. Make a list of three-digit numbers using the digits 1, 2, and 3. You may not repeat the same digit in any number.

You learned something new about finding equivalent fractions. To review, look at pages 284 and 285. Then use the new skill to write two equivalent fractions for each group.

7.   8. 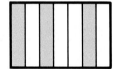   9. 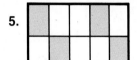

10. 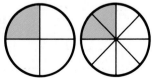   11.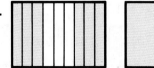

FOCUS   Review and test skills learned and practiced.

288

LOOKING AHEAD
Preparing for New Skills for Chapter 22

In the next chapter, you will focus on

- formulating problems.
- adding fractions.
- using measurement.

- subtracting fractions.
- a problem-solving strategy.
- how math is used in science.

New skills in adding and subtracting fractions will be easier to learn if you review what you already know about fractions. Study the model. Then do the PRACTICE exercises.

Model

A **fraction** is a part of a whole. Each circle is divided into equal parts. The fraction shows what part of the whole circle is shaded.

one half $\frac{1}{2}$ one third $\frac{1}{3}$ one fourth $\frac{1}{4}$ one fifth $\frac{1}{5}$ one sixth $\frac{1}{6}$ one eighth $\frac{1}{8}$

PRACTICE

Write the letter of the figure that answers the question.

1. Which figure shows $\frac{1}{5}$?

A B C

2. Which figure shows $\frac{1}{8}$?

A B C

3. Which figure shows $\frac{1}{6}$?

A B C

4. Which figure shows $\frac{1}{2}$?

A B C

Review NUMBER skills in preparation for learning a new skill.

FORMULATING PROBLEMS

CHAPTER 22

Addition and Subtraction of Fractions

DATA

Alaska

Winter

Hours of daylight	0–4
Hours of darkness	20–24
January temperature	11°F

Day with most darkness
   December 21

Snow season
   October 1–May 1

Amount of snow
   in one winter   100
                       inches

Summer

Hours of daylight	20–24
Hours of darkness	0–4
July temperature	60°F

Day with longest period of
   light
   June 21

Summer season
   May 1–October 1

Alaska is the biggest state in the United States. It's twice as big as Texas.

Alaska is the most northern state. It lies very close to the North Pole. Because of the way the Earth turns, the length of days and nights changes during the year. In Alaska, the sun doesn't really set during the summer months. The sky stays bright all night long. In the winter, the sun doesn't rise, so there's only a little light throughout the day.

Look at the picture and then look at the data. What do you think life is like in Alaska? Life during the long, dark winter is very different than life during the cool, light summer. What problems might people in Alaska solve in the winter? What problems might they solve in summer?

FRACTIONS
Adding Fractions With Like Denominators

A garden has 5 equal parts. Corn is planted in $\frac{1}{5}$ of the garden. Onions are planted in $\frac{2}{5}$ of the garden. What part of the whole garden is planted with corn and onions?

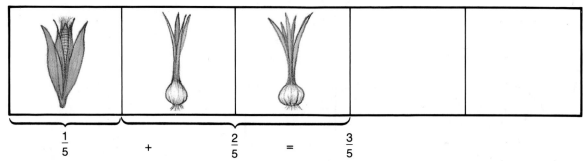

$$\frac{1}{5} \qquad + \qquad \frac{2}{5} \qquad = \qquad \frac{3}{5}$$

$\frac{3}{5}$ of the garden is planted with corn and onions.

GUIDED PRACTICE

Write the sum of the red and yellow parts.

1.

$$\frac{1}{3} + \frac{1}{3} = \frac{2}{3}$$

2.

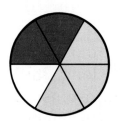

$$\frac{2}{6} + \frac{3}{6} = \frac{\blacksquare}{6}$$

3.

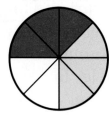

$$\frac{5}{10} + \frac{3}{10} = \frac{\blacksquare}{10}$$

4.

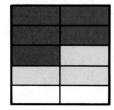

$$\frac{3}{8} + \frac{3}{8} = \frac{6}{\blacksquare}$$

5.

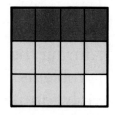

$$\frac{4}{12} + \frac{7}{12} = \frac{11}{\blacksquare}$$

6.

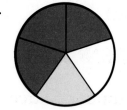

$$\frac{3}{5} + \frac{1}{5} = \frac{\blacksquare}{\blacksquare}$$

FOCUS Use NUMBER skills to add fractions with like denominators.

292

PRACTICE

Write the sum of the red and yellow parts.

7.

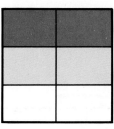

$$\frac{2}{6} + \frac{2}{6} = \frac{\blacksquare}{\blacksquare}$$

8.

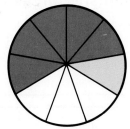

$$\frac{5}{9} + \frac{1}{9} = \frac{\blacksquare}{\blacksquare}$$

9.

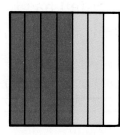

$$\frac{4}{7} + \frac{2}{7} = \frac{\blacksquare}{\blacksquare}$$

10.

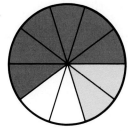

$$\frac{6}{10} + \frac{2}{10} = \frac{\blacksquare}{\blacksquare}$$

11.

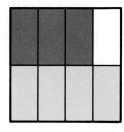

$$\frac{3}{8} + \frac{4}{8} = \frac{\blacksquare}{\blacksquare}$$

12.

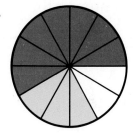

$$\frac{7}{12} + \frac{3}{12} = \frac{\blacksquare}{\blacksquare}$$

MIXED PRACTICE
Maintaining and Reviewing Skills

Write a fraction for the red part of the figure.

13.

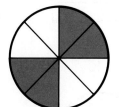

14.

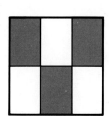

$\frac{4}{8}$

$\frac{3}{6}$

15.

$\frac{2}{4}$

16.

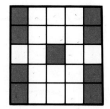

$\frac{9}{25}$

CHALLENGE

17. One ninth of a tree's leaves have turned orange.
Four ninths of the leaves have turned yellow.
What part of the tree's leaves have changed color?

$$\frac{1}{9} + \frac{4}{9} = \frac{5}{9}$$

of the tree

FRACTIONS

Adding Fractions With Like Denominators

Tracy ran $\frac{3}{10}$ of a mile. Then she ran another $\frac{1}{10}$ of a mile. How far did Tracy run?

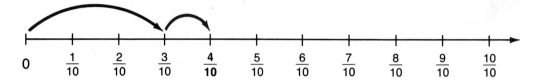

Add the numerators.

$$\frac{3}{10}$$
$$+\frac{1}{10}$$
$$\overline{\quad 4 \quad}$$

Write the same denominator.

$$\frac{3}{10}$$
$$+\frac{1}{10}$$
$$\overline{\frac{4}{10}}$$

Tracy ran $\frac{4}{10}$ of a mile.

PRACTICE

Add.

1. $\frac{2}{6}$ $+\frac{3}{6}$

2. $\frac{1}{3}$ $+\frac{1}{3}$

3. $\frac{4}{7}$ $+\frac{2}{7}$

4. $\frac{3}{5}$ $+\frac{1}{5}$

5. $\frac{6}{9}$ $+\frac{2}{9}$

6. $\frac{1}{4}$ $+\frac{2}{4}$

MIXED PRACTICE

Maintaining and Reviewing Skills

Add or subtract.

7. $\frac{1}{4} + \frac{1}{4}$

8. $\frac{2}{8} + \frac{5}{8}$

9. $16 - 9$

10. $23 - 6$

11. $75 + 8$

FOCUS   Use NUMBER skills to add fractions with like denominators.

APPLICATION
Using Measurement

This ruler has $\frac{1}{2}$ inch markings.

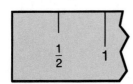

This ruler has $\frac{1}{4}$ inch markings.

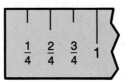

Use the rulers to add.

$$\frac{1}{2} + \frac{1}{2} = \frac{2}{2} = 1$$

$\frac{2}{2}$ is the same as 1

$$\frac{1}{4} + \frac{1}{4} + \frac{1}{4} + \frac{1}{4} = \frac{4}{4} = 1$$

$\frac{4}{4}$ is the same as 1

When the *numerator* and the *denominator* are the same, the fraction is equal to 1.

Add. Ring the sums that are equal to 1.

12. $\frac{2}{3}$ $+\frac{1}{3}$

13. $\frac{1}{6}$ $+\frac{4}{6}$

14. $\frac{3}{10}$ $+\frac{4}{10}$

15. $\frac{2}{5}$ $+\frac{3}{5}$

16. $\frac{5}{8}$ $+\frac{3}{8}$

17. $\frac{2}{4}$ $+\frac{2}{4}$

18. $\frac{1}{7}$ $+\frac{5}{7}$

19. $\frac{5}{12}$ $+\frac{7}{12}$

20. $\frac{1}{2}$ $+\frac{1}{2}$

21. $\frac{6}{11}$ $+\frac{3}{11}$

22. $\frac{2}{9}$ $+\frac{7}{9}$

23. $\frac{4}{5}$ $+\frac{1}{5}$

24. $\frac{4}{6} + \frac{2}{6}$

25. $\frac{3}{9} + \frac{2}{9}$

26. $\frac{4}{7} + \frac{3}{7}$

27. $\frac{5}{10} + \frac{5}{10}$

Solve the problem.

28. Nathan ran for $\frac{1}{5}$ of an hour, rode his bike for $\frac{2}{5}$ of an hour, and napped for $\frac{2}{5}$ of an hour. How long did he run, bike, and nap?

Use MEASUREMENT to add fractions with sums that are equal to 1.

FRACTIONS
Subtracting Fractions With Like Denominators

John cut a sandwich into 4 equal parts, or $\frac{4}{4}$. He ate $\frac{1}{4}$ of the sandwich. What part of the whole sandwich is left?

$$\frac{4}{4} - \frac{1}{4} = \frac{3}{4}$$

$\frac{3}{4}$ of the whole sandwich is left.

GUIDED PRACTICE

Write the difference.

1.

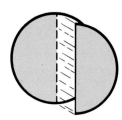

$$\frac{2}{2} - \frac{1}{2} = \frac{\blacksquare}{2}$$

2.

$$\frac{4}{6} - \frac{1}{6} = \frac{3}{\blacksquare}$$

3.

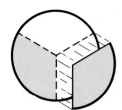

$$\frac{2}{3} - \frac{1}{3} = \frac{\blacksquare}{\blacksquare}$$

4.

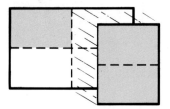

$$\frac{3}{4} - \frac{2}{4} = \frac{\blacksquare}{4}$$

5.

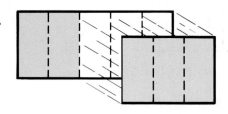

$$\frac{5}{5} - \frac{3}{5} = \frac{\blacksquare}{\blacksquare}$$

FOCUS   Use NUMBER skills to subtract fractions with like denominators.

296

PRACTICE

Write the difference.

6.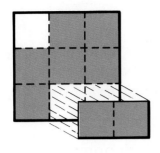

$$\frac{8}{9} - \frac{2}{9} = \frac{\blacksquare}{\blacksquare}$$

7.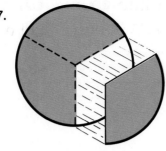

$$\frac{3}{3} - \frac{1}{3} = \frac{\blacksquare}{\blacksquare}$$

8.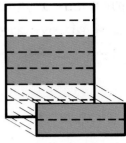

$$\frac{5}{7} - \frac{2}{7} = \frac{\blacksquare}{\blacksquare}$$

9.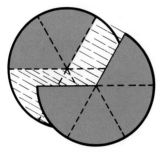

$$\frac{6}{6} - \frac{4}{6} = \frac{\blacksquare}{\blacksquare}$$

10.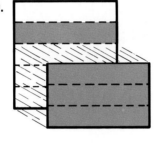

$$\frac{4}{5} - \frac{3}{5} = \frac{\blacksquare}{\blacksquare}$$

11.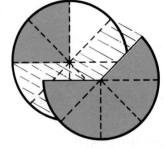

$$\frac{7}{8} - \frac{5}{8} = \frac{\blacksquare}{\blacksquare}$$

MIXED PRACTICE
Maintaining and Reviewing Skills

Write a fraction for the unshaded part of the figure.

12. 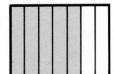 **13.**   **14.** 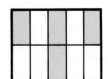 **15.**

CHALLENGE

16. Ellie read $\frac{7}{9}$ of a book. Brian read $\frac{3}{9}$ of that book. Who read more? How much more?

FRACTIONS

Subtracting Fractions With Like Denominators

Joshua has $\frac{7}{9}$ of a yard of ribbon. He used $\frac{5}{9}$ of a yard of ribbon. How much ribbon is left?

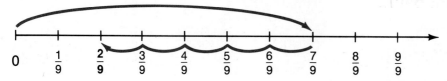

Subtract the numerators.   Write the same denominator.

$$\begin{array}{r} \frac{7}{9} \\ -\frac{5}{9} \\ \hline \frac{2}{} \end{array}$$

$$\begin{array}{r} \frac{7}{9} \\ -\frac{5}{9} \\ \hline \frac{2}{9} \end{array}$$

Joshua has $\frac{2}{9}$ of a yard of ribbon left.

PRACTICE

Subtract.

1. $\frac{2}{3}$
$-\frac{1}{3}$

2. $\frac{4}{5}$
$-\frac{2}{5}$

3. $\frac{6}{7}$
$-\frac{3}{7}$

4. $\frac{2}{4}$
$-\frac{1}{4}$

5. $\frac{6}{8}$
$-\frac{2}{8}$

6. $\frac{5}{6}$
$-\frac{2}{6}$

7. $\frac{11}{12} - \frac{9}{12}$

8. $\frac{7}{9} - \frac{4}{9}$

9. $\frac{8}{10} - \frac{3}{10}$

10. $\frac{10}{11} - \frac{5}{11}$

MIXED PRACTICE

Maintaining and Reviewing Skills

Add or subtract.

11. $\frac{3}{5} - \frac{1}{5}$

12. $\frac{2}{4} + \frac{1}{4}$

13. $\frac{5}{6} - \frac{4}{6}$

14. $\frac{4}{8} + \frac{4}{8}$

FOCUS   Use NUMBER skills to subtract fractions with like denominators.

APPLICATION

Problem Solving: Making a List

Remember to READ, KNOW, PLAN, SOLVE, and CHECK all problems. See the Five-Step Plan on page 425 in the Data Bank.

  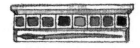 

There are 11 items on a table. There are 2 crayons, 5 pencils, 1 paintbox, and 3 erasers.

Copy and complete the list. Then use the list to solve each problem.

crayons: 2 out of 11 or $\frac{\blacksquare}{\blacksquare}$

pencils: ■ out of ■ or $\frac{\blacksquare}{\blacksquare}$

paintbox: ■ out of ■ or $\frac{\blacksquare}{\blacksquare}$

erasers: ■ out of ■ or $\frac{\blacksquare}{\blacksquare}$

15. Which part of the items is greater, the crayons or the pencils?

16. What part of the items on the table are crayons and erasers?

17. Which part of the items is greater, the paintbox or the pencils? How much greater?

18. What part of the items on the table are the pencils and the paintbox?

19. Which part of the items is greater, the paintbox or the erasers? How much greater?

20. What part of the items on the table are crayons and pencils?

Make a list and apply the Five-Step PROBLEM-SOLVING Plan.

Wind

When the air that surrounds the earth moves, wind occurs. Wind does many things. It makes a cold day feel even colder. Wind makes a hot day feel more comfortable. A hurricane, a very strong wind, can damage houses and trees. Windmills use wind to pump water and grind grain.

Wind brings rain clouds. Warm winds bring warm weather, and cold winds bring cold weather. If there were no wind, if the air and the earth stood still, there would be no weather.

The air moves and becomes wind because of the heating and cooling of the earth. When air is heated it rises. When it cools it falls. Look at the picture on page 301. It shows how the kind of wind called an on-shore breeze is made. The shore heats up more quickly than the water. When the sun shines, the land becomes hot while the lake stays cool. The air above the land also becomes warm and rises. Cool air above the lake moves in to take its place. This makes a wind—the on-shore breeze.

The on-shore breeze is mild, but sometimes wind can be very fierce. Winds of different strengths have different names. In 1805, a British admiral named Sir Francis Beaufort named winds of different speeds. These names are on the chart on page 301.

CRITICAL THINKING

1. What would the world be like if there were no wind?

2. According to the Beaufort Scale, what is a wind of 9 miles per hour called?
   A wind of 22 miles per hour?
   A wind of 27 miles per hour?
   A wind of 50 miles per hour?
   A wind of 75 miles per hour?

3. If the weather service predicts a gale, should you go outside?

4. What causes winds to form?
   a. heating and cooling of the earth
   b. rising air and falling air
   c. Sir Francis Beaufort
   d. windmills

FOCUS   Use LOGIC to understand wind and weather connections.

BEAUFORT WIND SCALE

Beaufort number	Name	Miles per hour	Effect on land
0	Calm	less than 1	Smoke rises straight up.
1	Light air	1-3	Smoke drifts a little.
2	Light breeze	4-7	Wind felt on face; leaves rustle.
3	Gentle breeze	8-12	Leaves move; flags extend from poles.
4	Moderate breeze	13-18	Small branches sway; paper blows about.
5	Fresh breeze	19-24	Small trees sway; waves break on inland waters.
6	Strong breeze	25-31	Large branches sway; umbrellas hard to use.
7	Moderate gale	32-38	Whole trees sway; difficult to walk against wind.
8	Fresh gale	39-46	Twigs break off trees; walking is difficult.
9	Strong gale	47-54	Slight damage to buildings.
10	Whole gale	55-63	Trees uprooted; some damage to buildings.
11	Storm	64-73	Widespread damage; very rare occurrence.
12-17	Hurricane	74 and above	Extreme damage occurs.

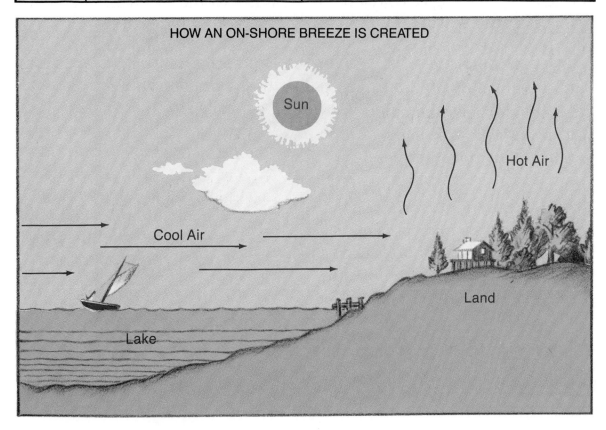

HOW AN ON-SHORE BREEZE IS CREATED

LOOKING BACK
Reviewing and Testing Chapter 22

In Chapter 22 you formulated problems about Alaska. Look at pages 290 and 291.

1. Write a sentence telling about the winter in Alaska.

You learned something new about adding fractions with like denominators. To review what you learned, study the sample problem on page 292. Then use the new skill to find the sum for examples 2 to 13.

2. $\frac{1}{4} + \frac{2}{4}$ 3. $\frac{3}{8} + \frac{4}{8}$ 4. $\frac{5}{12} + \frac{2}{12}$ 5. $\frac{6}{14} + \frac{3}{14}$

6. $\frac{3}{5} + \frac{1}{5}$ 7. $\frac{6}{9} + \frac{2}{9}$ 8. $\frac{4}{10} + \frac{1}{10}$ 9. $\frac{8}{11} + \frac{2}{11}$

10. $\frac{2}{7} + \frac{4}{7}$ 11. $\frac{1}{3} + \frac{1}{3}$ 12. $\frac{3}{6} + \frac{2}{6}$ 13. $\frac{2}{5} + \frac{2}{5}$

You learned something new about subtracting fractions with like denominators. To review, look at pages 296 and 297. Then use the new skill to find the difference for examples 14 to 25.

14. $\frac{8}{9} - \frac{4}{9}$ 15. $\frac{4}{7} - \frac{1}{7}$ 16. $\frac{6}{12} - \frac{3}{12}$ 17. $\frac{7}{15} - \frac{3}{15}$

18. $\frac{6}{8} - \frac{2}{8}$ 19. $\frac{7}{12} - \frac{6}{12}$ 20. $\frac{8}{13} - \frac{5}{13}$ 21. $\frac{8}{14} - \frac{7}{14}$

22. $\frac{9}{10} - \frac{7}{10}$ 23. $\frac{6}{6} - \frac{1}{6}$ 24. $\frac{9}{11} - \frac{4}{11}$ 25. $\frac{5}{9} - \frac{2}{9}$

You learned about types of wind. Look at page 300 to review the different types of wind.

26. What are some ways we can use wind?

FOCUS | Review and test skills learned and practiced.

LOOKING AHEAD

Preparing for New Skills for Chapter 23

In the next chapter you will focus on

- formulating problems.
- identifying tenths.
- comparing and ordering decimals.

- using measurement.
- a problem-solving strategy.
- identifying decimals greater than one.

Learning new skills about decimals will be easier if you review what you already know about fractions. Study the model. Then do the PRACTICE exercises. Check your work with the model.

Model

Each figure has ten equal parts. Each part is one tenth or $\frac{1}{10}$.

PRACTICE

Write the letter of the figures that show $\frac{1}{10}$.

A.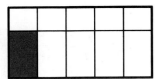

B.

C.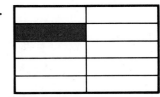

D.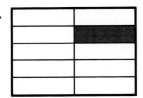

E.

F.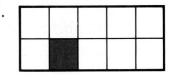

Review NUMBER skills in preparation for learning a new skill.

303

QUARTERLY REVIEW/TEST

Write the letter of the correct answer.

Multiply.

1.	6 ×5	A. 11 C. 30		B. 24 D. 36	

2.	8 ×8	E. 16 G. 48		F. 64 H. 72	

3.	7 ×9	A. 63 C. 42		B. 16 D. 56	

4.	6 ×4	E. 18 G. 10		F. 12 H. 24	

5.	9 ×8	A. 63 C. 81		B. 72 D. 17	

Divide.

6. 8)56   E. 7   F. 6
               G. 9   H. 8

7. 6)54   A. 6   B. 8
               C. 7   D. 9

8. 9)81   E. 7   F. 9
               G. 8   H. 6

9. 7)49   A. 9   B. 8
               C. 7   D. 6

10. 8)48   E. 8   F. 4
              G. 7   H. 6

What is the place value of the 5 in each number?

11. 4,572
    - A. ones
    - B. tens
    - C. hundreds
    - D. thousands

12. 3,850
    - E. ones
    - F. tens
    - G. hundreds
    - H. thousands

13. 5,169
    - A. ones
    - B. tens
    - C. hundreds
    - D. thousands

Add or subtract.

14.	6,324 +3,472	E. 9,792 G. 8,752	F. 9,796 H. 3,752

15.	8,509 + 683	A. 8,182 C. 8,192	B. 9,292 D. 9,192

16.	9,637 −2,530	E. 7,107 G. 8,007	F. 8,167 H. 7,137

17.	5,426 − 286	A. 5,260 C. 5,140	B. 4,240 D. 5,240

18.	7,075 −5,436	E. 2,441 G. 1,639	F. 2,639 H. 2,649

FOCUS   Review concepts and skills taught in Chapters 15 to 22.

How much of each shape is shaded?

19.
A. $\frac{2}{6}$

B. $\frac{6}{4}$

C. $\frac{4}{6}$

D. $\frac{6}{3}$

20.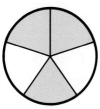
E. $\frac{3}{5}$

F. $\frac{5}{2}$

G. $\frac{5}{3}$

H. $\frac{2}{5}$

21.
A. $\frac{4}{6}$

B. $\frac{4}{8}$

C. $\frac{2}{2}$

D. $\frac{8}{4}$

What is the equivalent fraction?

22. $\frac{2}{4}$
E. $\frac{4}{4}$ F. $\frac{4}{6}$

G. $\frac{2}{2}$ H. $\frac{4}{8}$

23. $\frac{1}{3}$
A. $\frac{2}{6}$ B. $\frac{3}{6}$

C. $\frac{2}{3}$ D. $\frac{4}{9}$

24. $\frac{1}{2}$
E. $\frac{2}{2}$ F. $\frac{3}{8}$

G. $\frac{2}{4}$ H. $\frac{4}{4}$

Add or subtract.

25. $\frac{1}{3} + \frac{1}{3}$
A. $\frac{1}{6}$ B. $\frac{2}{6}$

C. $\frac{2}{3}$ D. $\frac{1}{3}$

26. $\frac{3}{5} + \frac{2}{5}$
E. $\frac{1}{5}$ F. $\frac{5}{5}$

G. $\frac{5}{10}$ H. $\frac{1}{10}$

27. $\frac{4}{9} + \frac{3}{9}$
A. $\frac{7}{9}$ B. $\frac{1}{9}$

C. $\frac{1}{18}$ D. $\frac{7}{18}$

28. $\frac{8}{10} - \frac{4}{10}$
E. $\frac{12}{10}$ F. $\frac{4}{20}$

G. $\frac{12}{20}$ H. $\frac{4}{10}$

29. $\frac{3}{4} - \frac{1}{4}$
A. $\frac{2}{4}$ B. $\frac{2}{8}$

C. $\frac{4}{8}$ D. $\frac{4}{4}$

30. $\frac{7}{8} - \frac{6}{8}$
E. $\frac{13}{16}$ F. $\frac{1}{8}$

G. $\frac{1}{16}$ H. $\frac{13}{8}$

Solve the problem.

31. Meyer knitted $\frac{1}{4}$ of a scarf the first week and knitted $\frac{2}{4}$ of the scarf the second week. How much of the scarf did he knit?

A. $\frac{2}{8}$ B. $\frac{3}{4}$

C. $\frac{3}{8}$ D. $\frac{2}{4}$

FOCUS   Formulate problems using picture cues, text, and data.

23

Meaning of Decimals

DATA

Target pitching from 25 feet
Red	0
Yellow	1
Blue	7

Fielding practice (throwing and catching ball off garage door)
Balls caught	32
Balls missed	15

Batting practice
Hits	3
Misses	35
Fouls	5

Time spent practicing
Week 1	2 hours
Week 2	3 hours
Week 3	5 hours
Week 4	6 hours

In most ways, Billy is like any other boy. He's pretty good at some things, and not so good at others. One of the things he's not so good at is baseball. But he wants to get good at it.

Billy made a practice plan to get ready for Little League. The garage door is one part of that plan. The data, kept in a daily log book, is another.

Look at the photo and the data. What else could Billy add to his practice? What problems might he still have? Think carefully. Then predict whether or not Billy's plan will work. Explain.

DECIMALS
Identifying Tenths

Nancy is making a blanket with 10 squares. What part of the whole blanket is blue?

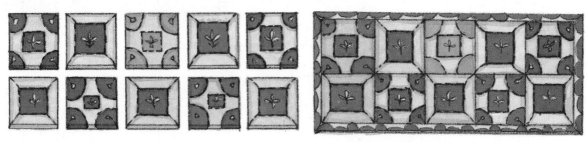

One tenth of the whole blanket is blue.

One tenth can be written as a fraction or as a **decimal.**

$$\frac{1}{10} \text{ or } 0 \overset{\uparrow}{.} 1$$

Decimal point

GUIDED PRACTICE

Complete the fraction and the decimal to name the shaded part.

1.

$$\frac{5}{10} = 0.5$$

2.

$$\frac{\blacksquare}{10} = 0.\blacksquare$$

3.

$$\frac{\blacksquare}{10} = 0.\blacksquare$$

4.

$$\frac{\blacksquare}{10} = 0.\blacksquare$$

5.

$$\frac{\blacksquare}{10} = 0.\blacksquare$$

6.

$$\frac{\blacksquare}{10} = 0.\blacksquare$$

FOCUS   Use NUMBER skills to write fractions and decimals for tenths.

308

PRACTICE

Write a decimal for the unshaded part.

7.

8.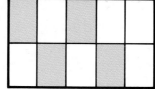

9.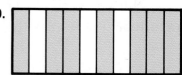

10.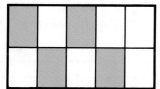

11.

12.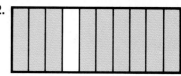

Write a decimal for the number name.

13. two tenths   **14.** four tenths   **15.** seven tenths

16. three tenths   **17.** nine tenths   **18.** six tenths

Write a number name for the decimal.

19. 0.8   **20.** 0.5   **21.** 0.1   **22.** 0.9   **23.** 0.4   **24.** 0.6

MIXED PRACTICE

Maintaining and Reviewing Skills

Write a fraction and a decimal for the shaded part.

25.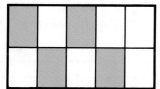

26.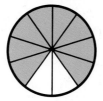

27.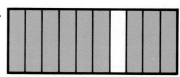

CHALLENGE

28. Draw a picture to show the decimal 0.6.

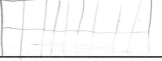

DECIMALS
Comparing and Ordering Decimals

Willis swam 0.5 of a mile. Lorraine swam 0.8 of a mile. Who swam the greater distance?

Compare 0.5 and 0.8.

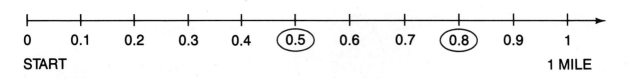

0.5 **is less than** 0.8   0.8 **is greater than** 0.5
      0.5 < 0.8   0.8 > 0.5

Lorraine swam the greater distance.

PRACTICE

Compare. Write < or >. Use the number line above to help you.

1. 0.1 < 0.2   **2.** 0.6 < 0.9   **3.** 0.4 < 0.5   **4.** 0.7 > 0.4

5. 0.3 < 0.7   **6.** 0.5 > 0.1   **7.** 0.2 < 0.6   **8.** 0.9 > 0.3

Write the decimals in order from least to greatest.

9. 0.7, 0.1, 0.5, 0.3   **10.** 0.6, 0.9, 0.4, 0.7   **11.** 0.2, 0.6, 0.8, 0.3

12. 0.4, 0.9, 0.8, 0.5   **13.** 0.2, 0.8, 0.6, 0.1   **14.** 0.5, 0.4, 0.3, 0.7

MIXED PRACTICE
Maintaining and Reviewing Skills

Compare. Write < or >.

15. 0.4 < 0.9   **16.** 0.8 > 0.6   **17.** $\frac{4}{5}$ > $\frac{2}{5}$ **18.** $\frac{6}{9}$ < $\frac{8}{9}$

| FOCUS | Use NUMBER skills to compare and order decimals. |

APPLICATION
Using Measurement

Ten dimes are equal to one dollar.

10¢   20¢   30¢   40¢   50¢

   =

60¢   70¢   80¢   90¢ $1.00

0.1 of one dollar = 10¢

What is 0.6 of one dollar?

Since 10¢ is equal to 0.1 of one dollar, then 60¢ is equal to 0.6 of one dollar, or $0.60.

Write each decimal part of one dollar in cents.

19. 0.4   **20.** 0.8   **21.** 0.5   **22.** 0.9   **23.** 0.7   **24.** 0.3

Write each money amount with a decimal point and a dollar sign.

25. 60¢   **26.** 10¢   **27.** 80¢   **28.** 20¢   **29.** 90¢   **30.** 50¢

Mental Arithmetic

See how quickly you can complete each pattern.

31. 10¢, 20¢, 30¢, ■, ■, ■, ■, ■, ■

32. 0.1, 0.2, 0.3, ■, ■, ■, ■, ■, ■

33. $\frac{1}{10}$, $\frac{2}{10}$, $\frac{3}{10}$, ■, ■, ■, ■, ■, ■

Use MEASUREMENT to equate dimes with tenths.
Use MENTAL ARITHMETIC to count by dimes and tenths.

PROBLEM SOLVING
Selecting a Strategy: Using a Formula

Using a formula is a strategy you can use to PLAN and SOLVE a problem. A formula is an equation that organizes the information you have. It uses letters to stand for numbers.

1. READ   Alan's lunch costs 10¢ more than Mae's lunch. How much does Alan's lunch cost if Mae's lunch costs 30¢?

2. KNOW   Ask yourself: What am I being asked to find? How much does Alan's lunch cost when Mae's lunch is 30¢? What **key facts** do I need? Alan's lunch costs 10¢ more than Mae's lunch.

3. PLAN   Select a strategy: try using a formula. Think: Alan's lunch is always 10¢ more than Mae's lunch.
Alan's lunch equals Mae's lunch plus 10¢.

The formula is $A = M + 10$.

4. SOLVE   Use the formula $A = M + 10$.
Replace **M** with the cost of Mae's lunch.
$A = \mathbf{30} + 10$
Solve the equation. $A = 40$
Alan's lunch costs 40¢.

5. CHECK   Ask yourself: Why is my answer reasonable?

Since $40 - 10 = 30$, 40¢ is a reasonable answer.

FOCUS | Evaluate information as part of the Five–Step PROBLEM–SOLVING Plan.

PRACTICE

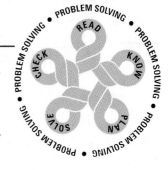

Use the formula to solve each problem. Remember to READ, KNOW, PLAN, SOLVE, and CHECK.

Use the formula: $A = M + 10$ to find the cost of Alan's lunch (A) when Mae's lunch (M) cost:

1. $M = 50¢$
2. $M = 34¢$
3. $M = 62¢$

4. $M = 47¢$
5. $M = 75¢$
6. $M = 83¢$

Use the formula: $M = A - 10$ to find the cost of Mae's lunch (M) when Alan's lunch (A) costs:

7. $A = 87¢$
8. $A = 63¢$
9. $A = 76¢$

10. $A = 44¢$
11. $A = 59¢$
12. $A = 39¢$

There are 4 glasses of milk in a bottle.
Use the formula: $G = B \times 4$ to find the number of glasses of milk (G) you can get when you have a different number of bottles (B).

13. $B = 9$ bottles
14. $B = 6$ bottles
15. $B = 5$ bottles

16. $B = 4$ bottles
17. $B = 8$ bottles
18. $B = 7$ bottles

Class Project

Work with a classmate. Write a formula to PLAN the problem below. Then use the formula to SOLVE the problem. CHECK your answer using another operation.

Jessica's allowance is always 50¢ more than her younger brother Wesley's allowance. How much allowance will Jessica get if Wesley gets 40¢?

DECIMALS
Identifying Decimals Greater Than One

Margaret made enough orange juice to fill two whole pitchers and three tenths of another pitcher. How much orange juice did Margaret make?

Margaret made two and three tenths pitchers of orange juice.

Two and three tenths can be written as a **mixed number** or as a **decimal.**

Mixed number		Decimal
$2\frac{3}{10}$	or	2.3

GUIDED PRACTICE

Complete the mixed number and the decimal to name the shaded part.

1.
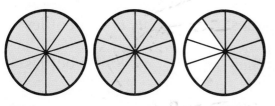

$$2\frac{7}{10} = 2.7$$

2.
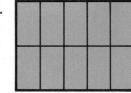

$$1\frac{\blacksquare}{10} = 1.\blacksquare$$

3.
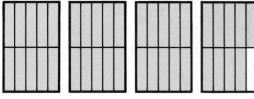

$$3\frac{\blacksquare}{10} = 3.\blacksquare$$

4.
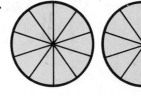

$$2\frac{\blacksquare}{10} = 2.\blacksquare$$

FOCUS Use NUMBER skills to identify decimals greater than one.

314

PRACTICE

Write a decimal for the shaded part.

5. 6.

7.

Write a decimal for the number name.

8. seven and six tenths

9. four and four tenths

10. two and three tenths

11. three and one tenth

12. eight and seven tenths

13. nine and five tenths

Write a number name for the decimal.

14. 6.7   15. 1.3   16. 5.5   17. 7.8   18. 6.9   19. 7.2

MIXED PRACTICE

Maintaining and Reviewing Skills

Write a fraction and a decimal for the shaded part.

20. 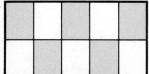   21.   22.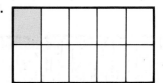

CHALLENGE

23. Draw a picture to show the decimal 6.5.

DECIMALS
Comparing and Ordering Decimals Greater Than One

The Fun Run is 3.8 km long. The Road Rally is 3.2 km long. Which race is longer?

Compare 3.8 and 3.2.

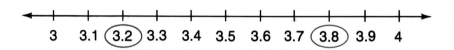

3.8 **is greater than** 3.2   3.2 **is less than** 3.8
3.8 > 3.2   3.2 < 3.8

The Fun Run is the longer race.

PRACTICE

Compare. Write < or >. Draw a number line to help you.

1. 2.6 ■ 2.4   **2.** 9.3 ■ 3.6   **3.** 4.5 ■ 4.1   **4.** 7.8 ■ 6.8

5. 6.9 ■ 9.5   **6.** 1.7 ■ 1.2   **7.** 8.4 ■ 7.3   **8.** 5.1 ■ 5.9

Write the decimals in order from greatest to least.

9. 5.6, 7.9, 3.2, 9.8   **10.** 1.2, 6.3, 8.2, 4.7   **11.** 2.5, 9.3, 5.4, 8.9

12. 4.9, 4.6, 4.3, 4.1   **13.** 7.5, 7.8, 7.2, 7.4   **14.** 1.1, 1.8, 1.6, 1.4

MIXED PRACTICE
Maintaining and Reviewing Skills

Compare. Write < or >.

15. 7.4 ■ 7.6   **16.** 9.1 ■ 1.9   **17.** 0.3 ■ 0.5   **18.** 0.8 ■ 0.7

FOCUS   Use NUMBER skills to compare and order decimals greater than one.

APPLICATION

Problem Solving: Using a Formula

Remember to READ, KNOW, PLAN, SOLVE, and CHECK all problems. See the Five–Step Plan on page 425 in the Data Bank.

Which number can the letter stand for?
Choose the number.

19. A is greater than 1.3
$A > 1.3$
1.4   1.2   1.1

20. B is less than 6.2
$B < 6.2$
7.4   5.9   8.3

21. C is less than 4.6
$C < 4.6$
4.7   5.0   3.6

22. D is greater than 2.0
$D > 2.0$
1.7   1.9   2.1

Which number can the letter stand for?
Choose the number and rewrite each formula.

23. A is greater than B
$A > B; B = 3.5$
4.0   3.4   1.5

24. C is less than D
$C < D; D = 2.7$
2.4   2.9   3.0

25. E is less than F
$E < F; E = 7.2$
7.4   7.1   6.9

26. G is greater than H
$G > H; G = 8.9$
8.8   9.0   9.3

Complete each formula by writing a number that each letter can stand for.

27. A is greater than 5.5
$A > 5.5$

28. B is less than 9.4
$B < 9.4$

29. C is less than 2.3
$C < 2.3$

30. D is greater than 4.1
$D > 4.1$

Use a formula and apply the Five–Step PROBLEM–SOLVING Plan.

LOOKING BACK
Reviewing and Testing Chapter 23

In Chapter 23 you formulated problems about practicing baseball. Look at pages 306 and 307.

1. Write a sentence telling how practicing would help you become better at something.

You learned something new about identifying tenths. To review what you learned, study the sample on page 308. Then use the new skill to write a decimal for the number name for examples 2 to 9.

2. nine tenths   3. two tenths   4. seven tenths   5. three tenths

6. eight tenths   7. five tenths   8. four tenths   9. six tenths

You learned how to use a formula to solve problems. To review what you learned look at pages 312 and 313. There are 4 quarters in 1 dollar. Use the formula: $D = Q \div 4$ to find the number of dollars if you have:

10. 8 quarters   11. 16 quarters   12. 24 quarters

You learned something new about identifying decimals greater than one. To review, look at pages 314 and 315. Then use the new skill to write a number name for the decimal for examples 13 to 23.

13. 5.4   14. 7.2   15. 8.3   16. 1.7   17. 6.3

18. 3.3   19. 2.9   20. 4.8   21. 9.2   22. 7.8

23. Write a decimal to show how much is shaded.

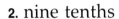

FOCUS   Review and test skills learned and practiced.

LOOKING AHEAD
Preparing for New Skills for Chapter 24

In the next chapter you will focus on

- formulating problems.
- adding decimals.
- adding dollars and cents.
- using measurement.

- subtracting decimals.
- subtracting dollars and cents.
- statistics and probability.
- math in technology.

New skills in adding and subtracting decimals will be easier to learn if you review what you already know about decimals. Study the model. Then do the PRACTICE exercises. Use the model to help you.

Model

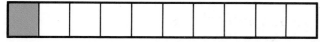

One tenth of the whole shape is shaded.
One tenth can be written as a decimal, 0.1.

↑
Decimal point

PRACTICE

Write a decimal for the shaded part.

1.    2.   3.   4.

5.   6.   7.   8.

Review NUMBER skills in preparation for learning a new skill.

FOCUS | Formulate problems using picture cues, text, and data.

DATA

Kind of pet	Kitten
Number of pets	3
Age of pets	4 months
Names of pets	Jo, Bo, Flo

Color of pets

Jo	White, gray
Bo	Black, white
Flo	Black, brown

Weight of pets

Jo	4 pounds
Bo	3 pounds
Flo	6 pounds

Amount each pet eats a day

Jo	2.5 ounces
Bo	2 ounces
Flo	3.5 ounces

Amount of water for each pet	2 ounces a day

CHAPTER 24

Addition and Subtraction of Decimals

Many people decide to get a pet because they fall in love with a puppy or kitten they have seen. When someone decides to have a pet, he or she must see that it grows up to be strong and healthy. In order for a baby animal to grow up strong and healthy, it must have the right kind of food. It must be given a comfortable and safe place to live. It must also be loved and wanted.

The kittens in the picture all need homes. As you can see from the data, each kitten is different. Notice how much each kitten eats, how much each kitten weighs, and what each kitten looks like. What problems might someone have in raising one of the kittens?

DECIMALS
Adding Tenths

In 1864, Charles Lawes set the world record for the one-mile run. His time was 4.9 minutes. In 1981, Sebastian Coe set a new world record for the one-mile run. His time was 3.7 minutes. What is their total running time?

Add the decimals to find the total running time.

Line up the decimal points.

```
  4.9
+ 3.7
```

Add the tenths. Regroup.

```
   1
  4.9      9 tenths
+ 3.7    + 7 tenths
  6       16 tenths
```

Regroup the 16 tenths as 1 one, 6 tenths.

Write the decimal point. Add the ones.

```
  1
  4.9
+ 3.7
  8.6
```

Their total running time is 8.6 minutes.

GUIDED PRACTICE

Add. Sometimes you will need to regroup.

1.
```
  3.2
+ 5.6
  8.8
```

2.
```
   1
  6.1
+ 0.4
  ▮.5
```

3.
```
  ☐
  2.5
+ 1.8
  ▮.3
```

4.
```
  ☐
  0.4
+ 2.9
  ▮.▮
```

5.
```
  ☐
  4.6
+ 4.6
  ▮.▮
```

6.
```
  ☐
  5.9
+ 0.7
  ▮.▮
```

7.
```
  0.2
+ 0.6
  ▮.▮
```

8.
```
  ☐
  7.5
+ 1.5
  ▮.▮
```

9.
```
  ☐
  5.4
+ 2.7
  ▮.▮
```

10.
```
  9.7
+ 0.1
  ▮.▮
```

11.
```
  ☐
  0.8
+ 0.5
  ▮.▮
```

12.
```
  6.3
+ 3.6
  ▮.▮
```

13.
```
  ☐
  1.9
+ 5.4
  ▮.▮
```

14.
```
  3.8
+ 2.1
  ▮.▮
```

15.
```
  0.3
+ 0.6
  ▮.▮
```

16.
```
  ☐
  4.5
+ 4.5
  ▮.▮
```

17.
```
  6.2
+ 2.6
  ▮.▮
```

18.
```
  ☐
  0.7
+ 7.8
  ▮.▮
```

FOCUS Use NUMBER skills to add tenths with and without regrouping.

PRACTICE

Add. Remember to write the decimal point in the
sum.

19.	5.2	20.	7.4	21.	6.3	22.	4.6	23.	0.9	24.	0.7
	+2.3		+0.9		+2.9		+0.7		+4.9		+0.6

25.	7.7	26.	1.6	27.	2.7	28.	1.3	29.	2.5	30.	7.1
	+2.2		+3.5		+2.1		+0.8		+3.5		+2.9

31.	4.7	32.	4.2	33.	1.8	34.	2.1	35.	6.4	36.	0.9
	+1.4		+3.1		+1.9		+1.7		+2.7		+3.8

37. 4.6 + 3.1　　　**38.** 3.2 + 3.9　　　**39.** 8.3 + 0.8　　　**40.** 6.7 + 2.8

Solve each problem.

41. Lauren ran two 1-km races. Her
time for the first race was 5.4
minutes. Her time for the
second race was 4.5 minutes.
What was her total running
time?

42. Isabel was in a high jump
contest. Her height for her first
jump was 1.2 m. Her height for
her second jump was 1.8 m.
What was her total height in
both jumps?

MIXED PRACTICE
Maintaining and Reviewing Skills

Add.

43. 5.2 + 3.7　　　**44.** 0.6 + 0.8　　　**45.** 73 + 25　　　**46.** 68 + 9

CHALLENGE

47. Leroy has 4.2 L of water in a pail. He puts twice
this amount of water in his pool. How many
liters of water does Leroy put in his pool?

DECIMALS
Adding Dollars and Cents

Angela bought a knapsack for $7.42 and a flashlight for $2.26. How much did she spend?

Add to find the total amount Angela spent.

Line up the decimal points.	Add the pennies.	Add the dimes. Write the decimal point.	Add the dollars. Write the dollar sign.
$7.42 +2.26	$7.42 +2.26 8	$7.42 +2.26 .68	$7.42 +2.26 $9.68

Angela spent nine dollars and sixty-eight cents.

PRACTICE

Add.

1. $5.61
 +2.33
2. $7.28
 +1.41
3. $3.64
 +1.25
4. $6.43
 +1.40
5. $4.25
 +3.42
6. $0.22
 +0.37

7. $8.38
 +1.40
8. $0.96
 +0.03
9. $5.80
 +1.10
10. $0.75
 +0.13
11. $2.53
 +0.46
12. $7.41
 +1.44

13. $5.36 + $1.53
14. $0.45 + $0.32
15. $2.68 + $6.30
16. $3.50 + $0.25

17. Larry has $1.30. He earned $2.55 babysitting. How much does Larry have altogether?

18. Jennifer spent $2.45 on a chain and $3.00 on beads. How much did she spend altogether?

MIXED PRACTICE
Maintaining and Reviewing Skills

Add or subtract.

19. $3.29 + $4.30
20. 56¢ − 31¢
21. $7.98 + $0.01
22. 98¢ − 7¢

FOCUS Use MEASUREMENT and NUMBER skills to add dollars and cents.

APPLICATION

Using Measurement

Stanley spent $1.43 on frog stickers and $1.45 on car stickers. About how much did he spend?

Estimate to find *about* how much he spent.

Step 1: Round each amount to the nearest ten cents.

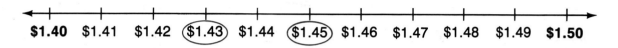

* $1.43 is between $1.40 and $1.50
* $1.43 is closer to $1.40
* $1.43 rounds down to $1.40

* $1.45 is halfway between $1.40 and $1.50
* $1.45 rounds up to $1.50

Step 2: Add the rounded amounts.

$$
\begin{array}{rl}
 & \text{Estimate} \\
\$1.43 \longrightarrow & \$1.40 \\
\$1.45 \longrightarrow & +1.50 \\
\hline
 & \$2.90
\end{array}
$$

Stanley spent *about* $2.90 on stickers.

Round each amount to the nearest ten cents.

23. $2.61   **24.** $5.92   **25.** $3.85   **26.** $7.17   **27.** $4.28   **28.** $8.54

Estimate each sum by rounding each amount to the nearest ten cents and adding.

29. $1.27 → $1.30
$7.62 → +7.60
$8.90

30. $3.15 → ■
$5.73 → +■
■

31. $7.21 → ■
$2.73 → +■
■

32. $5.47 → ■
$4.39 → +■
■

33. $2.56 → ■
$6.29 → +■
■

34. $8.32 → ■
$1.64 → +■
■

35. $4.38 → ■
$4.52 → +■
■

36. $6.11 → ■
$3.83 → +■
■

Use MEASUREMENT and NUMBER skills to estimate sums to the nearest ten cents.

DECIMALS
Subtracting Tenths

In 1962, Walter Schirra stayed up in space for 9.2 hours. In 1965, Virgil Grissom and John Young stayed up in space for 4.9 hours. How much longer did Walter Schirra stay up in space?

Subtract the decimals to find the difference between the length of times the astronauts were in space.

Line up the decimal points.	Regroup.	Subtract the tenths.	Write the decimal point. Subtract the ones.
9.2 −4.9	8 12 $\cancel{9}.\cancel{2}$ −4.9 Regroup 9 ones, 2 tenths as 8 ones, 12 tenths.	8 12 $\cancel{9}.\cancel{2}$ − 9 3	8 12 $\cancel{9}.\cancel{2}$ −4.9 4.3

Walter Schirra stayed up in space 4.3 hours longer than Virgil Grissom and John Young.

GUIDED PRACTICE

Subtract. Sometimes you need to regroup.

1. 5.6
  −3.1
  2.5

2. 9.8
  −2.6
  ▮.2

3. 6 13
  7.3
  −4.9
  ▮.4

4. 6.1
  −1.8
  ▮.▮

5. 7.4
  −0.5
  ▮.▮

6. 4.7
  −2.7
  ▮.▮

7. 0.9
  −0.6
  ▮.▮

8. 2.4
  −0.9
  ▮.▮

9. 8.2
  −6.3
  ▮.▮

10. 4.8
  −2.4
  ▮.▮

11. 3.5
  −1.6
  ▮.▮

12. 9.1
  −7.5
  ▮.▮

13. 7.3
  −3.8
  ▮.▮

14. 8.7
  −8.4
  ▮.▮

15. 1.6
  −0.7
  ▮.▮

16. 9.2
  −5.3
  ▮.▮

17. 6.8
  −5.8
  ▮.▮

18. 2.3
  −1.9
  ▮.▮

FOCUS | Use NUMBER skills to subtract tenths with and without regrouping.

326

PRACTICE

Subtract. Remember to write the decimal point in the difference.

| 19. | 7.5
−6.2 | 20. | 9.4
−3.8 | 21. | 6.7
−3.2 | 22. | 7.2
−4.5 | 23. | 4.9
−4.8 | 24. | 9.6
−1.6 |

| 25. | 7.8
−3.9 | 26. | 6.3
−1.7 | 27. | 5.5
−3.3 | 28. | 6.4
−4.5 | 29. | 3.2
−2.3 | 30. | 8.2
−4.1 |

| 31. | 2.6
−0.4 | 32. | 1.7
−1.6 | 33. | 8.4
−3.7 | 34. | 9.8
−2.4 | 35. | 6.8
−4.9 | 36. | 4.8
−2.1 |

37. $5.5 - 3.7$ 38. $7.2 - 3.6$ 39. $5.8 - 4.7$ 40. $8.8 - 5.4$

41. Alicia's paper airplane stayed in the air for 1.6 minutes. Rosa's paper airplane stayed in the air for 0.9 minute. How much longer did Alicia's airplane stay in the air than Rosa's?

42. Leila's glider stayed in the air for 8.4 seconds. Marlene's glider stayed in the air for 7.7 seconds. How many more seconds was Leila's glider in the air than Marlene's?

MIXED PRACTICE
Maintaining and Reviewing Skills

Subtract.

43. $0.8 - 0.7$ 44. $6.3 - 3.6$ 45. $52 - 13$ 46. $74 - 9$

CHALLENGE

47. Marco bought 2.3 L of grape juice on Monday. He bought 1.8 L of grape juice on Tuesday. He drank 2.9 L by Wednesday. How many liters of grape juice does Marco have left?

DECIMALS
Subtracting Dollars and Cents

Celeste has $8.65. She spent $6.25 on a record album.

Subtract to find the amount Celeste has left.

Line up the decimal points.	Subtract the pennies.	Subtract the dimes. Write the decimal point.	Subtract the dollars. Write the dollar sign.
$8.65 −6.25	$8.65 −6.25 0	$8.65 −6.25 .40	$8.65 −6.25 $2.40

Celeste has two dollars and forty cents left.

PRACTICE

Subtract.

1. $9.56
   −3.43

2. $8.25
   −4.20

3. $6.55
   −1.20

4. $9.70
   −6.70

5. $3.78
   −1.24

6. $1.82
   −0.21

7. $7.88
   −2.01

8. $5.95
   −2.22

9. $6.99
   −1.43

10. $8.59
    −3.25

11. $3.52
    −2.42

12. $7.67
    −6.53

13. $2.98 − $0.67   14. $9.55 − $2.25   15. $8.87 − $3.45   16. $4.52 − $2.21

17. Jose has $9.48. He spent $2.35 on a guitar book. How much does he have left?

18. Helen has $5.77. She bought a music book for $3.75. How much does she have left?

MIXED PRACTICE
Maintaining and Reviewing Skills

Add or subtract.

19. $4.36 − $2.25   20. $6.23 + $3.74   21. $7.68 − $5.68   22. $1.85 + $0.22

FOCUS   Use MEASUREMENT and NUMBER skills to subtract dollars and cents.

APPLICATION
Using Statistics and Probability

Here is a table of world swimming records. It shows women's and men's times for a 100-meter race using different strokes.

WORLD SWIMMING RECORDS FOR 100 METERS			
Stroke	Year	Name	Time
Freestyle	1980	Barbara Krause	54.8 seconds
	1981	Rowdy Gaines	49.4 seconds
Breast stroke	1983	Ute Geweniger	68.5 seconds
	1983	Steve Lundquist	62.3 seconds
Butterfly	1981	Mary Meagher	57.9 seconds
	1983	Matt Gribble	53.4 seconds
Backstroke	1980	Rica Reinisch	60.9 seconds
	1983	Rick Carey	55.2 seconds

Use the table to answer the questions.

23. What is the total swimming time of Barbara Krause and Rowdy Gaines?

24. How much longer did Mary Meagher swim than Matt Gribble?

25. How much less time did Rica Reinisch swim than Steve Lundquist?

26. What is the total swimming time of Ute Geweniger and Rick Carey?

27. Who swam the fastest race? What stroke was used? What was the year? What was the time?

28. Who swam the slowest race? What stroke was used? What was the year? What was the time?

Use STATISTICS AND PROBABILITY to read and interpret a table.
Use NUMBER skills to add and subtract decimals.

Computer Vocabulary

The secret to becoming good friends with your computer is in speaking its language.

A computer must be told how to do every job in detailed steps. Our description of what to do, written in the computer's language, is called a **computer program.** This and any other information we put into the computer is called **input.**

Sometimes, we give the computer very specific information such as the names and ages of all the children in the class. This type of input is called **data.**

After the computer has finished doing what the program tells it to, it usually has an answer, a picture, or some other result. This result is called **output.** We usually find output on the screen or printed on paper. **Graphics,** or pictures, are a type of output.

When a computer saves information, it is called **storing** the information. We save information in our memory. A computer stores information in its **memory,** just as we do. When a computer is asked to remember the stored information, it is said to be **recalling** the information.

Computers are made of a metal cover, wires, and boxes. A computer's hard outer cover and inside electronics are called **hardware.** The information that is not part of the computer's hardware is called **software.**

Finally, if you hear about a **bug** in the system, don't step on it! It only means there is a mistake in the program.

CRITICAL THINKING

1. If a computer could talk, would its words be called input or output?

2. If a computer could listen, would our words be called input or output?

3. Which of the following can we see and touch?
   hardware or memory

4. Why is it important for us to learn computer vocabulary?

| FOCUS | Use LOGIC to understand computer vocabulary. |

These students worked together to program this computer.

Students watch this turtle follow their LOGO commands.

LOOKING BACK
Reviewing and Testing Chapter 24

In Chapter 24 you formulated problems about cats. Look at pages 320 and 321.

1. Write a sentence telling what things you might think about before getting a cat.

You learned something new about adding tenths. To review what you learned, study the sample on page 322. Then use the new skill to find each sum for examples 2 to 12.

2. 4.3 +2.1	**3.** 6.8 +2.6	**4.** 5.5 +4.4	**5.** 1.7 +2.3	**6.** 3.4 +2.4	**7.** 2.4 +6.5

8. 3.8 + 3.7　　**9.** 2.7 + 3.8　　**10.** 5.7 + 3.4　　**11.** 7.3 + 1.2　　**12.** 4.2 + 2.1

You learned something new about subtracting tenths. To review, look at pages 326 and 327. Then use the new skill to find each difference for examples 13 to 28.

13. 5.6 −2.4	**14.** 7.7 −4.3	**15.** 9.9 −8.8	**16.** 5.3 −4.4	**17.** 8.2 −4.9	**18.** 6.7 −1.9

19. 9.8 − 9.6　　**20.** 2.7 − 1.2　　**21.** 7.8 − 4.3　　**22.** 8.6 − 5.9　　**23.** 9.7 − 7.8

24. 3.9 − 2.9　　**25.** 6.4 − 4.6　　**26.** 1.4 − 0.6　　**27.** 5.1 − 3.7　　**28.** 2.4 − 2.3

You learned about computer vocabulary. Look at page 330 to review what you learned.

29. Write the meaning of the words, *input, output,* and *memory.*

FOCUS　　Review and test skills learned and practiced.

LOOKING AHEAD

Preparing for New Skills for Chapter 25

In the next chapter you will focus on

- formulating problems.
- identifying line segments, angles, and right angles.
- using measurement.
- identifying polygons.
- classifying geometric shapes.
- using geometry.

New geometry skills will be easier to learn if you review geometry skills you already know.

Study Models A and B. Then complete the PRACTICE exercises. Use the models to help you.

Model A

Square

Circle

Triangle

Rectangle

Model B

 ← Side

↖ Corner

A square has 4 sides and 4 corners.

A circle has 0 sides and 0 corners.

PRACTICE

Write the name of each figure. Then write the number of sides and corners each figure has.

1.

2.

3.

4.

Review GEOMETRY in preparation for learning a new skill.

FOCUS | Formulate problems using picture cues, text, and data.

25

Geometry

DATA

Number of sheets of plywood	2
Number of boards	10
Number of nails	200
Height above ground of tree house	9 feet
Tools	
Hammers	2
Screwdrivers	1
Hand drills	1
Files	1

A tree house is a great place to spend time in the summer. It takes a lot of work to build a good tree house. As you can see from the picture, these children are doing their best. The data shows they have 2 big sheets of plywood for the floor of the tree house and 10 long boards to make the rest. Mother is there, too, to help them with the plans and to saw wood.

Using the data and the photograph, tell several different things you think they will do to build the tree house. How do you think they'll get up and down the tree to get to their tree house? What other problems will have to be solved? What do you think they will do when the tree house is finished?

GEOMETRY
Identifying Line Segments and Angles

Each side of this rectangle is a **line segment**.

A line segment is always straight. A line segment has two **endpoints**.

Each corner of this triangle is an **angle**.

When two sides have the same endpoint, it is called an **angle**.

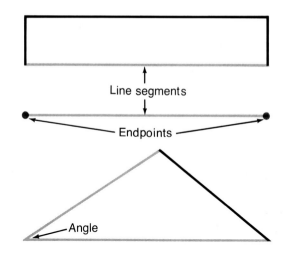

Line segments

Endpoints

Angle

GUIDED PRACTICE

Write whether each picture shows a line segment, an angle, or both.

1.

2.

3.

4.

5.

6.

FOCUS   Use GEOMETRY to identify line segments and angles.

PRACTICE

Which are line segments? Write *Y* (yes) or *N* (no).

7.

8.

9.

10.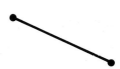

11.

12.

Which figures have angles? Write *Y* (yes) or *N* (no).

13.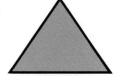

14.

15.

16.

17.

18.

MIXED PRACTICE
Maintaining and Reviewing Skills

Write the name of each solid figure. Then write the number of line segments each figure has.

19.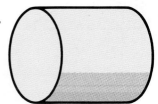

20.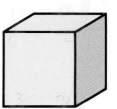

21.

CHALLENGE

22. Draw a figure with five line segments and five angles.

GEOMETRY
Identifying Right Angles

Each corner of this rectangle is a **right angle.**

When an angle forms a square corner it is called a **right angle.**

PRACTICE

Does the figure have at least one right angle? Write Y (yes) or N (no).

1.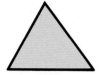

2.

3.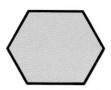

4.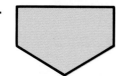

5.

6.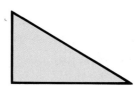

Write the number of right angles each figure has.

7.

8.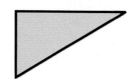

9.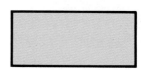

MIXED PRACTICE
Maintaining and Reviewing Skills

Label each as angle, right angle, or line segment.

10.

11.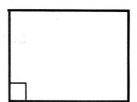

12.

APPLICATION
Using Measurement

The hands of a clock form an angle. When it is 3 o'clock, the angle is a right angle. Look at each clock below. If the angle is a right angle write *R*. If the angle is greater than a right angle write *G*. If the angle is less than a right angle write *L*.

13.

14.

15.

16.

17.

18.

19.

20.

21.

22. Copy this clock three times. Draw the hands on each clock so they form a right angle. Then write the time.

Use MEASUREMENT to relate angles to clock hands.

GEOMETRY
Identifying Polygons by the Number of Sides and Angles

A **polygon** is a figure formed by joining three or more line segments. The line segments are the sides of the polygon.

A polygon is named by the number of sides and angles it has.

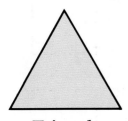

Triangle
3 sides
3 angles

Square
4 equal sides
4 right angles

Rectangle
4 sides
4 right angles

Pentagon
5 sides
5 angles

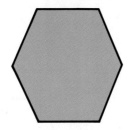

Hexagon
6 sides
6 angles

Octagon
8 sides
8 angles

GUIDED PRACTICE

Count the number of sides and angles. Then write the name of each polygon.

1.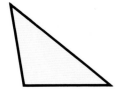

2.

3.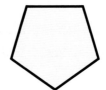

4.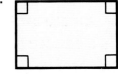

FOCUS   Use GEOMETRY to identify polygons by the number of sides and angles.

PRACTICE

Write the name of each polygon and the number of sides and angles each polygon has.

5.

6.

7.

8.

9.

10.

11.

12.

13.

14.

15.

16.

MIXED PRACTICE

Maintaining and Reviewing Skills

Write the name of each figure.

17.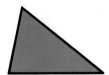

18.

19.

20.

21.

22.

23.

24.

CHALLENGE

25. A square and a rectangle are alike in many ways. Is a square also a rectangle? Is a rectangle also a square?

GEOMETRY

Classifying Geometric Shapes

A shape can be **open** or **closed.**

 This shape is **closed** because it begins and ends at the same point.

 This shape is **open** because it does not begin and end at the same point.

Look at the shapes below. Copy and complete this chart to show how many of each shape there are. Also record if each shape is open or closed.

	Figure	Number
1.	*Triangle*	■
2.	*Square*	■
3.	*Pentagon*	■
4.	*Hexagon*	■
5.	*Octagon*	■

6.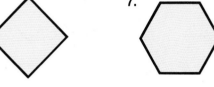

7.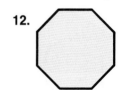

8.

9.

10.

11.

12.

13.

MIXED PRACTICE

Maintaining and Reviewing Skills

Is the figure *open*? Write *Y* (yes) or *N* (no). Write the name of each closed figure.

14.

15.

16.

17.

FOCUS   Use GEOMETRY to classify geometric shapes.

342

APPLICATION
Using Geometry

Trace this figure on a piece of paper. Cut it out and fold it in half.

Do the two parts match?

When a figure can be folded in half so the two parts match exactly it is **symmetric.** The line along the fold is called the **line of symmetry.**

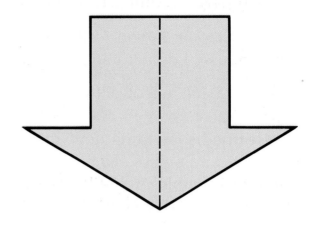

Is the red line a line of symmetry? Write Y (yes) or N (no).

18. 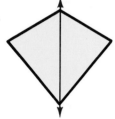   **19.** 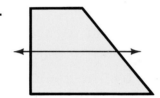   **20.**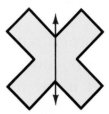

Do these figures have a line of symmetry? Write Y (yes) or N (no).

21.    **22.**    **23.**   **24.**

Copy these figures. Draw one line of symmetry through each figure.

25.    **26.**    **27.** 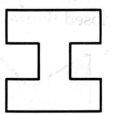   **28.**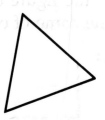

Use GEOMETRY to explore symmetry.

LOOKING BACK

Reviewing and Testing Chapter 25

In Chapter 25 you formulated problems about a tree house. Look at pages 334 and 335.

1. Draw a picture of a tree house.

You learned something new about identifying line segments and angles. To review what you learned, study the sample problem on page 336. Then use the new skill to write which is a line segment.

2.

3.

4.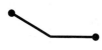

5.

You learned something new about measurement. To review, look at page 339. Then use the new skill to label if the angle formed by the hands of the clock is a right angle (*R*), or greater than (*G*), or less than a right angle (*L*) for examples 6 to 9.

6.

7.

8.

9.

You learned something new about identifying shapes by the number of sides and angles. To review, look at pages 340 and 341. Then use the new skill to name each shape for examples 10 to 13.

10.

11.

12.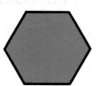

13.

| FOCUS | Review and test skills learned and practiced. |

344

LOOKING AHEAD

Preparing for New Skills for Chapter 26

In the next chapter, you will focus on

- formulating problems.
- multiplying with and without regrouping.
- using measurement.

- estimating products.
- using algebra.
- how math is used in art.

New multiplication skills will be easier to learn if you review the multiplication table. Complete the PRACTICE exercises.

x	0	1	2	3	4	5	6	7	8	9
0	0	0	0	0	0	0	0	0	0	0
1	0	1	2	3	4	5	6	7	8	9
2	0	2	4	6	8	10	12	14	16	18
3	0	3	6	9	12	15	18	21	24	27
4	0	4	8	12	16	20	24	28	32	36
5	0	5	10	15	20	25	30	35	40	45
6	0	6	12	18	24	30	36	42	48	54
7	0	7	14	21	28	35	42	49	56	63
8	0	8	16	24	32	40	48	56	64	72
9	0	9	18	27	36	45	54	63	72	81

PRACTICE

Multiply. Review the multiplication table.

1. 2×4 2. 4×6 3. 0×5 4. 3×7 5. 8×2

6. 5×5 7. 1×9 8. 7×7 9. 4×8 10. 6×3

Review NUMBER skills in preparation for learning a new skill.

Formulate problems using picture cues, text, and data.

26

DATA

Game   Scavenger hunt

Each team gets 1 hour

Time left   30 minutes

Teams
  Ron and Carla
  Linda and Aretha
  Nils and Jose

List of items to be found
  1 hammer
  1 flower vase
  1 trumpet
  1 hard-boiled egg
  1 pair of ice skates
  2 pieces of rope
  1 garden hose
  Something that catches
    flies

Multiplication by a 1-Digit Number

Do you know what a scavenger hunt is? It is a fun and easy game that you can play. A group of people get together and form teams. Each team is given a list of things to find. The teams are only allowed a certain amount of time to find the things. The team that finds everything on the list first wins.

The list can include anything, from a flower vase to a hard-boiled egg. It can also include things in the form of a riddle. You must figure out the riddle in order to know what object to find.

After you have looked at the picture and the data, think about the scavenger hunt. Where might each team look for the things on the list? Think of some other things you might have to look for in a scavenger hunt.

MULTIPLICATION
Multiplying Tens and Hundreds

The grocer unpacks 2 crates of grapefruits. Each crate has 40 grapefruits. How many grapefruits does the grocer unpack?

Multiply to find the total number of grapefruits.

$$
\begin{array}{r} 4 \text{ tens} \\ \times 2 \\ \hline 8 \text{ tens} \end{array}
\qquad
\begin{array}{r} 40 \\ \times\ 2 \\ \hline 80 \end{array}
$$

The grocer unpacks 80 grapefruits.

The grocer unpacks 2 crates of grapes. Each crate has 400 grapes. How many grapes does the grocer unpack?

Multiply to find the total number of grapes.

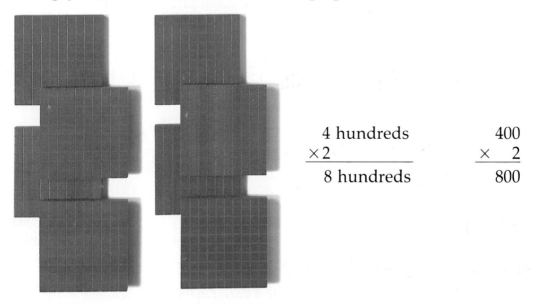

$$
\begin{array}{r} 4 \text{ hundreds} \\ \times 2 \\ \hline 8 \text{ hundreds} \end{array}
\qquad
\begin{array}{r} 400 \\ \times\ 2 \\ \hline 800 \end{array}
$$

The grocer unpacks 800 grapes.

| FOCUS | Use NUMBER skills to multiply tens and hundreds. |

348

GUIDED PRACTICE

Copy and complete.

1. 2 tens   20
    ×3   × 3
    ■ tens   ■0

2. 8 tens   80
    ×2   × 2
    ■ tens   ■0

3. 6 hundreds   600
    ×4   × 4
    ■ hundreds   ■00

PRACTICE

Multiply.

4.   10
    × 5

5.   30
    × 7

6.   70
    × 6

7.   20
    × 8

8.   10
    × 4

9.   40
    × 5

10.   200
     × 3

11.   600
     × 2

12.   100
     × 7

13.   500
     × 5

14.   700
     × 6

15.   300
     × 4

16. 70 × 2

17. 300 × 3

18. 10 × 9

19. Trudy unpacked 4 boxes with 60 apples in each box. How many apples did she unpack?

20. Ben ordered 5 boxes with 200 cherries in each box. How many cherries did he order?

MIXED PRACTICE
Maintaining and Reviewing Skills

Multiply.

21.   60
     × 2

22.   10
     × 7

23.   200
     × 9

24.   7
     ×6

25.   5
     ×8

26.   9
     ×9

CHALLENGE

27. The grocer sold 30 bags of rice each month for 3 months. Each bag has 9 pounds of rice. How many pounds of rice were sold altogether?

MULTIPLICATION
Multiplying Without Regrouping

Mrs. Taber is planning a trip. She will drive for 2 days. She plans to drive 124 miles each day. How many miles is she planning to drive?

Multiply to find the total number of miles.

Multiply the ones by 2.

H	T	O
1	2	4
×		2
		8

$$\begin{array}{r} 4 \\ \times 2 \\ \hline 8 \end{array}$$

Multiply the tens by 2.

H	T	O
1	2	4
×		2
	4	8

$$\begin{array}{r} 2 \text{ tens} \\ \times 2 \\ \hline 4 \text{ tens} \end{array}$$

Multiply the hundreds by 2.

H	T	O
1	2	4
×		2
2	4	8

$$\begin{array}{r} 1 \text{ hundred} \\ \times 2 \\ \hline 2 \text{ hundreds} \end{array}$$

Mrs. Taber plans to drive 248 miles in 2 days.

PRACTICE

Multiply.

1. $\begin{array}{r} 23 \\ \times\ 3 \\ \hline \end{array}$
2. $\begin{array}{r} 64 \\ \times\ 2 \\ \hline \end{array}$
3. $\begin{array}{r} 31 \\ \times\ 3 \\ \hline \end{array}$
4. $\begin{array}{r} 43 \\ \times\ 2 \\ \hline \end{array}$
5. $\begin{array}{r} 24 \\ \times\ 2 \\ \hline \end{array}$
6. $\begin{array}{r} 44 \\ \times\ 2 \\ \hline \end{array}$

7. $\begin{array}{r} 13 \\ \times\ 3 \\ \hline \end{array}$
8. $\begin{array}{r} 112 \\ \times\ \ 3 \\ \hline \end{array}$
9. $\begin{array}{r} 531 \\ \times\ \ 3 \\ \hline \end{array}$
10. $\begin{array}{r} 232 \\ \times\ \ 2 \\ \hline \end{array}$
11. $\begin{array}{r} 313 \\ \times\ \ 3 \\ \hline \end{array}$
12. $\begin{array}{r} 212 \\ \times\ \ 3 \\ \hline \end{array}$

13. $\begin{array}{r} 12 \\ \times\ 4 \\ \hline \end{array}$
14. $\begin{array}{r} 221 \\ \times\ \ 2 \\ \hline \end{array}$
15. $\begin{array}{r} 423 \\ \times\ \ 3 \\ \hline \end{array}$
16. $\begin{array}{r} 83 \\ \times\ 3 \\ \hline \end{array}$
17. $\begin{array}{r} 144 \\ \times\ \ 2 \\ \hline \end{array}$
18. $\begin{array}{r} 73 \\ \times\ 2 \\ \hline \end{array}$

MIXED PRACTICE
Maintaining and Reviewing Skills

Multiply.

19. 14×2
20. 213×3
21. 8×4
22. 5×6
23. 22×4

FOCUS — Use NUMBER skills to multiply two-digit and three-digit numbers by a one-digit number, without regrouping.

APPLICATION

Using Measurement

The apple tree in Bill's backyard is 4 m tall. How many centimeters tall is the apple tree?

Since 1 m = 100 cm, multiply 4 × 100.

The apple tree is 400 cm tall.

Copy and complete the table to show how many centimeters tall each tree is.

NORTH AMERICAN TREES			
Name	State	Height in Meters	Height in Centimeters
Rusty Blackhaw	Arkansas	8 m	24. ■
Silver Buffaloberry	Oregon	7 m	25. ■
Aloe Yucca	Florida	5 m	26. ■
Tesota	Arizona	9 m	27. ■
Poison Sumac	New York	6 m	28. ■

Mental Arithmetic

See how quickly you can multiply.

29.
$$\begin{array}{ccccccccc} 10 & 10 & 10 & 10 & 10 & 10 & 10 & 10 & 10 \\ \times 1 & \times 2 & \times 3 & \times 4 & \times 5 & \times 6 & \times 7 & \times 8 & \times 9 \end{array}$$

30.
$$\begin{array}{ccccccccc} 100 & 100 & 100 & 100 & 100 & 100 & 100 & 100 & 100 \\ \times 6 & \times 3 & \times 8 & \times 2 & \times 5 & \times 9 & \times 4 & \times 1 & \times 7 \end{array}$$

31.
$$\begin{array}{ccccccccc} 100 & 200 & 300 & 400 & 500 & 600 & 700 & 800 & 900 \\ \times 9 & \times 9 & \times 9 & \times 9 & \times 9 & \times 9 & \times 9 & \times 9 & \times 9 \end{array}$$

32. 50 × 5   60 × 5   70 × 5   80 × 5   90 × 5

Use MEASUREMENT and NUMBER skills to convert meters to centimeters.
Use MENTAL ARITHMETIC to multiply by tens and hundreds.

MULTIPLICATION
Multiplying With Regrouping

The Toppal family is moving. A mover carries 2 boxes to the van. Each box weighs 57 pounds. How many pounds does the mover carry?

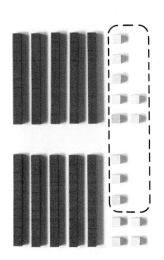

Multiply the ones by 2. Regroup.

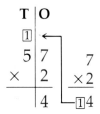

```
   T | O
   1 | ←
   5 | 7         7
 × |   2        ×2
   ---          ---
     4          1 4
```

Regroup 14 ones as 1 ten, 4 ones.

Multiply the tens by 2.

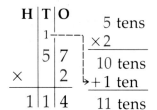

```
 H | T | O           5 tens
     1                ×2
   5 | 7             ------
 × |   | 2          10 tens
 -----------        +1 ten
 1 | 1 | 4          ------
                    11 tens
```

The mover carries 114 pounds.

The Toppals have 3 dressers. Each dresser weighs 146 pounds. How many pounds do the 3 dressers weigh?

Multiply the ones by 3. Regroup.

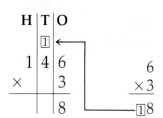

```
 H | T | O
     1 | ←
   1 | 4 | 6         6
 × |   | 3          ×3
 -----------        ---
         8          1 8
```

Regroup 18 ones as 1 ten, 8 ones.

Multiply the tens by 3. Regroup.

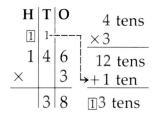

```
 H | T | O          4 tens
     1 | 1           ×3
   1 | 4 | 6        ------
 × |   | 3          12 tens
 -----------        +1 ten
   3 | 8            ------
                    1 3 tens
```

Regroup 13 tens as 1 hundred, 3 tens.

Multiply the hundreds by 3.

```
 H | T | O          1 hundred
 1 | 1               ×3
 1 | 4 | 6          ------
 × |   | 3          3 hundreds
 -----------        +1 hundred
 4 | 3 | 8          ------
                    4 hundreds
```

The 3 dressers weigh 438 pounds.

FOCUS | Use NUMBER skills to multiply two-digit and three-digit numbers by a one-digit number, with regrouping.

GUIDED PRACTICE

Copy and complete.

1.
```
   T O
    1
   3 8
 ×   2
 ▪ ▪ 6
```

2.
```
 H T O
   2
 2 7 1
 ×   3
 ▪ ▪ 1 3
```

3.
```
 Th H T O
    □   1
    2 8 3
 ×      4
 ▪  ▪ ▪ 2
```

PRACTICE

Multiply.

4.   19
   × 3

5.   24
   × 4

6.   33
   × 3

7.   45
   × 4

8.   27
   × 7

9.   64
   × 5

10.   324
    × 3

11.   193
    × 3

12.   417
    × 4

13.   271
    × 2

14.   583
    × 7

15.   482
    × 2

16.   22
    × 6

17.   150
    × 5

18.   93
    × 6

19.   493
    × 7

20.   76
    × 5

21.   817
    × 3

22. 42×3

23. 171×2

24. 602×4

25. 93×6

MIXED PRACTICE
Maintaining and Reviewing Skills

Multiply.

26. 18×3

27. 139×2

28. 200×6

29. 90×4

CHALLENGE

30. The teacher orders 3 cartons of chalk. Each carton has 24 boxes. Each box has 10 pieces. How many pieces of chalk does she order?

MULTIPLICATION
Estimating Products

Ted reads 3 poems every day. About how many poems does he read in the 31 days of May?

Estimate to find *about* how many poems he reads.

Step 1: Round the greater factor to the nearest ten.

$$
\begin{array}{r}
31 \longrightarrow 30 \\
3 \longrightarrow \underline{\times\ 3} \\
90
\end{array}
$$

Step 2: Multiply.

Ted reads *about* 90 poems in May.

PRACTICE

Round the greater factor to the nearest ten or to the nearest hundred. Estimate the product.

1. $26 \longrightarrow \blacksquare$
   $2 \longrightarrow \times \blacksquare$
   $\blacksquare$

2. $14 \longrightarrow \blacksquare$
   $7 \longrightarrow \times \blacksquare$
   $\blacksquare$

3. $55 \longrightarrow \blacksquare$
   $4 \longrightarrow \times \blacksquare$
   $\blacksquare$

4. $139 \longrightarrow \blacksquare$
   $6 \longrightarrow \times \blacksquare$
   $\blacksquare$

5. $253 \longrightarrow \blacksquare$
   $3 \longrightarrow \times \blacksquare$
   $\blacksquare$

6. $782 \longrightarrow \blacksquare$
   $6 \longrightarrow \times \blacksquare$
   $\blacksquare$

7. Cecily reads 2 short stories a day for 28 days. About how many stories does she read?

8. Bryan listens to 4 new songs a day for 365 days. About how many songs does he listen to?

MIXED PRACTICE
Maintaining and Reviewing Skills

Estimate.

9. 22×3 10. 126×8 11. $73¢ + 19¢$ 12. $87¢ - 35¢$ 13. 46×4

FOCUS | Use NUMBER skills to estimate products.

354

APPLICATION

Using Algebra

One pencil has a mass of 4 grams. What is the mass of 15 pencils?

Multiply to find the total mass.

The mass of one pencil is 1×4 or 4 g, so 15 pencils are 15×4 or 60 g.

Fifteen pencils have a mass of 60 grams.

Write a number sentence to solve each problem.

14. A dog has a mass of 25 kg. What is the mass of 5 of these dogs?

15. One penny has a mass of 2 g. What is the mass of 200 pennies?

16. A leopard has 315 spots. How many spots are on 6 of these leopards?

17. A tree has 581 leaves. How many leaves do 2 of these trees have?

18. A box has eight glasses. How many glasses are in twelve of these boxes?

19. One day has twenty-four hours. How many hours are in seven days?

Patterns and Functions

Multiply the factors. Then add the three products.
What do you notice about the sum?

20.
$$\begin{array}{cccc} 100 & 10 & 1 & 111 \\ \times\ 5 & \times\ 5 & \times 5 & \times\ 5 \\ \hline \end{array}$$
$$500 + 50 + 5 = \blacksquare$$

21.
$$\begin{array}{cccc} 200 & 30 & 4 & 234 \\ \times\ 2 & \times\ 2 & \times 2 & \times\ 2 \\ \hline \end{array}$$
$$\blacksquare + \blacksquare + \blacksquare = \blacksquare$$

22.
$$\begin{array}{cccc} 300 & 20 & 6 & 326 \\ \times\ 3 & \times\ 3 & \times 3 & \times\ 3 \\ \hline \end{array}$$
$$\blacksquare + \blacksquare + \blacksquare = \blacksquare$$

23.
$$\begin{array}{cccc} 100 & 0 & 9 & 109 \\ \times\ 4 & \times 4 & \times 4 & \times\ 4 \\ \hline \end{array}$$
$$\blacksquare + \blacksquare + \blacksquare = \blacksquare$$

Use ALGEBRA to translate a word problem into a number sentence.
Use PATTERNS AND FUNCTIONS to relate place value to three-digit multiplication.

Adinkra Cloth of Ghana

The Asante people of Ghana, Africa, make Adinkra cloth. Adinkra means *goodbye*. Long ago it was only worn when people said goodbye to someone. Now it is worn any time.

Many different designs are stamped onto a piece of Adinkra cloth. Patterns are carved out of a hard squash shell. Handles are attached to the shell, and then the patterns are dipped into a dye and stamped on the cloth. Adinkra cloth may be black, red, white, yellow, green, or purple.

A pattern is repeated many times. Adinkra makers must plan their work so that each pattern fits into its space correctly.

How many times can the design be repeated in one row? How many rows will fit in the space? The artist must figure this out before beginning the design. All the designs have meanings. This design is called the Akoma:

The Akoma design means *take heart* or *have patience*. If you fold the heart in half on the dotted line, one half matches the other half:

This line is called a **line of symmetry.** It divides the heart into two equal parts. Many Adinkra designs are symmetrical.

CRITICAL THINKING

1. Find the heart section on the Adinkra cloth. What is the shape of the box?

2. How many rows across of the heart pattern are there?

3. How many times is the heart pattern repeated in each row?

4. Do all the rows have the same number of hearts?

5. Draw a triangle-shaped pattern. Draw the line of symmetry through it.

FOCUS Use GEOMETRY and PATTERNS to appreciate and analyze the mathematical principles used by makers of Adinkra cloth.

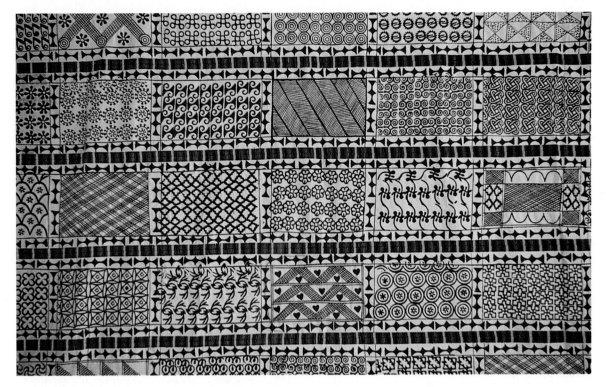

Adinkra artists work freehand, without the use of geometric tools.

These stamps were used to design part of this cloth.

LOOKING BACK
Reviewing and Testing Chapter 26

In Chapter 26 you formulated problems about a scavenger hunt. Look at pages 346 and 347.

1. Make a list of things to look for on a scavenger hunt.

You learned something new about multiplying tens and hundreds. To review what you learned, study the sample problem on page 348. Then use the new skill to find each product for examples 2 to 12.

| 2. 30
$\times\ 4$ | 3. 40
$\times\ 2$ | 4. 200
$\times\ 3$ | 5. 500
$\times\ 5$ | 6. 70
$\times\ 4$ | 7. 400
$\times\ 2$ |

8. 60×5 9. 100×8 10. 20×8 11. 300×3 12. 80×6

You learned something new about multiplying with regrouping. To review, look at pages 352 and 353. Then use the new skill to find each product for examples 13 to 28.

| 13. 17
$\times\ 4$ | 14. 36
$\times\ 2$ | 15. 173
$\times\ 4$ | 16. 324
$\times\ 3$ | 17. 93
$\times\ 5$ | 18. 137
$\times\ 6$ |

19. 28×3 20. 121×6 21. 63×5 22. 452×2 23. 76×3

24. 318×3 25. 49×4 26. 272×2 27. 81×5 28. 109×8

You learned about Adinkra Cloth of Ghana. Look at page 356 to review the patterns and what a line of symmetry is.

29. Draw a square. Draw one line of symmetry through the square.

FOCUS | Review and test skills learned and practiced.

LOOKING AHEAD
Preparing for New Skills for Chapter 27

In the next chapter you will focus on

- formulating problems.
- dividing with a remainder.
- checking division.

- using measurement.
- a problem-solving strategy.
- estimating quotients.

New division skills will be easier to learn if you review division skills you already know. First review the basic division facts on page 425 in the Data Bank. Then study Models A and B. Complete the PRACTICE exercises. Use the models to help you.

Model A

$12 \div 3 = 4$ $21 \div 7 = 3$ $48 \div 6 = 8$ $14 \div 2 = 7$

$30 \div 5 = 6$ $8 \div 1 = 8$ $16 \div 4 = 4$ $72 \div 9 = 8$

Model B

$4\overline{)24}$ = 6 $6\overline{)30}$ = 5 $3\overline{)27}$ = 9 $1\overline{)7}$ = 7 $2\overline{)16}$ = 8

$8\overline{)56}$ = 7 $2\overline{)18}$ = 9 $7\overline{)28}$ = 4 $5\overline{)15}$ = 3 $9\overline{)63}$ = 7

PRACTICE

Divide. Review Model A or Model B.

1. $12 \div 2$ **2.** $24 \div 6$ **3.** $42 \div 7$ **4.** $18 \div 3$ **5.** $16 \div 8$

6. $35 \div 5$ **7.** $27 \div 9$ **8.** $6 \div 1$ **9.** $32 \div 4$ **10.** $56 \div 7$

11. $6\overline{)18}$ **12.** $3\overline{)21}$ **13.** $5\overline{)45}$ **14.** $2\overline{)10}$ **15.** $8\overline{)48}$ **16.** $9\overline{)36}$

17. $4\overline{)20}$ **18.** $8\overline{)64}$ **19.** $9\overline{)81}$ **20.** $6\overline{)54}$ **21.** $1\overline{)9}$ **22.** $7\overline{)49}$

Review NUMBER skills in preparation for learning a new skill.

FORMULATING PROBLEMS

FOCUS Formulate problems using picture cues, text, and data.

27

<u>Division</u>

DATA

Project
  Gift for Bill's sister

Time   6 hours

Materials   Assorted lumber
            Nails
            Screws
            Glue
            Sandpaper
            Paint
            3 wooden wheels

Dad's tools Hammer
            Ruler
            Saw
            Screwdriver
            Clamp

Bill's tools Paintbrush
             Pencil

Decorations
  2 birthday balloons
  Wrapping paper
  Ribbon

It can be very rewarding to make things for other people. Today Bill is planning to make a birthday present for his 14-year-old sister. Before he started, he collected all the materials he could find around the house. But now he has to figure out what to make.

Using the data, tell what problems Bill must solve before he makes his sister's present. Using the photograph, tell what he decided to make. Why did he do this?

DIVISION
Dividing With a Remainder

Felicia made a book for her stickers. The book has 5 pages. She has 17 stickers. She puts the same number of stickers on each page.

How many stickers are on each page?
How many stickers are left over?

Divide 17 by 5 to answer the questions.

Estimate how many 5s are in 17.

Can she put
1 on each page? $1 \times 5 = 5$ Yes
2 on each page? $2 \times 5 = 10$ Yes
3 on each page? $3 \times 5 = 15$ Yes
4 on each page? $4 \times 5 = 20$ No

The estimate is 3.

Multiply and subtract.

$$5\overline{)17} \qquad 5\overline{)17}$$

Remainder┘
(number left)

Write the remainder.

$$5\overline{)17}$$

Felicia puts 3 stickers on each page.
She has 2 stickers left over.

GUIDED PRACTICE

Copy and complete.

1. $3\overline{)19}$ 6 R ▮
   -18
   1

2. $4\overline{)3}$ 0 R ▮
   -0
   3

3. $7\overline{)16}$ 2 R ▮
   -14
   ▮

4. $2\overline{)13}$ 6 R ▮
   $-▮$
   ▮

5. $6\overline{)25}$ ▮ R ▮
   $-▮$
   ▮

6. $9\overline{)38}$ ▮ R ▮
   $-▮$
   ▮

7. $5\overline{)3}$ ▮ R ▮
   $-▮$
   ▮

8. $8\overline{)44}$ ▮ R ▮
   $-▮$
   ▮

FOCUS Use NUMBER skills to divide with a nonzero remainder.

362

PRACTICE

Divide and find the remainder.

9. $7 \overline{)23}$ 10. $6 \overline{)25}$ 11. $4 \overline{)27}$ 12. $8 \overline{)6}$ 13. $9 \overline{)30}$

14. $7 \overline{)41}$ 15. $8 \overline{)26}$ 16. $7 \overline{)60}$ 17. $3 \overline{)28}$ 18. $5 \overline{)41}$

19. $2 \overline{)9}$ 20. $7 \overline{)4}$ 21. $8 \overline{)62}$ 22. $4 \overline{)33}$ 23. $9 \overline{)40}$

24. $3 \overline{)11}$ 25. $6 \overline{)51}$ 26. $7 \overline{)50}$ 27. $8 \overline{)2}$ 28. $5 \overline{)49}$

29. $23 \div 5$ 30. $30 \div 7$ 31. $64 \div 7$ 32. $88 \div 9$

Solve each problem.

33. Lou has a stamp album with 9 pages. He has 65 stamps. He puts the same number of stamps on each page. How many stamps does he put on each page? How many stamps are left?

34. Ruby has a sticker book. She wants to divide her 29 stickers equally onto the 7 pages of her book. How many stickers does she put on each page? How many stickers are left?

MIXED PRACTICE
Maintaining and Reviewing Skills

Multiply or divide.

35. $8 \overline{)33}$ 36. $5 \overline{)32}$ 37. $\begin{array}{r} 6 \\ \times 5 \end{array}$ 38. $\begin{array}{r} 9 \\ \times 3 \end{array}$ 39. $4 \overline{)40}$ 40. $\begin{array}{r} 7 \\ \times 8 \end{array}$

CHALLENGE

41. If you divide by 5, what is the largest remainder you could have?

42. If you divide by 9, what is the largest remainder you could have?

DIVISION
Checking Division

There are 26 ribbons for Sports Day. There will be 8 races. How many ribbons will be given after each race? How many ribbons will be left?

Divide to find the number of ribbons given after each race.

$$\text{Quotient} \rightarrow 3 \text{ R } 2 \leftarrow \text{Remainder}$$
$$\text{Divisor} \rightarrow 8 \overline{)26}$$
$$\underline{-24}$$
$$2$$

Three ribbons will be given after each race.
Two ribbons will be left over.

Check the division problem.

Multiply the divisor and the quotient.

$$\begin{array}{r} 3 \\ \times 8 \\ \hline 24 \end{array}$$

Add the remainder.

$$\begin{array}{r} 24 \\ + 2 \\ \hline 26 \end{array}$$

PRACTICE

Divide. Then check each quotient.

1. $4\overline{)37}$ 2. $9\overline{)69}$ 3. $5\overline{)47}$ 4. $2\overline{)15}$ 5. $7\overline{)59}$ 6. $3\overline{)19}$

7. $2\overline{)19}$ 8. $6\overline{)38}$ 9. $8\overline{)58}$ 10. $3\overline{)29}$ 11. $9\overline{)37}$

12. $5\overline{)22}$ 13. $9\overline{)85}$ 14. $7\overline{)48}$ 15. $4\overline{)18}$ 16. $8\overline{)76}$

MIXED PRACTICE
Maintaining and Reviewing Skills

Multiply or divide.

17. $6\overline{)40}$ 18. $7\overline{)68}$ 19. 7×6 20. 9×3 21. $5\overline{)45}$

22. 8×5 23. 9×9 24. $3\overline{)13}$ 25. $8\overline{)49}$ 26. $4\overline{)26}$

| FOCUS | Use NUMBER skills to check division. |

APPLICATION

Using Measurement

Jayne has 2 quarters, 1 dime, and 1 nickel. She sees that comic books are 9¢ each. How many can she buy? How much money will she have left?

Count Jayne's money. Then divide to find how many comic books she can buy. The remainder will be the amount of money Jayne has left.

$$25¢ + 25¢ + 10¢ + 5¢ = 65¢$$

$$
\begin{array}{r}
7\,\text{R}\,2 \\
9\overline{)65} \\
-63 \\
\hline
2
\end{array}
$$

Jayne can buy 7 comic books. She will have 2¢ left.

Write the number of items you can buy and the amount you have left.

	Money You Have	Price of Item	Number of Items You Can Buy	Money You Have Left
27.	1 quarter, 2 dimes *45¢*	8¢	■ 5	■ 5
28.	3 dimes, 1 nickel *35¢*	6¢	■ 5	■ 5
29.	5 nickels, 6 pennies *26¢*	5¢	■ 5	■ 1
30.	1 half dollar, 1 dime	9¢	■ 6	■
31.	1 quarter, 1 dime, 8 pennies	7¢	■	■
32.	1 half dollar, 1 quarter, 3 pennies	8¢	■	■

Use MEASUREMENT and NUMBER skills to divide with a nonzero remainder.

PROBLEM SOLVING
Selecting a Strategy: Using Guess and Test

Guess and test is a strategy you can use when you PLAN and SOLVE a problem.

1. READ In the equation $2 + A + 9 = 19$, what number does A stand for to make the equation true?

2. KNOW Ask yourself: What am I being asked to find? What does A stand for in the equation $2 + A + 9 = 19$? What **key facts** do I need? The A stands for a number that makes the equation true.

3. PLAN Select a strategy: try using guess and test. Guess a number and then test to see if it is correct.

4. SOLVE Guess a number: 10

$2 + \mathbf{10} + 9 = 21$

5. CHECK Ask yourself: Is 10 a reasonable answer? No, the sum is greater than 19.

SOLVE and CHECK again. What information from your first guess can you use to help you solve the equation?

4. SOLVE Guess a number: Since 19 is 2 less than 21, your next guess should be 2 less than your first guess.

Try 8: $2 + \mathbf{8} + 9 = 19$

5. CHECK Ask yourself: Why is 8 a reasonable answer? It makes the equation true.

FOCUS	Evaluate information as part of the Five–Step PROBLEM–SOLVING Plan.

PRACTICE

Remember to READ, KNOW, PLAN, SOLVE, and CHECK all problems. Replace each letter with a number. Guess and test until you find the number that makes the equation true.

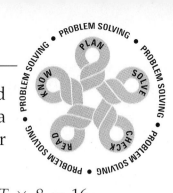

1. $A + 8 = 10$

2. $R - 9 = 8$

3. $T \times 8 = 16$

4. $12 \div F = 6$

5. $6 + W = 18$

6. $13 - N = 5$

7. $Z \times 8 = 56$

8. $14 \div E = 2$

9. $B + 7 = 13$

There are two letters in each equation. Replace each letter with a number to make the equation true. If the letters are the same you must use the same number. If the letters are different you must use different numbers. Guess and test until you find the numbers that make the equation true.

10. $B + B = 18$

11. $U \div F = 6$

12. $P - P = 0$

13. $A - H = 13$

14. $X + X = 12$

15. $L \times T = 42$

16. $R \times R = 16$

17. $G - S = 9$

18. $Z \div Z = 1$

Class Project

Form a group with several classmates. If you shake hands with each person in the group one time, how many handshakes will there be? Guess and test to solve. Now guess which member in the group has the longest arm span. To test, have a friend measure the distance from the fingertips on your left hand to the fingertips on your right hand. Write the length of your arm span. Compare all the lengths to see if your guess is correct.

DIVISION
Finding Two-Digit Quotients With Remainders

At camp 42 boys want to ride in a boat. Each boat can hold 3 boys. How many boats are needed?

Divide to find the total number of boats.

Estimate the tens digit.	Multiply and subtract.	Bring down the 2 ones.	Estimate the ones digit.	Multiply and subtract.

1 ten × 3 = 3 tens
  The tens digit could be 1.
2 tens × 3 = 6 tens
  TOO BIG!
  The tens digit is 1.

```
        T|O              T|O                              T|O
         1|               1|                              1|4
      3)4|2            3)4|2                            3)4|2
       -3|             -3| ↓                            -3|
        1|              1|2          4 × 3 = 12          1|2
                                                        -1|2
                                                          |0
```

The boys will need 14 boats.

There are 95 girls who want to run in a race. Only 4 girls can run in each race. How many races will be run? How many girls will not run?

Divide to find the total number of races.

Estimate the tens digit.	Multiply and subtract.	Bring down the ones.	Estimate the ones digit.	Multiply and subtract. Write the remainder.

1 ten × 4 = 4 tens
  The tens digit could be 1.
2 tens × 4 = 8 tens
  The tens digit could be 2.
3 tens × 4 = 12 tens
  TOO BIG!
  The tens digit is 2.

```
        T|O              T|O                              T|O
         2|               2|         3 × 4 = 12           2|3  R 3
      4)9|5            4)9|5          Could be 3.       4)9|5     ↑
       -8|             -8| ↓         4 × 4 = 16         -8|
        1|              1|5          TOO BIG!            1|5
                                    The ones           -1|2
                                    digit is 3.          |3 ---
```

In all 23 races will be run; 3 girls will not run.

FOCUS | Use NUMBER skills to divide with a nonzero remainder and a two-digit quotient.

GUIDED PRACTICE

Copy and complete.

1.
```
      18
   2 ) 36
    - 2
      16
    - 16
       ▮
```

2.
```
      1▮ R ▮
   5 ) 58
    - 5
      08
    - 5
       ▮
```

3.
```
      1▮
   4 ) 76
    - ▮
      ▮▮
      ▮▮
       ▮
```

4.
```
      ▮▮ R ▮
   3 ) 68
    - ▮
      ▮▮
      ▮
       ▮
```

PRACTICE

Divide. Then check each quotient.

5. 6) 72   6. 8) 98   7. 4) 50   8. 6) 60   9. 3) 43

10. 7) 77   11. 4) 72   12. 3) 91   13. 6) 88   14. 4) 47

15. 9) 97   16. 3) 75   17. 7) 85   18. 5) 96   19. 6) 93

20. 5) 63   21. 8) 96   22. 7) 93   23. 2) 67   24. 4) 97

25. $87 \div 7$ 26. $27 \div 2$ 27. $77 \div 4$ 28. $43 \div 3$

MIXED PRACTICE
Maintaining and Reviewing Skills

Multiply or divide.

29. 4) 84   30. 6) 68   31. 9×9 32. 7×6 33. 8) 85

CHALLENGE

34. There are 34 sandwiches on one tray and 25 sandwiches on another tray. The same number of sandwiches are to go on each of 4 tables. How many sandwiches will go on each table? How many sandwiches will be left over?

DIVISION
Estimating Quotients

Maggie wants to make 6 necklaces. She wants to put about the same number of beads on each necklace. She has 57 beads. About how many beads will she put on each necklace?

Estimate to find *about* how many beads she will put on each necklace.

Step 1: Round the greater number to the nearest ten.

$$57 \rightarrow 60$$

Step 2: Divide $60 \div 6 = 10$

Maggie will put *about* 10 beads on each necklace.

PRACTICE

Round the greater number to the nearest ten. Then divide to estimate each quotient.

1. $19 \div 2$ 2. $42 \div 4$ 3. $13 \div 5$ 4. $25 \div 6$

5. $22 \div 5$ 6. $75 \div 8$ 7. $32 \div 3$ 8. $86 \div 9$

9. $68 \div 7$ 10. $58 \div 6$ 11. $76 \div 2$ 12. $37 \div 8$

13. $81 \div 4$ 14. $91 \div 3$ 15. $59 \div 2$ 16. $39 \div 5$

MIXED PRACTICE
Maintaining and Reviewing Skills

Estimate.

17. $21 \div 4$ 18. 44×3 19. 68×4 20. $38 \div 5$

21. 16×7 22. $29 \div 6$ 23. $19 \div 5$ 24. 74×8

FOCUS | Use NUMBER skills to estimate quotients.

APPLICATION
Using a Calculator

The circus is in town. There are three rings under the big tent. Fifteen clowns are in each ring. How many clowns are in all of the rings?

25. Use a **calculator** to solve this problem.

● Which operation will you use to solve the problem?

● Which number key(s) do you press first?

● Which operation key do you press?

● Which number key(s) do you press second?

● Which key do you press to find the answer?

● Check your answer using pencil and paper.

● Which key do you press last?

Since $15 \times 3 = 45$, 45 clowns are in all of the rings.

Draw the keys you would use to solve each problem. Then use a calculator to find the answers. Check to see if your answer is reasonable.

26. Twenty-two clowns are happy. Sixteen clowns are sad. How many more clowns are happy than sad?

27. Twelve clowns can fit in one clown car. How many clowns can fit in nine clown cars?

28. Five hundred eight women and four hundred ninety-one men are in clown school. How many women and men in all are in clown school?

29. It took Leo fifty-six hours to sew eight clown costumes. If he worked the same number of hours on each costume, how many hours did it take to sew one costume?

Use a CALCULATOR to solve problems.

LOOKING BACK
Reviewing and Testing Chapter 27

In Chapter 27 you formulated problems about making a birthday present. Look at pages 360 and 361.

1. Write a sentence telling what you could build for a friend's birthday present.

You learned something new about dividing with a remainder. To review what you learned, study the sample problem on page 362. Then use the new skill to find each quotient for examples 2 to 12.

2. $6\overline{)25}$ **3.** $5\overline{)42}$ **4.** $9\overline{)8}$ **5.** $3\overline{)13}$ **6.** $8\overline{)30}$ **7.** $2\overline{)17}$

8. $37 \div 6$ **9.** $52 \div 8$ **10.** $27 \div 4$ **11.** $76 \div 9$ **12.** $45 \div 6$

You learned how to guess and test to solve problems. To review what you learned look at pages 366 and 367. Replace each letter with a number. Guess and test until you find the number that makes the equation true.

13. $T + 3 = 11$ **14.** $Z - 9 = 26$ **15.** $B \times 8 = 56$

You learned something new about finding two-digit quotients with remainders. To review, look at pages 368 and 369. Then use the new skill to find each quotient for examples 16 to 32.

16. $5\overline{)62}$ **17.** $3\overline{)61}$ **18.** $7\overline{)92}$ **19.** $4\overline{)72}$ **20.** $7\overline{)83}$ **21.** $5\overline{)68}$

22. $6\overline{)78}$ **23.** $8\overline{)92}$ **24.** $4\overline{)86}$ **25.** $2\overline{)29}$ **26.** $3\overline{)53}$ **27.** $9\overline{)97}$

28. $93 \div 8$ **29.** $43 \div 2$ **30.** $62 \div 6$ **31.** $55 \div 5$ **32.** $37 \div 3$

| FOCUS | Review and test skills learned and practiced. |

LOOKING AHEAD
Preparing for New Skills for Chapter 28

In the next chapter you will focus on

- formulating problems.
- identifying inches, feet, yards, and miles.
- estimating measures.
- statistics and probability.
- reading and graphing Fahrenheit temperatures.
- math in consumer education.

New measurement skills will be easier to learn if you review the measurement skills that you already know. Study the model. You can review facts about measurement on page 427 in your Data Bank. Complete the PRACTICE exercises. Check your work with the model.

Model

Inches and **feet** are used to measure the length of objects.

An **inch** is used to measure the length of short objects. Use an inch to measure the length of a nail.

A **foot** is used to measure the length of long objects. Use a foot to measure the length of a saw.

PRACTICE

Write whether you would use inches or feet to measure each length.

1. a key
2. a classroom
3. a swimming pool

4. a bed
5. a banana
6. a toothbrush

7. your finger
8. a window
9. your shoe

10. a watermelon
11. your math book
13. your leg

Review MEASUREMENT in preparation for learning a new skill.

FORMULATING PROBLEMS

FOCUS Formulate problems using picture cues, text, and data.

CHAPTER **28**

Measurement of Length and Temperature

DATA

Event
   Fourth of July picnic

Game   Sack race

Equipment
   needed   Burlap sacks

Racers in lead so far
   First   Sue
   Second   Jane
   Third   Tom

Length of race-
   course   100 yards

Yards left in
   race   50 yards

First Prize   Blue ribbon

Have you ever been to a summertime picnic? Picnics are a lot of fun. At some picnics, people play games. You don't need a lot of equipment to play these games. One exciting game is the sack race. The only equipment you need is a bunch of old burlap sacks.

It takes skill to win a sack race. You have to be fast, too. Using this action photograph and the data, tell several ways that this race might end.

First, decide what you think will happen next. What problems might the sack racers have? Who do you think will win the race? Give your reasons.

MEASUREMENT
Identifying Inch, Foot, Yard, and Mile

The inch, foot, yard, and mile are standard units of length. Each unit is always the same length.

Inches	1	2	3	4	5	6

The **inch** is used for measuring small objects.

A **foot** is equal to 12 inches.

> A ruler is 12 inches, or 1 foot long.

A **yard** is equal to 3 feet, or 36 inches.

> A yardstick is 36 inches, 3 feet, or 1 yard long.

A **mile** is equal to 5,280 feet.

> Long distances are measured in miles.

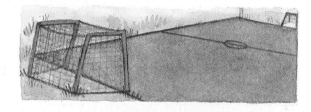

GUIDED PRACTICE

Which unit would you use to measure the following?
Write *inches*, *feet*, *yards*, or *miles*.

1. your feet

2. a hockey stick

3. a ladder

4. a bus

5. the distance from China to Egypt

6. the distance from Butte to Fargo

7. a football field

8. a worm

FOCUS | Use MEASUREMENT to identify inches, feet, yards and miles.

376

PRACTICE

Which unit would you use to measure the following?
Write *inches, feet, yards* or *miles.*

9. a television tube

10. how far an airplane flies

11. a pencil

12. a bed

13. a shovel

14. a paper clip

15. an airplane

16. the height of a door

17. your sleeve

18. a baseball diamond

Write *true* or *false.*

19. A whole crayon is longer than an inch.

20. Your hand is longer than a foot.

21. An airplane is shorter than a mile.

22. Your little toe is about 1 inch long.

MIXED PRACTICE
Maintaining and Reviewing Skills

Add, subtract, multiply, or divide.

23. $\frac{3}{5} + \frac{1}{5}$

24. $2\overline{)20}$

25. $\frac{7}{8} - \frac{3}{8}$

26. $\begin{array}{r} 320 \\ -166 \end{array}$

27. 9×4

28. $64 \div 8$

29. $273 + 156$

30. $4 \times \blacksquare = 20$

CHALLENGE

31. A football field is 120 yards long. How many feet long is a football field?

MEASUREMENT

Estimating Length in Inches

Estimate the length of each object. Then measure the actual length with an inch ruler.

1.

   Estimate ■   Actual ■

2.

   Estimate ■   Actual ■

3. ▰▰▰▰▰▰▰▰▰▰▰▰▰▰

   Estimate ■   Actual ■

Measure the line segments to the nearest inch.

4. —————— ■ in.

5. ———————————— ■ in.

6. ——————————————————— ■ in.

MIXED PRACTICE

Maintaining and Reviewing Skills

Add, subtract, multiply, or divide.

7. $\begin{array}{r} 413 \\ 26 \\ +145 \\ \hline \end{array}$

8. $\begin{array}{r} 700 \\ -\ 63 \\ \hline \end{array}$

9. $\begin{array}{r} ■ \\ \times 9 \\ \hline 81 \end{array}$

10. $8\overline{)56}$

11. $\frac{6}{11} - \frac{4}{11}$

| FOCUS | Use MEASUREMENT to estimate length. |

378

APPLICATION

Using Statistics and Probability

The **grid** below shows a map of Home Town.

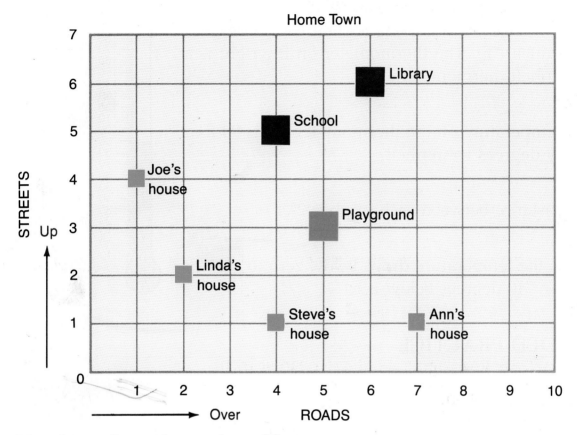

Home Town

Use the grid to solve each problem.

12. What is at Road 5, Street 3?
Step 1: Start at zero.
Step 2: Move over to Road 5.
Step 3: Move up to Street 3.

13. What is at Road 4, Street 5?
Step 1: Start at zero.
Step 2: Move over to Road 4.
Step 3: Move up to Street 5.

14. Where is Ann's house?
Step 1: Start at Ann's house.
Step 2: Look down to find the road number.
Step 3: Look over to find the street number.

15. Where is the library?
Step 1: Start at the library.
Step 2: Look down to find the road number.
Step 3: Look over to find the street number.

Use STATISTICS AND PROBABILITY to locate and name points on a grid.

MEASUREMENT
Reading Fahrenheit Temperature

A thermometer measures temperature. Temperature is measured in **degrees**. A **Fahrenheit thermometer** shows the temperature in degrees Fahrenheit (°F). The thermometer on the right is a Fahrenheit thermometer.

The temperature on the thermometer reads 90°F or ninety degrees Fahrenheit.

The distance between each mark is 2°.

When the temperature drops below zero to −10°F, we say "10 degrees below zero."

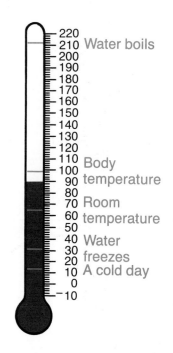

GUIDED PRACTICE

Write each temperature in degrees Fahrenheit.

1.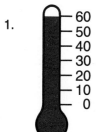

2.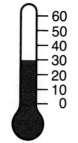

3.

4.

5.

6.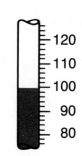

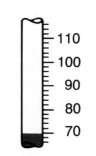

FOCUS   Use MEASUREMENT to read a thermometer in degrees Fahrenheit.

380

PRACTICE

Write each temperature in degrees Fahrenheit.

7.
```
110
105
100
95
90
```

8.
```
15
10
5
0
-5
```

9.
```
70
65
60
55
50
```

10.
```
85
80
75
70
65
```

11.
```
30
25
20
15
10
```

12.
```
30
25
20
15
10
```

13.
```
85
80
75
70
65
```

14.
```
105
100
95
90
85
```

Write the name of an activity you could do at each
temperature. Use the thermometer on page 380 to
help you.

15. 85°F   **16.** 32°F   **17.** 50°F

MIXED PRACTICE
Maintaining and Reviewing Skills

Add, subtract, multiply, or divide.

18. ■ $\times$ 8 = 72   **19.** ■ $\div$ 6 = 9   **20.** 363 + 17 + 41 **21.** 821 − 647

CHALLENGE

22. Terry's thermometer read 80°F. Draw a picture
of her thermometer. Draw a picture of an activity
Terry could do at this temperature and what she
is wearing.

MEASUREMENT
Reading and Graphing Temperatures

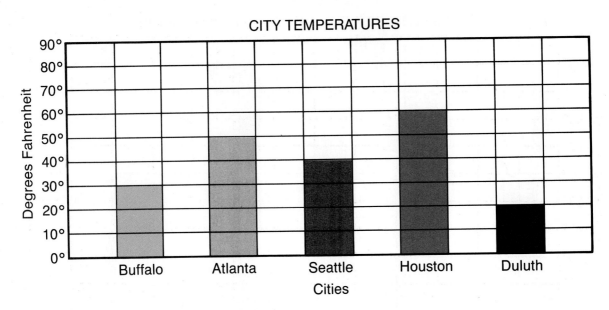

CITY TEMPERATURES

Write the temperature for each city.

1. Buffalo   2. Seattle   3. Duluth

4. Atlanta   5. Houston

Use the graph to answer the questions.

6. Which city has the highest temperature?

7. Which city has the lowest temperature?

8. What is the difference between temperatures in Houston and Duluth?

MIXED PRACTICE
Maintaining and Reviewing Skills

Add or subtract.

9. $432 + 187$ 10. $956 - 78$ 11. $3.4 - 1.3$ 12. $\frac{2}{5} + \frac{1}{5}$

FOCUS | Use STATISTICS AND PROBABILITY to read and interpret a bar graph.

382

APPLICATION
Using Statistics and Probability

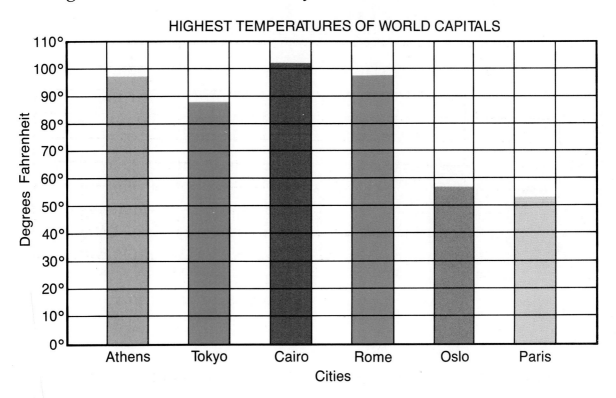

HIGHEST TEMPERATURES OF WORLD CAPITALS

Use the graph to answer the questions.

13. Which city had the highest temperature?

14. Which city had the lowest temperature?

15. Which cities had the same high temperature?

16. Which cities had a higher temperature than Tokyo?

Make your own graph.

17. Measure the temperature outside your classroom at the same time every day for 1 week. Then use your information to make a bar graph.

Use MEASUREMENT to measure temperature.
Use STATISTICS AND PROBABILITY to read and interpret a bar graph and to create a bar graph.

Reading Labels

Careful shoppers read labels on the packages of food they buy.

Here are two cans of soup:

can A   can B

Can *B* is larger than Can *A*. It looks like it will have more soup. Does it? To find out you must read the labels carefully.

Can *A* is smaller than Can *B* but it contains **condensed** soup. This means that liquid should be added to it. With one 8-ounce can of water, Can *A* makes more soup than Can *B*. Can *B* makes only the amount of soup in the can.

The *Serving Size Information* on the back of the labels tells how many servings each can contains or makes. It also tells the size of each serving. So don't be fooled, even though Can *A* is smaller, it makes more soup than Can *B*.

Look at the two cans of tomatoes on the next page. They are the same size and the same **net weight,** the weight of everything in the can (in this case, 28 ounces). But the two cans do not have the same amount of tomatoes. Read the ingredients list. Both have tomatoes and tomato juice, but in different amounts. Can *B* contains 5 ounces more tomatoes than Can *A*.

Read the labels on these pages, then answer the questions.

CRITICAL THINKING

1. How many ounces of chicken noodle soup does Can *A* make when water is added?

2. How many ounces of vegetable soup are in each can? How many servings are in each can? Which soup has more vegetables? How do you know?

3. How many servings of fruit cocktail are in each can? How many ounces are in each serving? Are the ingredients different?

FOCUS   Use NUMBER skills and LOGIC to understand and analyze product labels.

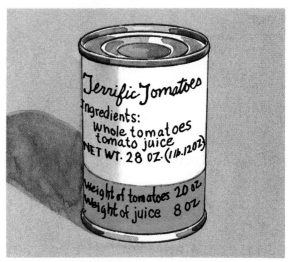

LOOKING BACK
Reviewing and Testing Chapter 28

In Chapter 28 you formulated problems about a sack race. Look at pages 374 and 375.

1. Write a sentence telling what skills are needed to win a sack race.

You learned something new about identifying inch, foot, yard, and mile. To review what you learned, study the sample problem on page 376. Then use the new skill to choose the correct unit of measure for examples 2 to 9.

2. pencil

3. bus

4. paper clip

5. your height

6. distance between cities

7. sofa

8. bulletin board

9. shoe

You learned something new about reading Fahrenheit temperature. To review, look at page 380. Use the new skill to write the temperature in degrees Fahrenheit for examples 10 to 14.

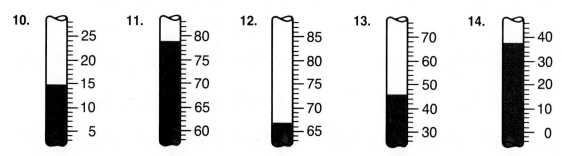

10.   11.   12.   13.   14.

You learned about reading labels. Look at page 384 to review the importance of reading labels.

15. How does reading labels help you make the best choice?

LOOKING AHEAD

Preparing for New Skills for Chapter 29

In the next chapter you will focus on

- formulating problems.
- identifying ounces and pounds.
- adding measures.

- statistics and probability.
- identifying cup, pint, quart, and gallon.
- estimating measures.

New measurement skills will be easier to learn if you review the measurement skills that you already know. Study Models A and B. You can review the facts about measurement on page 427 in the Data Bank. Complete the PRACTICE exercises and check your work with the models.

Model A
Ounces and **pounds** are used to measure the weight of objects. A loaf of bread weighs about 1 pound.

Model B
Cups, pints, quarts, and **gallons** are used to measure how much liquid is in a container. A drinking glass holds about 1 cup.

PRACTICE

What is being measured? Write *weight* or *liquid.*

1. How much does a glass hold?

2. How heavy is an elephant?

3. How light is a cotton ball?

4. How much is in that bottle?

5. How many pounds is a desk?

6. How many quarts are in a jar?

7. How many cups of juice are in a can?

8. How many ounces is the napkin?

9. How many gallons of water are in the swimming pool?

10. How many pounds of potatoes can you carry?

Review MEASUREMENT in preparation for learning a new skill.

29

Customary Measurement: Weight and Capacity

DATA

Activity	Painting a picture
Place	After-school art class
Painter	Reggie
Paint colors	Yellow
	Red
	Blue
	Brown
	Green
	Purple

Things Reggie likes

Cars and trucks
Trees and flowers
Ice skating

Did you ever paint a picture? What was it like? Maybe it showed a yellow sun and some green grass. There might have been red and purple flowers in the grass. A picture can show what you see around you. It can tell other people what things you like. You might even paint a picture of yourself!

A painter has many things to choose from. Reggie is about to start painting. She has many colors of paint. She also knows a few things that she likes, such as cars and trucks.

Can you think of what Reggie must decide before she begins to paint? What problems will she solve after she finishes the painting?

MEASUREMENT
Weighing in Ounces and Pounds

Ounces and pounds are standard units of weight.

A slice of cheese weighs about **1 ounce (1 oz)**.

Four sticks of margarine weigh about **1 pound (1 lb)**.

One pound equals 16 ounces.
1 lb = 16 oz

Look at the scale. What is the weight of the cheese?

The cheese weighs 1 lb 8 oz.

GUIDED PRACTICE

Which unit would you use to measure the weight of each object? Write *ounce* or *pound*.

1.

2.

3.

FOCUS   Use MEASUREMENT to weigh objects in ounces and pounds.

390

PRACTICE

Look at the scale. Write how much each item weighs.

4.

5.

Write the unit of measure you would use to weigh the following items. Write *ounce* or *pound.*

6.

7.

8.

9.

10.

11.

MIXED PRACTICE
Maintaining and Reviewing Skills

Add, subtract or multiply.

12. 7×2 **13.** 5×6 **14.** $\begin{array}{r} 109 \\ -\ 67 \end{array}$ **15.** $\begin{array}{r} 370 \\ +299 \end{array}$ **16.** $\frac{8}{10} - \frac{3}{10}$

17. $663 + 231 + 28$ **18.** $\frac{2}{9} + \frac{3}{9} + \frac{3}{9}$ **19.** $\frac{1}{4} + \frac{3}{4}$

CHALLENGE

20. Pablo has 7 ounces of chili. How many more ounces does he need to have 1 pound?

MEASUREMENT

Adding Ounces and Pounds

Ed is at the post office mailing two books. One book weighs 1 lb 6 oz. The other book weighs 2 lb 1 oz. How much do the two books weigh?

Add to find the total weight.

Add the ounces first, then add the pounds. Always label your work.

$$\begin{array}{r} 1 \text{ lb } 6 \text{ oz} \\ +2 \text{ lb } 1 \text{ oz} \\ \hline 3 \text{ lb } 7 \text{ oz} \end{array}$$

The two books weigh 3 lb 7 oz.

PRACTICE

Add to solve.

1. $\begin{array}{r} 4 \text{ lb } 6 \text{ oz} \\ +3 \text{ lb } 8 \text{ oz} \\ \hline \end{array}$

2. $\begin{array}{r} 3 \text{ lb } 3 \text{ oz} \\ +3 \text{ lb } 9 \text{ oz} \\ \hline \end{array}$

3. $\begin{array}{r} 12 \text{ lb } 7 \text{ oz} \\ + \ \ 6 \text{ lb } 5 \text{ oz} \\ \hline \end{array}$

4. $\begin{array}{r} 1 \text{ lb } 3 \text{ oz} \\ +2 \text{ lb } 1 \text{ oz} \\ \hline \end{array}$

5. Cory's bookbag weighs 3 lb 5 oz. Tim's bookbag weighs 5 lb 9 oz. How many pounds do both bookbags weigh?

6. Mrs. Ford buys a chicken that weighs 4 lb 8 oz. She buys a ham that weighs 7 lb 7 oz. How much do the chicken and the ham weigh altogether?

MIXED PRACTICE

Maintaining and Reviewing Skills

Add, subtract, multiply, or divide.

7. $\begin{array}{r} 608 \\ -389 \\ \hline \end{array}$

8. $\begin{array}{r} 410 \\ +634 \\ \hline \end{array}$

9. $\begin{array}{r} \blacksquare \\ \times 7 \\ \hline 49 \end{array}$

10. $7\overline{)70}$

11. $\dfrac{3}{4} - \dfrac{2}{4}$

FOCUS Use MEASUREMENT and NUMBER skills to add ounces and pounds.

APPLICATION
Using Statistics and Probability

The chart shows the weight of 6 students in Arlene's class.

A bar graph was made from the information on the class chart.

Name	Weight
Karl	65 lb
Helene	45 lb
Peter	70 lb
Tara	60 lb
Arlene	65 lb
Bill	80 lb

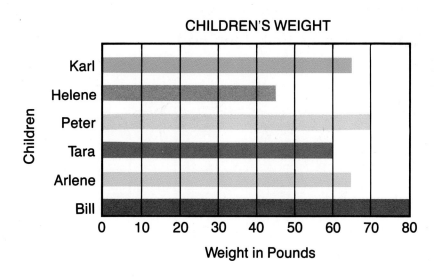

CHILDREN'S WEIGHT

Use the bar graph to solve each problem.

12. Who weighs the most?

13. Who weighs the least?

14. How much heavier is Peter than Tara?

15. Who weighs the same?

Ellen made this chart. It shows the weight of 6 children in her class.

16. Draw a bar graph using the information from Ellen's chart. Remember to title your graph and to write labels on the left side and the bottom.

Name	Weight
Ellen	60 lb
Todd	80 lb
Dave	70 lb
Yoko	65 lb
Gina	50 lb
Noel	70 lb

Use STATISTICS AND PROBABILITY to read, interpret, and create a bar graph.

MEASUREMENT
Identifying Units of Capacity

These are some of the standard units for measuring liquid.

Cup (c)   Pint (pt)   Quart (qt)   Gallon (gal)

 =

1 gallon = 4 quarts

 =   =

1 quart = 2 pints   1 pint = 2 cups

GUIDED PRACTICE

Which unit would you use to measure the capacity of each container? Write *gallon*, *quart*, *pint*, or *cup*.

1.    2.    3.    4.

FOCUS   Use MEASUREMENT to determine capacity.

PRACTICE

Choose the best measuring unit for each container.

5. a fish tank
   quart or gallon

6. a tea kettle
   cup or gallon

7. a large can of paint
   pint or gallon

8. a baby's bottle
   quart or pint

9. a big bottle of
   shampoo
   quart or cup

10. a glass
    cup or pint

CAPACITY MEASURED IN CUPS

Complete.

11. 1 gallon = ■ quarts

12. 1 quart = ■ pints

13. 1 pint = ■ cups

14. 2 gallons = ■ quarts

MIXED PRACTICE
Maintaining and Reviewing Skills

Add, subtract, multiply, or divide.

15.
$$\begin{array}{r} 600 \\ -345 \\ \hline \end{array}$$

16.
$$\begin{array}{r} 418 \\ +\ 99 \\ \hline \end{array}$$

17. $6\overline{)42}$

18.
$$\begin{array}{r} 7 \\ \times 4 \\ \hline \end{array}$$

19. $\frac{3}{12} + \frac{7}{12}$

CHALLENGE

20. How many cups fill 1 gallon?

MEASUREMENT
Estimating Capacity

Sarah estimates how many bowls of soup the pot holds. Then she uses a soup bowl to measure the actual amount of soup the pot holds.

Sarah estimates that the pot holds about 20 bowls of soup. She measures the pot. She finds that it holds 16 bowls of soup. The difference between Sarah's estimate and the actual amount is four bowls of soup.

PRACTICE

The bowl holds 1 cup. Estimate how many bowls will fill each pot. Then write the actual number of cups.

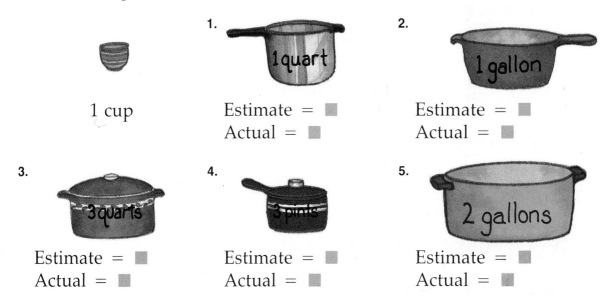

1 cup

1. 1 quart

Estimate = ■
Actual = ■

2. 1 gallon

Estimate = ■
Actual = ■

3. 3 quarts

Estimate = ■
Actual = ■

4. 3 pints

Estimate = ■
Actual = ■

5. 2 gallons

Estimate = ■
Actual = ■

MIXED PRACTICE
Maintaining and Reviewing Skills

Multiply.

6. 243×6 **7.** 327×4 **8.** 118×7 **9.** 236×6

FOCUS   Use MEASUREMENT to estimate capacity.

APPLICATION

Using Measurement

Read each problem. Choose the best unit of measure to solve.

10. Katie wants to measure the length of her yard. Which unit of measurement should she use?

    feet   gallons   ounces

11. Pedro is going on a trip to Argentina. He is allowed to take a suitcase that weighs 44 ▓.

    inches   pounds   quarts

12. John is going to wash clothes. He needs to fill his washing machine with water. His machine holds 20 ▓ of water.

    feet   pounds   gallons

13. Maya bought a roll of giftwrap to wrap a present. The length of the paper was 36 ▓.

    pints   pounds   inches

14. Alex made a pitcher of ice tea. The capacity of the pitcher is 3 ▓.

    miles   ounces   quarts

15. Linda's cat weighs 14 ▓.

    ounces   feet   pounds

16. Ms. Findorak measured her desk. It is about 2 ▓ long.

    miles   pounds   feet

Use MEASUREMENT to determine the correct unit of measure.

LOOKING BACK
Reviewing and Testing Chapter 29

In Chapter 29 you formulated problems about paintings. Look at pages 388 and 389.

1. Write about a painting you would like to hang in your bedroom.

You learned something new about weighing in ounces and pounds. To review what you learned, study the sample problem on page 390. Then use the new skill to choose either ounces or pounds for examples 2 to 9. Then solve examples 10 and 11.

2. feather

3. bag of potatoes

4. pencil

5. carrot

6. watermelon

7. turkey

8. orange

9. an adult male

10. Debbie has 11 ounces of salad. How many more ounces does she need to have 1 pound?

11. Jack has 2 pounds of fruit. How many ounces of fruit does Jack have?

You learned something new about units of capacity. To review, look at pages 394 and 395. Then use the new skill to write the better unit of measure for examples 12 to 15. Then solve examples 16 and 17.

12. a glass of juice

ounce   or   quart

13. a small can of paint

pint   or   quart

14. a bowl of soup

ounce   or   quart

15. a large bottle of shampoo

cup   or   quart

16. Iris has 2 gallons of paint. How many quarts of paint does she have?

17. Eliot has 8 pints of milk. How many quarts of milk does he have?

LOOKING AHEAD

Preparing for New Skills for Chapter 30

In the next chapter you will focus on

- formulating problems.
- learning probability terms.
- representing probability with fractions.
- a problem-solving strategy.

- predicting outcomes.
- combinations.
- using statistics and probability.
- how math is used in music.

New skills in probability will be easier to learn if you review what you already know about probability. Study the model. Then complete the PRACTICE exercises. Use the model to help you.

Model

The spinner has 4 parts. What is the chance of spinning red?

The chance of spinning red is 2 out of 4.

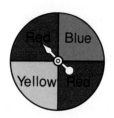

PRACTICE

Complete each sentence to show the chance of picking a cube from the bag without looking.

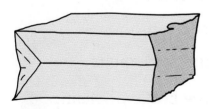

1. The chance of picking a red cube is ■ out of ■.

2. The chance of picking a yellow cube is ■ out of ■.

3. The chance of picking a blue cube is ■ out of ■.

4. The chance of picking a green cube is ■ out of ■.

Review STATISTICS AND PROBABILITY in preparation for learning a new skill.

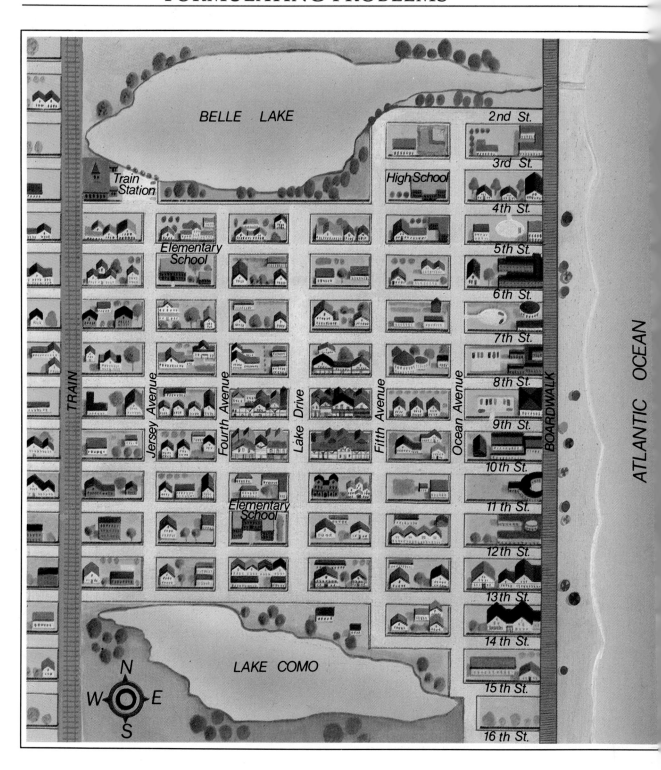

30

Probability

DATA

Town	Belle Lake
Location	On the the coast of the Atlantic Ocean
Area	4 square miles
Population	12,000 winter 30,000 summer
Length of beach	2.5 miles
Length of boardwalk	2 miles
Schools	1 high school 2 elementary schools
Hospital	3 miles north of town
Hotels and small inns	15
Shopping center	1
Lakes	Belle Lake Lake Como

Belle Lake is a resort town on the coast of the Atlantic Ocean. It's a good town for a resort because it has two lakes and a long stretch of ocean beach. Many people vacation in Belle Lake during the warm summer months. The population grows and business booms during the busy season.

The town of Belle Lake is well-planned. The streets are numbered and lettered. The houses are numbered to follow the streets. There are many hotels and restaurants along the ocean front.

Look at the data. How many people live in the town all year round? What problems would these people have in the summer? What problems would the people who come for a vacation have to solve? Would the picture map help them?

PROBABILITY
Learning Terms

At a school fair, Juan played a game with a spinner. He saw that there were four sections, each with a different number. There were four different places the arrow could land when spun. These were the **possible outcomes.** Juan wanted the arrow to land on the number 2. There was only one **favorable outcome** for Juan. Juan's chance of winning was 1 out of 4.

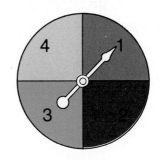

Number of sections?   4
Number with 2?   1
Chance of spinning a 2?
    1 out of 4

Celia played the same game. She wanted to spin and get an odd number. There were two favorable outcomes for Celia, the 1 or the 3. Celia's chances of winning were 2 out of 4.

Number of sections?   4
Number with odd numbers?   2
Chance of spinning an odd number?
    2 out of 4

GUIDED PRACTICE

1.

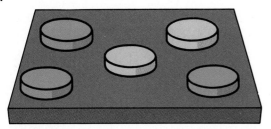

Number of discs?   5
Number of green discs?   3
Chances of picking a green disc?
3 out of ■

2.

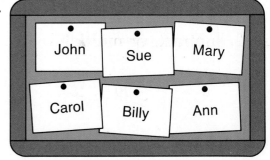

Number of names?   ■
Number of boys' names?   ■
Chances of picking a boy's name?
■ out of ■

FOCUS   Learn the vocabulary of probability. Use PROBABILITY to predict outcomes.

PRACTICE

Look at each picture. Then answer each question
for exercises 3–6.

- What are the total possible outcomes?
- What are the favorable outcomes?
- What is the chance of choosing a favorable outcome?

3.

Chance of landing on RED?

4.

Chance of picking a black marble?

5.

Chance of choosing an English or spelling book?

6.

Chance of choosing a striped sock or a green sock?

MIXED PRACTICE
Maintaining and Reviewing Skills

Add, subtract, or multiply.

7. $\frac{5}{8} + \frac{1}{8}$ **8.** $\frac{7}{10} - \frac{2}{10}$ **9.** 8×5 **10.** $486 - 317$ **11.** $167 + 248$

CHALLENGE

12. Lori played a spinner game with her brother Sam. Sam chose the color BLUE and Lori chose the color RED. Who had a better chance to win? Why?

EXTRA PRACTICE—page 424

PROBABILITY

Representing Probability With Fractions

When we spin the arrow we can show the chance of getting any of the numbers as a fraction.

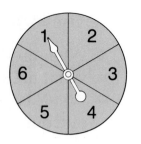

- The chance of getting a 5 is 1 out of 6 or $\frac{1}{6}$.
- The chances of getting an even number are 3 out of 6 or $\frac{3}{6}$.

PRACTICE

Write a fraction to show the probability for each event. Each pick is made without looking.

1. Picking a red marble

2. Spinning an odd number

3. Picking a Ⓖ

4.  Spinning a green

5. Picking a blue disc

6. Picking a vowel

MIXED PRACTICE

Maintaining and Reviewing Skills

Add, subtract, multiply, or divide.

7. $3\overline{)27}$ 8. 5×10 9. $18 - 12$ 10. $32 + 15$ 11. $28 \div 4$

FOCUS   Use fractions to represent probability.

Problem Solving: Using Guess and Test

To record how many times something happens, you can use a **tally chart**.

Make 1 tally mark for each time something happens. The fifth tally crosses the first four. Here is how to show something happening 6 times:

Use tally marks to record the results of each experiment.

12. Make a spinner with a circle of cardboard, a fastener, and a half-opened paper clip. Fill in the colors as in the picture.

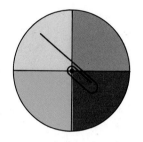

If you spin the spinner 20 times, what color should come up most often?

Spin the spinner 20 times. Copy this chart and use it to record the color of each spin. What color did you get most often?

Red	Green	Yellow	Blue

13. If you roll a number cube (numbers 1 to 6) 20 times will you get more odd numbers than even numbers? Roll the cube 20 times. Copy this chart and record your results. Did you roll more odd numbers or more even numbers?

Odd number	
Even number	

14. Copy this chart to record your results. Get a bag with 3 red, 2 blue, and 1 white marble. Choose a marble without looking. Record its color. Put it back. Do this 30 times. What color did you get most often?

Red	
Blue	
White	

Use Guess and Test and apply the Five-Step PROBLEM SOLVING Plan.

PROBABILITY
Predicting Outcomes

One day Jamie did this experiment. He tossed a coin 50 times. He recorded the results on a tally chart. He noticed that the outcome for heads was almost the same as the outcome for tails. The more he tossed, the closer he came to getting heads half the time and tails the other half.

Heads	Tails
𝓣𝓗𝓛	𝓣𝓗𝓛
𝓣𝓗𝓛	𝓣𝓗𝓛
𝓣𝓗𝓛	𝓣𝓗𝓛
𝓣𝓗𝓛	𝓣𝓗𝓛
///	𝓣𝓗𝓛
	//
23	27

GUIDED PRACTICE

Imagine doing each of these experiments. Predict what the results will be.

1. Spin 20 times.

Which color will come up most often? Why?

2. Pick a letter 20 times.

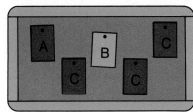

Which letter will come up most often? Why?

3. Roll the cube 50 times.

Number cube with numbers 1 to 6.

Which number will come up most often? Why?

4. Spin 20 times.

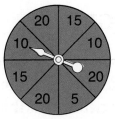

Which number will come up most often? Why?

FOCUS Use PROBABILITY to predict outcomes.

PRACTICE

Predict the outcome of each experiment if it is repeated 100 times. There may be more than one correct answer.

5. Pick a marble

most: ■ least: ■

6. Spin a number

most: ■ least: ■

7. Pick a name

most: ■ least: ■

8. Pick a letter

most: ■ least: ■

9. Pick a slip

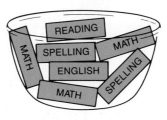

most: ■ least: ■

10. Roll a letter

Letter cube with letters A, E, I, O, U, A

most: ■ least: ■

MIXED PRACTICE
Maintaining and Reviewing Skills

Add, subtract, multiply, or divide.

11. $387 + 462$ **12.** $592 - 137$ **13.** 6×4 **14.** $5\overline{)40}$ **15.** $29 - 15$

CHALLENGE

16. Make a list of all the letters of the alphabet from A to Z. Draw a tally mark next to a letter each time it appears on this page. Which 5 letters appear most often? Which 5 letters appear least often?

PROBABILITY
Combinations

Keith, Lenny, Wally, and Danny want to ride the roller coaster. They see that each car on the ride holds two people. The boys figured out all the different ways that two of them can be seated in one car.

KEITH and LENNY   LENNY and WALLY

KEITH and WALLY   LENNY and DANNY

KEITH and DANNY   WALLY and DANNY

There are six different ways the boys can pair up.

Remember: the combination of KEITH and LENNY is the same as LENNY and KEITH.

PRACTICE

1. Jana has a red sweater, a yellow sweater, and a green sweater. She has a pair of jeans and a blue skirt. List the outfits Jana can make using one sweater and either the jeans or the skirt.

2. Joe's Deli makes sandwiches using two different kinds of cold cuts. List the different sandwich combinations they can make using bologna, ham, cheese, salami, and turkey.

MIXED PRACTICE
Maintaining and Reviewing Skills

Add, subtract, multiply, or divide.

3. 18×4 4. $372 + 498$ 5. $807 - 39$ 6. $7\overline{)68}$ 7. 59×8

FOCUS Use PROBABILITY to make combinations.

APPLICATION
Using Statistics and Probability

Paulo made this **tree diagram** to show all the different combinations of pizzas that you can get with one topping.

Pizza	Toppings
small large	cheese green peppers mushrooms

COMBINATIONS OF SIZES AND TOPPINGS

Combinations

small cheese
small green peppers
small mushrooms
large cheese
large green peppers
large mushrooms

Tree Diagrams

small ⟨ cheese / green peppers / mushrooms

large ⟨ cheese / green peppers / mushrooms

He can make 6 different pizzas.

Draw a tree diagram to show the combinations for the problems below. Do not combine two like things.

8. combinations of hats and ties

9. combinations of shirts and pants

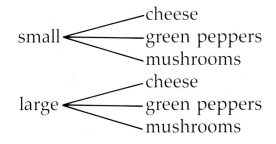

10. combinations of vegetable and flower seeds

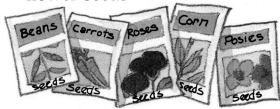

11. combinations of boys' names and girls' names

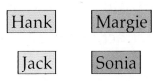

Hank   Margie

Jack   Sonia

Use STATISTICS AND PROBABILITY to show combinations.

Pitch

The musical instrument on the next page is a banjo. Each banjo string has a tuning peg. By turning the peg, the sound of the string can be made higher or lower.

A whistle makes a high sound. A big drum makes a low sound. A siren makes a sound that goes up high and down low. Sound has a changing **pitch.** A tune has sounds of different pitches.

Sound is caused by a back and forth motion called a vibration. The faster the vibration, the higher the pitch. Strings, columns of air, and bars of wood or metal can be made to vibrate and make sounds of different pitches. Here is how.

Sound is made on a banjo by strumming its strings. A short string sounds higher than a long string. A tight string sounds higher than a loose string. A lightweight string sounds higher than a heavy string.

Sound is made on a recorder by blowing air into it. A short column of air sounds higher than a long column of air.

Sound is made on a xylophone by striking bars of hardwood or metal. A short bar sounds higher than a long bar.

Smaller, lighter objects vibrate faster than larger, heavier objects, and have a higher pitch.

CRITICAL THINKING

1. How does a banjo player make a string sound higher?

2. On a xylophone which bar should be struck to make a high sound? A low sound?

3. The holes of a recorder are covered by the fingertips to change the pitch. Is the pitch higher or lower with all the holes covered?

FOCUS | Use LOGIC to understand musical pitch.

Henry Tanner, an American artist, painted *The Banjo Lesson*.

LOOKING BACK
Reviewing and Testing Chapter 30

In Chapter 30 you formulated problems about a resort town. Look at pages 400 and 401.

1. Write a sentence telling how weather affects a beach resort town.

You learned something new about probability. To review what you learned, study the sample problem on page 402. Then use the new skill to complete the probability chart.

2.

	Total Possible Outcomes	Favorable Outcomes	Chance of Choosing a Favorable Outcome

Chance of landing on an even number

You learned something new about predicting outcomes. To review, look at pages 406 and 407. Then use the new skill to predict the outcome of each experiment if it is repeated 100 times for examples 3 to 5.

3. **Spin a Number**

 most
least

4. **Spin a Color**

 most
least

5. **Pick a Marble**

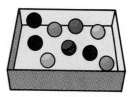 most
least

You learned about the way instruments make sounds. Look at page 410 to review the pitch of an instrument.

6. Write a sentence to tell why a lighter instrument has a higher pitch than a heavier instrument.

FOCUS | Review and test skills learned and practiced.

LOOKING AHEAD
Preparing for Next Year

This year you focused on

- **NUMBER SKILLS**
- **GEOMETRY**
- **ALGEBRA**
- **LOGIC**

- **MEASUREMENT**
- **PATTERNS AND FUNCTIONS**
- **STATISTICS AND PROBABILITY**

It will be easier for you to get a good start next year if you keep your math skills sharp while you are not at school. Here are some things to do on your vacation to stay mathematically powerful.

NUMBER SKILLS
Estimate the number of red cars that pass your house every hour. First count the number of red cars that go by in 5 minutes. Then multiply this number by 12. What other things can you estimate?

ALGEBRA
Open the refrigerator and get out a carton of eggs. Use this formula to find the missing number of eggs:
12 − eggs you see = eggs used

MEASUREMENT
Have a friend check these lengths. Are they the same?

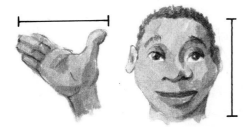

GEOMETRY
Find a partner and play the "I Spy Geometry" game. Look around wherever you are and find a shape. Then say, "I spy with my little eye, a ___." Fill in the blank with the shape you see. Then give your partner 10 guesses to find the exact location of your shape. Take turns.

PATTERNS AND FUNCTIONS
Mark a starting line. Take steps using the code below. Then mark where you stop.

1 = hop one step
2 = jump one step
3 = walk one step

Try these patterns:
1, 1, 2, 2, 3, 3
1, 2, 3, 1, 2, 3

Did you go the same distance both times?

Prepare for next year.

QUARTERLY REVIEW/TEST

Write the letter of the correct answer.

Which decimal names the shaded part?

1.

    A. 0.7   **B.** 0.5   **C.** 0.3   **D.** 0.1

2.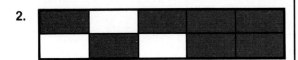

    E. 7.0   **F.** 0.3   **G.** 0.9   **H.** 0.7

3.

    A. 0.6   **B.** 1.4   **C.** 1.6   **D.** 2.4

4.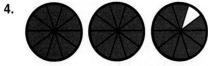

    E. 3.0   **F.** 2.1   **G.** 0.9   **H.** 2.9

Add.

5.   0.3
  +0.6   **A.** 0.3   **B.** 9
              C. 0.9   **D.** 0.6

6.   2.2
  +1.5   **E.** 1.7   **F.** 3.7
              G. 37   **H.** 0.7

7.   4.9
  +3.8   **A.** 7.7   **B.** 87
              C. 8.7   **D.** 7.1

Subtract.

8.   0.7
  −0.5   **E.** 12   **F.** 0.2
              G. 1.2   **H.** 2

9.   8.6
  −0.7   **A.** 8.1   **B.** 8.9
              C. 7.9   **D.** 89

10.   9.0
   −4.3   **E.** 53   **F.** 4.3
              G. 5.7   **H.** 4.7

11. Which is a line segment?

Name each polygon.

12.

    E. pentagon
    F. octagon
    G. hexagon
    H. polygon

13.

    A. square
    B. pentagon
    C. hexagon
    D. octagon

FOCUS   Review concepts and skills taught in Chapters 23 to 30.

Multiply.

14. $\begin{array}{r} 10 \\ \times\ 5 \end{array}$ E. 5   F. 50
                                 G. 500   H. 5,000

15. $\begin{array}{r} 300 \\ \times\ 2 \end{array}$ A. 6   B. 60
                                 C. 600   D. 6,000

16. $\begin{array}{r} 13 \\ \times\ 3 \end{array}$ E. 39   F. 16
                                 G. 19   H. 93

17. $\begin{array}{r} 231 \\ \times\ 2 \end{array}$ A. 492   B. 462
                                 C. 264   D. 262

18. $\begin{array}{r} 28 \\ \times\ 4 \end{array}$ E. 82   F. 96
                                 G. 116   H. 112

19. $\begin{array}{r} 126 \\ \times\ 5 \end{array}$ A. 530   B. 630
                                 C. 500   D. 600

Divide.

20. $6\overline{)38}$ E. 6 R2   F. 6
                         G. 8 R3   H. 7 R2

21. $9\overline{)49}$ A. 4 R9   B. 6 R3
                         C. 5 R4   D. 5

22. $7\overline{)82}$ E. 9 R7   F. 11 R5
                         G. 10 R2   H. 12

23. $5\overline{)95}$ A. 19   B. 19 R2
                         C. 21   D. 18 R5

24. $3\overline{)76}$ E. 28   F. 23
                         G. 25 R1   H. 25 R2

What is the correct unit of measure?

25. the weight of a bathtub
    A. lb   B. gal   C. oz   D. pt

26. the water in a pool
    E. gal   F. c   G. pt   H. qt

27. the length of a carrot
    A. oz   B. in.   C. qt   D. ft

What is the temperature?

28.   E. 16°F
                             F. 24°F
                             G. 15°F
                             H. 25°F

What is the chance of spinning red?

29. 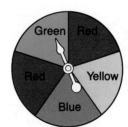   A. $\frac{5}{5}$
                             B. $\frac{2}{5}$
                             C. $\frac{1}{5}$
                             D. $\frac{3}{5}$

Which outcome is the most favorable?

30. 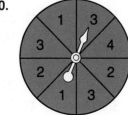   E. 1
                             F. 2
                             G. 3
                             H. 4

FINAL REVIEW/TEST

Write the letter of the correct answer.

Add or subtract.

1. $\begin{array}{r} 59 \\ +35 \\ \hline \end{array}$ A. 24   B. 84   C. 94   D. 76

2. $\begin{array}{r} 321 \\ +442 \\ \hline \end{array}$ E. 121   F. 663   G. 753   H. 763

3. $\begin{array}{r} 692 \\ +\ 35 \\ \hline \end{array}$ A. 627   B. 727   C. 557   D. 687

4. $\begin{array}{r} 1,528 \\ +2,151 \\ \hline \end{array}$ E. 5,493   F. 3,579   G. 3,679   H. 623

5. $\begin{array}{r} 2,746 \\ +\ \ 429 \\ \hline \end{array}$ A. 3,175   B. 3,157   C. 2,156   D. 2,165

6. $\begin{array}{r} 86 \\ -59 \\ \hline \end{array}$ E. 27   F. 33   G. 145   H. 37

7. $\begin{array}{r} 452 \\ -231 \\ \hline \end{array}$ A. 221   B. 123   C. 683   D. 231

8. $\begin{array}{r} 430 \\ -\ 51 \\ \hline \end{array}$ E. 397   F. 481   G. 389   H. 379

9. $\begin{array}{r} 5,297 \\ -1,165 \\ \hline \end{array}$ A. 6,461   B. 4,142   C. 4,132   D. 3,132

10. $\begin{array}{r} 9,700 \\ -6,245 \\ \hline \end{array}$ E. 15,945   F. 3,455   G. 3,545   H. 945

Multiply or divide.

11. $\begin{array}{r} 4 \\ \times 8 \\ \hline \end{array}$ A. 24   B. 32   C. 12   D. 72

12. $\begin{array}{r} 31 \\ \times\ 7 \\ \hline \end{array}$ E. 217   F. 38   G. 147   H. 271

13. $\begin{array}{r} 432 \\ \times\ \ 2 \\ \hline \end{array}$ A. 684   B. 764   C. 434   D. 864

14. $\begin{array}{r} 79 \\ \times\ 6 \\ \hline \end{array}$ E. 487   F. 85   G. 474   H. 73

15. $\begin{array}{r} 298 \\ \times\ \ 5 \\ \hline \end{array}$ A. 293   B. 1,490   C. 1,480   D. 303

16. $6\overline{)54}$ E. 8   F. 9   G. 12   H. 6

17. $8\overline{)65}$ A. 8 R1   B. 8   C. 8 R2   D. 7 R1

18. $7\overline{)86}$ E. 12 R2   F. 13   G. 21 R2   H. 1 R6

Solve the problem.

19. Al has 146 marbles. He buys 215 more marbles. How many marbles does Al have now?
    A. 61 marbles   B. 69 marbles   C. 351 marbles   D. 361 marbles

FOCUS   Review concepts and skills taught in Chapters 2 to 30.

How much of the shape is shaded?

20.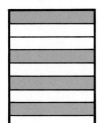
E. $\frac{4}{9}$

F. $\frac{5}{9}$

G. $\frac{9}{4}$

H. $\frac{6}{9}$

What is the equivalent fraction?

21. $\frac{1}{4}$
A. $\frac{2}{8}$
B. $\frac{2}{4}$

C. $\frac{4}{4}$
D. $\frac{3}{6}$

Add or subtract.

22. $\frac{4}{8} + \frac{2}{8}$
E. $\frac{6}{16}$
F. $\frac{6}{8}$

G. $\frac{2}{8}$
H. $\frac{1}{16}$

23. $\frac{9}{10} - \frac{6}{10}$
A. $\frac{15}{20}$
B. $\frac{3}{10}$

C. $\frac{3}{20}$
D. $\frac{15}{10}$

Which decimal names the shaded part?

24.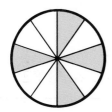

E. 0.4   F. 0.3   G. 0.6   H. 0.5

25.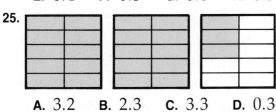

A. 3.2   B. 2.3   C. 3.3   D. 0.3

Add or subtract.

26.
$$\begin{array}{r} 4.1 \\ +0.5 \end{array}$$
E. 4.6   F. 46
G. 4.7   H. 4.4

27.
$$\begin{array}{r} 0.6 \\ -0.4 \end{array}$$
A. 0.2   B. 2
C. 0.6   D. 1.6

28.
$$\begin{array}{r} 3.6 \\ +2.7 \end{array}$$
E. 1.1   F. 7.2
G. 6.3   H. 0.3

29.
$$\begin{array}{r} 4.5 \\ -1.9 \end{array}$$
A. 2.4   B. 6.4
C. 5.4   D. 2.6

How many faces does the solid figure have?

30.
E. 5
F. 6
G. 8
H. 4

Name the figure.

31.
A. polygon
B. pentagon
C. hexagon
D. octagon

Solve the problem.

32. Amanda ate $\frac{1}{8}$ of a pizza on Monday and ate $\frac{2}{8}$ of the pizza on Tuesday. What part of the pizza did Amanda eat?

E. $\frac{3}{16}$ F. $\frac{1}{8}$ G. $\frac{3}{4}$ H. $\frac{3}{8}$

EXTRA PRACTICE

Chapter 2 (page 16) Add or subtract.

1.	2.	3.	4.	5.	6.	7.
3 +3	6 +2	5 +4	7 +8	9 +6	8 +9	4 +7

8.	9.	10.	11.	12.	13.	14.
9 −7	10 − 8	8 −4	16 − 8	17 − 9	14 − 7	12 − 5

Chapter 3 (page 30) Write the place value of the underlined digit.

1. 5̲43   2. 7̲4̲2   3. 2̲91   4. 56̲7   5. 8̲2̲6   6. 48̲2̲   7. 3̲39

8. 76̲6̲   9. 9̲45   10. 51̲8̲   11. 30̲5̲   12. 2̲72   13. 71̲6̲   14. 6̲06

Chapter 4 (page 48) Add.

1.	2.	3.	4.	5.	6.	7.
82 +17	47 +30	66 +19	94 +82	31 +19	79 +63	58 +95

8.	9.	10.	11.	12.	13.	14.
516 +143	482 +317	721 +129	666 +258	540 + 97	285 + 8	839 + 65

15. 342 + 250   16. 18 + 81   17. 208 + 475   18. 96 + 36   19. 656 + 98

Chapter 5 (page 64) Subtract.

1.	2.	3.	4.	5.	6.	7.
98 −17	66 −33	84 −65	50 −27	35 − 8	72 −64	40 − 9

8.	9.	10.	11.	12.	13.	14.
674 −342	807 −213	538 −229	960 −855	200 − 67	408 −218	711 −548

15. 673 − 253   16. 84 − 79   17. 375 − 289   18. 700 − 196   19. 84 − 28

EXTRA PRACTICE

Chapter 6 (page 72) Write *centimeter* or *meter* to measure each length.

1. shoe   2. door   3. pencil   4. paper clip   5. flagpole

6. ceiling   7. rug   8. eraser   9. airplane   10. calculator

Chapter 7 (page 86) Write *gram* or *kilogram* to measure each mass.

1. eagle   2. feather   3. table   4. pen   5. car

6. grape   7. pin   8. bowling ball   9. elephant   10. leaf

Chapter 8 (page 100) Write the name of each figure.

1. 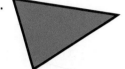   2.   3.   4.

5.   6.   7.    8.

Chapter 9 (page 120) Multiply.

1. $\begin{array}{r}3\\ \times 7\\ \hline\end{array}$	2. $\begin{array}{r}2\\ \times 4\\ \hline\end{array}$	3. $\begin{array}{r}9\\ \times 2\\ \hline\end{array}$	4. $\begin{array}{r}3\\ \times 8\\ \hline\end{array}$	5. $\begin{array}{r}2\\ \times 6\\ \hline\end{array}$	6. $\begin{array}{r}4\\ \times 3\\ \hline\end{array}$	7. $\begin{array}{r}3\\ \times 6\\ \hline\end{array}$
8. $\begin{array}{r}2\\ \times 2\\ \hline\end{array}$	9. $\begin{array}{r}8\\ \times 3\\ \hline\end{array}$	10. $\begin{array}{r}2\\ \times 5\\ \hline\end{array}$	11. $\begin{array}{r}3\\ \times 2\\ \hline\end{array}$	12. $\begin{array}{r}7\\ \times 2\\ \hline\end{array}$	13. $\begin{array}{r}3\\ \times 5\\ \hline\end{array}$	14. $\begin{array}{r}2\\ \times 3\\ \hline\end{array}$
15. $\begin{array}{r}8\\ \times 2\\ \hline\end{array}$	16. $\begin{array}{r}6\\ \times 2\\ \hline\end{array}$	17. $\begin{array}{r}9\\ \times 3\\ \hline\end{array}$	18. $\begin{array}{r}3\\ \times 3\\ \hline\end{array}$	19. $\begin{array}{r}2\\ \times 7\\ \hline\end{array}$	20. $\begin{array}{r}2\\ \times 9\\ \hline\end{array}$	21. $\begin{array}{r}7\\ \times 3\\ \hline\end{array}$

22. 9×2 23. 5×3 24. 7×3 25. 9×3 26. 8×2

EXTRA PRACTICE

Chapter 10 (page 132) Multiply.

| 1. | 4
×5 | 2. | 5
×4 | 3. | 7
×5 | 4. | 4
×3 | 5. | 5
×9 | 6. | 5
×5 | 7. | 8
×4 |

| 8. | 6
×4 | 9. | 4
×4 | 10. | 5
×2 | 11. | 9
×4 | 12. | 4
×7 | 13. | 6
×5 | 14. | 5
×3 |

| 15. | 7
×4 | 16. | 5
×8 | 17. | 4
×9 | 18. | 8
×5 | 19. | 5
×6 | 20. | 3
×4 | 21. | 9
×5 |

22. 2×4 **23.** 8×5 **24.** 6×4 **25.** 5×4 **26.** 9×5

Chapter 11 (page 146) Divide.

1. $14 \div 2$ 2. $12 \div 3$ 3. $6 \div 3$ 4. $8 \div 2$ 5. $9 \div 3$

6. $3\overline{)15}$ 7. $2\overline{)16}$ 8. $3\overline{)3}$ 9. $2\overline{)6}$ 10. $2\overline{)12}$ 11. $3\overline{)21}$ 12. $2\overline{)10}$

13. $3\overline{)27}$ 14. $2\overline{)4}$ 15. $3\overline{)18}$ 16. $3\overline{)12}$ 17. $2\overline{)2}$ 18. $2\overline{)18}$ 19. $3\overline{)24}$

Chapter 12 (page 158) Divide.

1. $20 \div 5$ 2. $16 \div 4$ 3. $12 \div 4$ 4. $25 \div 5$ 5. $8 \div 4$

6. $4\overline{)24}$ 7. $4\overline{)32}$ 8. $5\overline{)10}$ 9. $4\overline{)20}$ 10. $5\overline{)30}$ 11. $5\overline{)40}$ 12. $4\overline{)28}$

13. $4\overline{)36}$ 14. $5\overline{)45}$ 15. $5\overline{)15}$ 16. $4\overline{)4}$ 17. $4\overline{)32}$ 18. $5\overline{)5}$ 19. $5\overline{)35}$

Chapter 13 (page 168) Copy and complete.

1. ■ × 2 = 12
   12 ÷ 2 = ■

2. ■ × 4 = 28
   28 ÷ 4 = ■

3. ■ × 3 = 27
   27 ÷ 3 = ■

4. ■ × 5 = 40
   40 ÷ 5 = ■

5. ■ × 3 = 18
   18 ÷ 3 = ■

6. ■ × 2 = 16
   16 ÷ 2 = ■

7. ■ × 5 = 30
   30 ÷ 5 = ■

8. ■ × 4 = 24
   24 ÷ 4 = ■

9. ■ × 5 = 35
   35 ÷ 5 = ■

10. ■ × 3 = 24
    24 ÷ 3 = ■

11. ■ × 4 = 32
    32 ÷ 4 = ■

12. ■ × 2 = 18
    18 ÷ 2 = ■

EXTRA PRACTICE

Chapter 14 (page 182) Write the time in two ways.

1.
2.
3.
4.

Chapter 15 (page 202) Multiply.

1. 6
   ×0
2. 3
   ×7
3. 7
   ×8
4. 6
   ×6
5. 6
   ×5
6. 7
   ×1
7. 8
   ×6

8. 9
   ×7
9. 6
   ×7
10. 6
    ×1
11. 4
    ×7
12. 7
    ×0
13. 6
    ×9
14. 7
    ×7

Chapter 16 (page 214) Divide.

1. 6) 12
2. 6) 24
3. 7) 28
4. 7) 7
5. 7) 14
6. 6) 42
7. 6) 18

8. 7) 63
9. 6) 6
10. 6) 48
11. 7) 49
12. 6) 36
13. 6) 54
14. 7) 56

Chapter 17 (page 230) Multiply.

1. 1
   ×8
2. 9
   ×8
3. 4
   ×9
4. 8
   ×0
5. 9
   ×3
6. 5
   ×8
7. 8
   ×8

8. 9
   ×0
9. 4
   ×9
10. 8
    ×6
11. 9
    ×9
12. 7
    ×8
13. 8
    ×9
14. 9
    ×7

Chapter 18 (page 242) Divide.

1. 9) 45
2. 8) 32
3. 8) 56
4. 9) 63
5. 8) 24
6. 9) 72
7. 9) 36

8. 8) 48
9. 9) 81
10. 8) 64
11. 9) 36
12. 8) 72
13. 9) 27
14. 8) 40

EXTRA PRACTICE

Chapter 19 (page 252) Write the number.

1. 8 thousands 4 hundreds 2 tens 5 ones

2. 2 thousands 0 hundreds 3 tens 0 ones

3. 6 thousands 6 hundreds 6 tens 6 ones

4. 1 thousand 2 hundreds 0 tens 4 ones

5. 4 thousands 8 hundreds 1 ten 2 ones

Chapter 20 (page 268) Add or subtract.

1.	3,242 +1,746	2.	6,677 −3,462	3.	7,240 + 658	4.	2,380 −2,265	5.	5,642 +2,159
6.	9,605 −3,294	7.	4,444 +3,962	8.	1,000 − 342	9.	8,471 + 980	10.	6,329 −5,839

11. $5,421 + 4,389$ 12. $7,050 - 349$ 13. $2,960 + 878$ 14. $9,782 - 998$

Chapter 21 (page 284) Copy and complete the equivalent fractions.

1. $\frac{1}{3} = \frac{\blacksquare}{9}$ 2. $\frac{2}{4} = \frac{\blacksquare}{8}$ 3. $\frac{3}{4} = \frac{\blacksquare}{12}$ 4. $\frac{2}{3} = \frac{\blacksquare}{6}$ 5. $\frac{1}{2} = \frac{\blacksquare}{10}$

6. $\frac{1}{8} = \frac{2}{\blacksquare}$ 7. $\frac{1}{\blacksquare} = \frac{2}{14}$ 8. $\frac{1}{4} = \frac{2}{\blacksquare}$ 9. $\frac{1}{6} = \frac{2}{\blacksquare}$ 10. $\frac{1}{2} = \frac{\blacksquare}{6}$

Chapter 22 (page 296) Add or subtract.

1. $\frac{4}{6} + \frac{1}{6}$ 2. $\frac{3}{3} - \frac{1}{3}$ 3. $\frac{4}{7} + \frac{2}{7}$ 4. $\frac{6}{10} - \frac{4}{10}$ 5. $\frac{8}{9} - \frac{2}{9}$

6. $\frac{2}{8} - \frac{1}{8}$ 7. $\frac{6}{11} - \frac{2}{11}$ 8. $\frac{6}{9} + \frac{2}{9}$ 9. $\frac{7}{12} + \frac{5}{12}$ 10. $\frac{3}{4} - \frac{1}{4}$

11. $\frac{6}{10} + \frac{3}{10}$ 12. $\frac{3}{5} - \frac{2}{5}$ 13. $\frac{10}{12} - \frac{7}{12}$ 14. $\frac{4}{11} + \frac{6}{11}$ 15. $\frac{5}{8} + \frac{2}{8}$

EXTRA PRACTICE

Chapter 23 (page 314) Write a decimal for the shaded part.

1.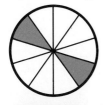
2.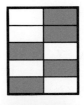
3.

4.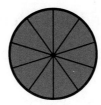
5.

Chapter 24 (page 326) Add or subtract.

1. 3.6 +2.3	**2.** 7.3 −2.1	**3.** 4.6 −2.7	**4.** 1.8 +3.9	**5.** 6.7 +3.1	**6.** 9.8 −2.8
7. 5.2 −3.9	**8.** 6.4 −2.8	**9.** 3.9 +4.9	**10.** 5.1 +4.8	**11.** 1.6 +1.6	**12.** 8.7 −5.8

13. 4.6 + 3.2   **14.** 9.9 − 5.5   **15.** 6.2 − 3.3   **16.** 2.7 + 2.9   **17.** 1.4 − 0.5

Chapter 25 (page 340) Write the name of each polygon.

1.
2.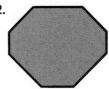
3.
4.

Chapter 26 (page 352) Multiply.

1. 43 × 2	**2.** 36 × 1	**3.** 27 × 8	**4.** 38 × 4	**5.** 93 × 2	**6.** 80 × 5
7. 333 × 3	**8.** 417 × 4	**9.** 173 × 2	**10.** 212 × 5	**11.** 326 × 4	**12.** 437 × 3

EXTRA PRACTICE

Chapter 27 (page 368) Divide.

1. $2\overline{)9}$ 2. $5\overline{)17}$ 3. $9\overline{)29}$ 4. $3\overline{)19}$ 5. $4\overline{)21}$ 6. $8\overline{)25}$ 7. $6\overline{)37}$

8. $4\overline{)38}$ 9. $7\overline{)53}$ 10. $3\overline{)16}$ 11. $8\overline{)54}$ 12. $5\overline{)34}$ 13. $9\overline{)76}$ 14. $7\overline{)59}$

15. $6\overline{)75}$ 16. $7\overline{)77}$ 17. $8\overline{)89}$ 18. $3\overline{)90}$ 19. $2\overline{)62}$ 20. $4\overline{)86}$ 21. $5\overline{)75}$

22. $2\overline{)38}$ 23. $5\overline{)63}$ 24. $3\overline{)74}$ 25. $9\overline{)93}$ 26. $6\overline{)85}$ 27. $8\overline{)96}$ 28. $2\overline{)93}$

Chapter 28 (page 376) Write *inch*, *foot*, or *yard* to measure length.

1. record   2. shoe   3. briefcase   4. ceiling   5. bus

6. eraser   7. truck   8. belt   9. tree   10. bed

Chapter 29 (page 394) Copy and complete.

1. 1 gallon = ■ quarts   2. 1 gallon = ■ pints

3. 1 quart = ■ pints   4. 1 pint = ■ cups

5. 2 gallons = ■ pints   6. 2 quarts = ■ cups

7. 1 pound = ■ ounces   8. 3 pounds = ■ ounces

Chapter 30 (page 402) Copy and complete the probability chart.

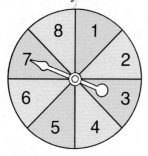

Total Possible Outcomes	Favorable Outcomes	Chance of Choosing a Favorable Outcome
1.	2.	3.

Chance of landing on an odd number.

DATA BANK

Five-Step Problem Solving Plan

1. READ	Do I know the meaning of each word?
2. KNOW	What am I being asked to find? Which **key facts** do I need to answer the question?
3. PLAN	Which operation should I use? Which strategy should I use?
4. SOLVE	Carry out the plan. Can I write a number sentence? What is my answer?
5. CHECK	Why is my answer reasonable? Does it answer the question?

Table of Geometric Shapes

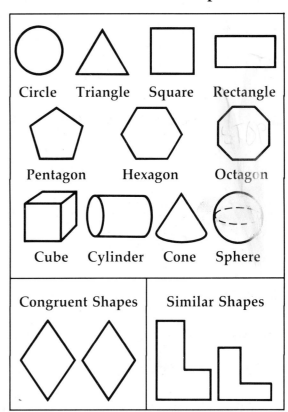

Circle   Triangle   Square   Rectangle

Pentagon   Hexagon   Octagon

Cube   Cylinder   Cone   Sphere

Congruent Shapes   Similar Shapes

Addition/Subtraction Table

	0	1	2	3	4	5	6	7	8	9
0	0	1	2	3	4	5	6	7	8	9
1	1	2	3	4	5	6	7	8	9	10
2	2	3	4	5	6	7	8	9	10	11
3	3	4	5	6	7	8	9	10	11	12
4	4	5	6	7	8	9	10	11	12	13
5	5	6	7	8	9	10	11	12	13	14
6	6	7	8	9	10	11	12	13	14	15
7	7	8	9	10	11	12	13	14	15	16
8	8	9	10	11	12	13	14	15	16	17
9	9	10	11	12	13	14	15	16	17	18

Multiplication/Division Table

	0	1	2	3	4	5	6	7	8	9
0	0	0	0	0	0	0	0	0	0	0
1	0	1	2	3	4	5	6	7	8	9
2	0	2	4	6	8	10	12	14	16	18
3	0	3	6	9	12	15	18	21	24	27
4	0	4	8	12	16	20	24	28	32	36
5	0	5	10	15	20	25	30	35	40	45
6	0	6	12	18	24	30	36	42	48	54
7	0	7	14	21	28	35	42	49	56	63
8	0	8	16	24	32	40	48	56	64	72
9	0	9	18	27	36	45	54	63	72	81

Table of Metric Measures

Length

1 centimeter (cm) = 10 millimeters (mm)

1 decimeter (dm) = { 100 millimeters
10 centimeters

1 meter (m) = { 1 000 millimeters*
100 centimeters
10 decimeters

1 kilometer (km) = 1 000 meters

Area

1 square centimeter = 100 square millimeters

Volume

1 cubic centimeter = { 1 000 cubic millimeters
1 milliliter

Capacity

1 liter (L) = { 1 000 milliters (mL)
1 000 cubic centimeters

Mass

1 gram (g) = 1 000 milligrams (mg)
1 kilogram (kg) = 1 000 grams
1 metric ton (t) = 1 000 kilograms

Temperature

Water freezes at 0 degrees Celsius (0°C).
Water boils at 100 degrees Celsius (100°C).

* According to the United States Metric Association,
spaces are used instead of commas in metric measurements.

DATA BANK

Table of Customary Measures

Length

1 foot (ft) = 12 inches (in.)

1 yard (yd) = $\begin{cases} 3 \text{ feet} \\ 36 \text{ inches} \end{cases}$

1 mile (mi) = $\begin{cases} 1{,}760 \text{ yards} \\ 5{,}280 \text{ feet} \end{cases}$

Area

1 square foot = 144 square inches
1 square yard = 9 square feet
1 acre = 4,840 square yards

Volume

1 cubic foot = 1,728 cubic inches
1 cubic yard = 27 cubic feet

Capacity

1 cup (c) = 8 fluid ounces (fl oz)

1 pint (pt) = $\begin{cases} 16 \text{ fluid ounces} \\ 2 \text{ cups} \end{cases}$

1 quart (qt) = $\begin{cases} 32 \text{ fluid ounces} \\ 4 \text{ cups} \\ 2 \text{ pints} \end{cases}$

1 gallon (gal) = $\begin{cases} 128 \text{ fluid ounces} \\ 16 \text{ cups} \\ 8 \text{ pints} \\ 4 \text{ quarts} \end{cases}$

Weight

1 pound (lb) = 16 ounces (oz)
1 ton (T) = 2,000 pounds

Temperature

Water freezes at 32 degrees Fahrenheit (32°F).
Water boils at 212 degrees Fahrenheit (212°F).

Table of Measure

Time
1 minute (min)	=	60 seconds (s)
1 hour (h)	=	60 minutes
1 day	=	24 hours
1 week	=	7 days
1 month is about 4 weeks		
1 year	=	{ 365 days / 52 weeks / 12 months
1 leap year	=	366 days
1 decade	=	10 years
1 century	=	100 years

Thirty days hath September,
April, June, and November,
February has twenty-eight alone,
All the rest have thirty-one;
Excepting leap year—that's the time
When February's days are twenty-nine.

Place-Value Chart

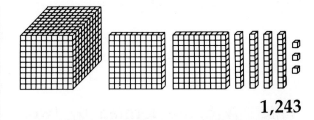

1,243

Thousands	Hundreds	Tens	Ones
1	2	4	3

one thousand two hundred forty-three

Digit	Place	Value
1	Thousands	1,000
2	Hundreds	200
4	Tens	40
3	Ones	3

Table of Symbols

+	plus		
−	minus		
×	times; multiplied by		
÷	divided by		
=	is equal to		
≠	is not equal to		
>	is greater than		
<	is less than		
( )	Parentheses mean "do this operation first."		
¢	cents		
$	dollars		
△	triangle		
□	square		
▭	rectangle		
°	degree		
∟	right angle		
s	second		
min	minute		
h	hour		
y	year		

Customary Measure

Length
in. inch
ft foot
yd yard
mi mile

Capacity
c cup
pt pint
qt quart
gal gallon

Weight
oz ounce
lb pound
T ton

Temperature
°F degree Fahrenheit

Metric Measure

Length
mm millimeter
cm centimeter
dm decimeter
m meter
km kilometer

Capacity
mL milliliter
L liter

Mass
mg milligram
g gram
kg kilogram
t ton

Temperature
°C degree Celsius

GLOSSARY

addend   Any number to be added.

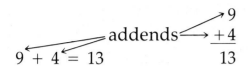

$$9 + 4 = 13$$

angle   A figure formed by two rays that have the same endpoint.

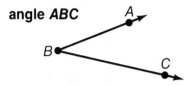

area   The number of square units inside a figure. The area of this figure is 6 square units.

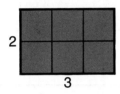

circle   A flat figure formed with all points the same distance from a center point.

command   An instruction given to a computer.

cone   A solid figure with one circular face and one vertex.

congruent figures   Figures with the same size and shape.

cube   A solid figure with six faces that are all congruent squares.

cylinder   A solid figure with two faces that are congruent circles.

decimal   A number written with a decimal point to show place value.

degree Celsius (°C)   A unit in the metric system used to measure temperature.

degree Fahrenheit (°F)   A unit in the customary system used to measure temperature.

difference   The answer to a subtraction problem.

digit   Any of the symbols 0, 1, 2, 3, 4, 5, 6, 7, 8, and 9.

disk   A device for storing computer information.

dividend   A number that is divided. In $16 \div 2$, or $2\overline{)16}$, the dividend is 16.

divisor   A number that divides the dividend. In $16 \div 2$, or $2\overline{)16}$, the divisor is 2.

edge   The line segment formed when two faces meet in a solid figure.

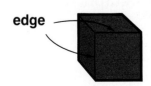

endpoint The point at the end of a segment or a ray.

equivalent fractions Fractions that name the same number or amount.

estimate To find an answer that is close to the actual answer.

even number A whole number with 0, 2, 4, 6, or 8 in the ones place.

face A flat surface of a solid figure.

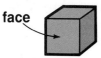
face

factor A number that is to be multiplied.

flowchart A diagram that shows the flow of steps in a process.

fraction A number that names part of a whole or group, written with a numerator and a denominator.

$$3 \leftarrow \text{numerator}$$
$$4 \leftarrow \text{denominator}$$

graph A picture used to show information. Examples are bar graph, line graph, circle graph, and picture graph.

graphics Pictures drawn by a computer.

greater than (>) A comparison of two numbers where one is larger than the other.

$7 > 5$ "7 is greater than 5"

grouping property The sum or the product of three addends or three factors is the same, no matter how they are grouped.

hardware The physical parts of a computer such as the keyboard, monitor, and cover.

keyboard A device used for typing information into a computer.

less than (<) A comparison of two numbers where one is less than the other.

$6 < 7$ "6 is less than 7"

line of symmetry A line on which a figure can be folded so that one part matches the other part exactly.

line segment Part of a line that joins two points.

line segment

monitor A computer screen.

number line A line that shows numbers in order.

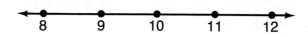

number sentence An inequality or an equation.

$$17 > 12 \qquad 4 + 3 = 7$$

odd number A whole number with 1, 3, 5, 7, or 9 in the ones place.

order property The sum or the product is the same when the order of the addends or the factors is changed.

$$5 + 7 = 7 + 5 \qquad 8 \times 3 = 3 \times 8$$

ordinal number A number used to tell order or position, such as *first*, *second*, or *third*.

perimeter The distance around a figure.

place value The value of the place of a digit in a number.

34.5
TENS ——⌐ | |
ONES ————⌐ |
TENTHS ————⌐

polygon A closed figure formed by three or more line segments.

product The answer to a multiplication problem.

program A list of instructions that tells a computer what to do.

quotient The answer to a division problem.

rectangle A polygon with four sides and four right angles.

remainder The number that is left over after a division is completed.

$$5\overline{)17} \quad \begin{array}{r} 3\,\text{R}2 \leftarrow \textbf{Remainder} \\ -15 \\ \hline 2 \end{array}$$

right angle An angle that forms a square corner.

similar figures Figures that are the same shape but not necessarily the same size.

software Information that a computer receives and uses. A computer program is software.

sphere A solid figure with all points the same distance from a center point.

square A rectangle with four congruent sides.

sum The answer to an addition problem.

triangle A three–sided figure.

volume The number of cubic units that fit inside a solid figure. The volume of this figure is 6 cubic units.

INDEX

A

Addition
associative/commutative properties of, 18
basic facts, 6, 16–19, 41, 67
basic facts table, 19, 425
calculator problems, 67, 131, 371
of decimal tenths, 322–323, 329
of dollars and cents, 51, 324
estimating sums in, 47, 51, 266, 325
of four-digit numbers, 264–267
of fractions with like denominators, 292–295
of money, 47, 51, 312–313, 324–325
of more than two addends, 18, 111, 123, 125, 131
of ounces/pounds, 392
of three-digit numbers, 6, 48–49, 261, 267
of two-digit numbers, 6, 41, 44–45, 123, 267
using a bar graph, 16–17
Algebra, 5, 11
finding missing factors in, 115, 147, 169, 241
inequalities (<, >) in, 11, 22, 32, 38, 258, 286, 310, 316–317
sign for "not equal to" (≠) in, 233
translating word problems into number sentences in, 355
Angles
classifying, 338–339
of polygons, 337–338, 340–341
right, 338–339
Applications. *See* Problem-Solving Applications.
Area, 76–79, 173, 427–428
Associative property of addition, 18

B

Associative property of multiplication, 174–175

Bar graphs, 10, 16–17, 75, 188, 382–383, 393

C

Calculator problems
in addition, 67, 131
in division, 371
identifying keys, 67
in multiplication, 131, 371
in subtraction, 67, 149
Calendar, 149, 205
Capacity, 83, 88–89, 387, 394–397, 426–427
Celsius temperatures, 186–189, 426
Centimeter, 69, 72–75, 78–79
Checking division with multiplication, 364
Circle, 8, 95, 102–103, 333
Combinations, 408–409
Commutative property of addition, 18
Commutative property of multiplication, 115–116, 174–175
Comparing and ordering decimals, 310, 316–317
four-digit numbers, 258, 259
fractions, 286
measurements, 75, 188, 382–383, 393
three-digit numbers, 11, 32
two-digit numbers, 11, 22
values of money, 38–39
Computer(s)
flowcharts, 136–137
graphics, 218–219, 330
programs, 136–137, 330
uses of, 52–53
vocabulary of, 330–331
Cone, 95, 100–102
Congruent figures, 104–105
Critical Thinking, 24, 52, 80,

Critical Thinking (*continued*)
108, 136, 162, 190, 218, 246, 272, 300, 330, 356, 384, 410
Cube, 95, 100–102
Cubic centimeter, 92–93
Cup, 387, 394–396
Customary measurement
of area, 427
of capacity, 384–387, 394–396
choosing the appropriate unit in, 373, 376–377, 387, 397
of length, 373, 376–378
table of symbols for, 428
table of units in, 427
of temperature, 380–383
of volume, 427
of weight, 387, 390–393
Cylinder, 95, 100

D

Data bank, 425–428
Decimals. *See also* Money.
adding dollars and cents, 324
adding tenths, 322–323, 329
comparing and ordering, 310, 316
identifying tenths, 303, 308–309, 311, 314–315, 319
subtracting dollars and cents, 328
subtracting tenths, 326–327, 329
Diagrams, 172–173, 177, 189, 227, 409
Division
checking, 364
by eights, 238–241
estimating quotients, 370
finding equal parts of a group, 139, 151, 165
by fives, 151, 158–160, 161
by fours, 151, 154–157, 160, 165

Art Credits

Betsy Day: 7, 10, 11, 18, 33, 39, 47, 51, 72-74, 76, 78, 86-89, 93, 100, 111, 120, 125, 128, 139, 151, 160, 165, 170, 176, 193, 202, 207, 210, 212-214, 221, 224, 230, 235, 244, 267, 278, 280, 287, 292, 299, 308, 314, 336, 376, 378-379, 390-391, 394-396, 408-409.

Lois Ehlert: 8, 114.

Tom Leonard: 81, 116, 205, 401.

Al Fiorentino: 384-385.

Dick Sanderson: 61, 190, 191, 247.

Photo Credits

The following abbreviations indicate the position of the photographs on the page: *t*, top; *b*, bottom; *l*, left; *r*, right; *c*, center.

Glyn Cloyd: 22, 67, 142(b), 146(b), 146(b), 154(b), 158(b), 214, 238, 242(b).

Ken Karp/OPC: 122, 130, 144, 148, 200, 204, 226, 233, 242(t).

Ken Lax: 142(t), 158(t), 240, 241, 252, 284, 296, 306, 331, 340, 360, 410(t).

John Lei/OPC: 8, 9, 20, 21, 27, 30, 31, 41, 44, 55, 58, 103, 120, 132, 146(t), 154(t), 156, 168, 198, 216, 249, 348, 352.

2(tl), Ira Block/The Image Bank; 2(tr) Cameron Davidson/Bruce Coleman; 2(bl), Dick Luria/The Stock Shop; 2(br), Focus on Sports; 4(tl), Ann Hagen Griffith/OPC; 4(tr), Bruce Roberts/Photo Researchers; 4(bl), Frank Keating/Photo Researchers; 4(br), Ann Hagen Griffith/OPC; 14, R. Steedman/The Stock Market; 24, Larousse/Photo Researchers; 25, Michael Holford; 35(l), Knott's Berry Farm; 35(r), Stuart Craig/ Bruce Coleman; 42, Gregory G. Dimijian, M.D./Photo Researchers; 53(t), Chuck Fishman/ Woodfin Camp and Associates; 53(b), David Burnett/ Contact; 56, M.P. Kahl/Bruce Coleman; 70, Craig Aurness/Woodfin Camp and Associates; 80, Philipa Scott/ Photo Researchers; 81, Claire Brett Smith/Bruce Coleman; 84, Horst Munzig/Woodfin Camp and Associates; 98, Gabe Palmer/The Stock Market; 109, New York State Museum; 112, Richard Hutchings/Photo Researchers; 126, Ken Sherman/Bruce Coleman; 140, Stuart Cohen/ The Stock Market; 152, Arthur d'Arazien/The Image Bank; 163(t), Art Resource/EPA; 163(bl), Harold Sund/ The Image Bank; 163(br), The Granger Collection; 166, Erica Stone/Peter Arnold; 180, D. Herman/Leo de Wys; 185, Norman Owen Tomalin/Bruce Coleman; 191, Tom McHugh/Photo Researchers; 196, Diana Walker/Gamma Liaison; 208, Erwin and Peggy Bauer/Bruce Coleman; 219, Chuck O'Rear/Woodfin Camp and Associates; 222, Charles Gupton/The Stock Market; 236, Clyde H. Smith/ Peter Arnold; 246, The Granger Collection; 250, Tom McGuire/Art Resource; 262, Michael Melford/Wheeler Pictures; 273, George Catlin/Art Resource; 273, Museum of the American Indian; 276, Victoria Beller-Smith; 282, Bjorn Bolstad/Peter Arnold; 290, Keith Gunman/Bruce Coleman; 320, Hans Reinhard/Bruce Coleman; 334, Whitney Lane/The Image Bank; 346, Peter Vadnai/The Stock Market; 357(t) The British Museum; 357(b), John Moss/Photo Researchers; 374, Pam Hasagawa/Taurus Photos; 388, Richard Hutchings/Photo Researchers; 410(b), Steve Skloot/Photo Researchers; 411, Henry O. Tanner/Hampton University, Virginia.